Black in America

Black in America
The Paradox of the Color Line

Enobong Hannah Branch

Christina Jackson

polity

The right of Enobong Hannah Branch and Christina Jackson to be identified as Authors of this Work has been asserted in accordance with the UK Copyright, Designs and Patents Act 1988.

First published in 2020 by Polity Press

Polity Press
65 Bridge Street
Cambridge CB2 1UR, UK

Polity Press
101 Station Landing
Suite 300
Medford, MA 02155, USA

ISBN-13: 978-1-5095-3138-7
ISBN-13: 978-1-5095-3139-4(pb)

A catalog record for this book is available from the British Library.

Library of Congress Cataloging-in-Publication Data
Names: Branch, Enobong Hannah, 1983- author. | Jackson, Christina Renee, author.
Title: Black in America : the paradox of the color line / Enobong Hannah Branch, Christina Jackson.
Other titles: Paradox of the color line
Description: Cambridge, UK ; Medford, MA : Polity, 2019. | Includes bibliographical references and index. | Summary: "To be Black in America is to exist amongst myriad contradictions: racial progress and regression, abject poverty amidst profound wealth, discriminatory policing yet equal protection under the law. This book explores these contradictions to provide a sociology of Black lives in America today"-- Provided by publisher.
Identifiers: LCCN 2019023981 (print) | LCCN 2019023982 (ebook) | ISBN 9781509531387 (hardback) | ISBN 9781509531394 (paperback) | ISBN 9781509531417 (epub)
Subjects: LCSH: African Americans--Social conditions. | Racism--United States. | United States--Race relations.
Classification: LCC E185.86 .B693 2019 (print) | LCC E185.86 (ebook) | DDC 305.896/073--dc23
LC record available at https://lccn.loc.gov/2019023981
LC ebook record available at https://lccn.loc.gov/2019023982

Typeset in 10.5 on 12pt Plantin by
Servis Filmsetting Ltd, Stockport, Cheshire
Printed and bound by CPI Group (UK) Ltd, Croydon

For further information on Polity, visit our website: politybooks.com

Between me and the other world there is ever an unasked question: unasked by some through feelings of delicacy; by others through the difficulty of rightly framing it. All, nevertheless, flutter round it. They approach me in a half-hesitant sort of way, eye me curiously or compassionately, and then, instead of saying directly, How does it feel to be a problem? they say, I know an excellent colored man in my town; or, I fought at Mechanicsville; or, Do not these Southern outrages make your blood boil? At these I smile, or am interested, or reduce the boiling to a simmer, as the occasion may require. To the real question, How does it feel to be a problem? I answer seldom a word.

W. E. B. Du Bois, *The Souls of Black Folk*

Contents

Spotlights on Resistance

Case Studies

About the Contributors

Authors

Enobong Hannah Branch is a professor of Sociology and Vice Chancellor for Diversity, Inclusion, and Community Engagement, at Rutgers University–New Brunswick. Her research interests are in race, racism, and inequality; intersectional theory; work and occupations; and diversity in science. She is the author of *Opportunity Denied: Limiting Black Women to Devalued Work* (2011), and the editor of *Pathways, Potholes, and the Persistence of Women in Science: Reconsidering the Pipeline* (2016), as well as several journal articles and book chapters that explore the historical roots and contemporary underpinnings of inequality.

Christina Jackson is an assistant professor of Sociology at Stockton University in New Jersey. Her research interests are primarily in the intersections of race, class, and gender; social inequality; urban spaces; social movements; and the politics of redevelopment and gentrification. She is the co-author of *Embodied Difference: Divergent Bodies in Public Discourse* with Jamie A. Thomas (2019), as well as several journal articles and book chapters.

Contributing authors to chapters

Emmanuel Adero is a senior director in the Office of Equity and Inclusion at the University of Massachusetts–Amherst. He has conducted research on race and inequality, Black masculinity, fatherhood, and the family. He has previously served in numerous research and analytical roles related to demography, public policy, and crime analysis.

Lucius Couloute is an assistant professor of Sociology at Suffolk University in Boston, MA. His research interests are in race and racism, class, gender, prisoner re-entry, criminalization, insecure work experiences, and organizations. He has also served as a policy analyst with the Prison Policy Initiative and has authored three policy reports related to the re-entry challenges of formerly incarcerated people.

Candace S. King is a Ph.D. student in the W. E. B. DuBois Department of Afro-American Studies at the University of Massachusetts–Amherst. She is also an Emmy award-winning journalist (2017) for her coverage of the water crisis affecting predominantly Black communities in Flint, Michigan. Her research interests are in formations of Black female identities and misrepresentations in mainstream media.

Introduction:
Are We "Post-racial" Yet?

Post-racial. *adjective*: having overcome or moved beyond racism: having reached a stage or time at which racial prejudice no longer exists or is no longer a major social problem.[1]

America is far from a post-racial society. Racial inequality is in fact our defining social problem. From rates of mass incarceration to infant mortality, health disparities to unemployment, staggering inequality along racial lines is as American as apple pie, so much so that sociologist Andrew Hacker penned a book in 1995 entitled *Two Nations: Black and White, Separate, Hostile, and Unequal*.

Yet, despite this stubborn reality, many Americans largely desire to live in a post-racial society. In a 2015 survey conducted by MTV, 91 percent of young people between the ages of 18 and 24 said they believed in racial equality. The vast majority of them (68 percent) said focusing on race "prevents society from becoming colorblind." Persistent inequality, in their view, is caused by focusing on race too much. The problem, as they see it, is America's preoccupation with race, so if we ignored it, society would be better off. The questions seem to be: What's up with race? Why can't we all just get along?

In *The Souls of Black Folk*, one of the defining works on the Black experience in America, W. E. B. Du Bois opened with conviction and certainty declaring "the problem of the Twentieth Century is the problem of the color line" (1903:7). To our great disappointment, he was right. It is a saddening reality that, well into the twenty-first century, Du Bois' clarion call still rings true. The problem of the color line remains. While the line itself is increasingly variegated as more racial and ethnic groups call America home,

Black Americans retain an unwelcome distinction as America's problem.

Yet, this idea was met with resistance at the start of the twentieth century when Du Bois uttered those words and it still is *today*. For many, Black success negates this truth. How can the color line be the problem, if evidence of Black progress is all around? At the start of the twenty-first century, words like post-racial and colorblind overtook the American lexicon, drowning out words like racism and discrimination, hiding – if only temporarily – the inconvenience of deep racial disparity. This is the quintessential American paradox, our embrace of the ideals of meritocracy and America as the land of opportunity, despite the systemic racial advantages and disadvantages accrued across generations that have denied this opportunity to Black people. To be Black in America is to exist among a myriad of contradictions: racial progress and regression, abject poverty amidst profound wealth, discriminatory policing yet equal protection under the law. The desire to focus on race less avoids the discomfort of this reality.

Allan G. Johnson in *Privilege, Power, and Difference* argues difference is not the problem, privilege and power are. In this sense, there is nothing wrong with racial difference itself, but with the way that race is used to structure and organize society. Yet just talking about the reality of racial inequality makes most Americans uncomfortable. Even among young people, who largely believe in racial equality, only 37 percent "were raised in households that talked about race." Even fewer, 20 percent, "felt comfortable talking about biases against specific groups." In this vacuum of belief in equality, but avoidance of racial bias as a cause of inequality, racial difference itself becomes the problem. Without discussing the racial privilege that structures American life, simply being Black becomes the problem, not the poverty, marginalization, or racism that scaffolds it.

Racial inequality is a social fact, but how should we understand race itself as contributing to or producing this inequality? The answer depends on one's conception of race. Race can be defined as an *ideology*, a manner of thinking, a system of complex ideas about power that justifies who should have it along racial lines (Fields 1990). Or race can be defined as an *ideological construct*, a shared societal understanding of racial ideologies that manifest materially and socially within society, resulting in differential power along racial lines. Race can also be defined as a *sociohistorical construct*, developed over hundreds of years, producing a shared global understanding and reinforcement of relationships of domination and subordination along racial lines (Winant 2000a). Finally, **race**[*] can be defined as an *objective fact*: one is simply their race.

Sociologist Howard Winant emphasizes the importance of not treating race as an ideology to be discarded or as an objective fact to be factored into sociological analysis, but instead he argues we must "recognize the importance of historical context and contingency in the framing of racial categories and the social construction of racially defined experiences" (Winant 2000a:185). Yet, Winant notes, "much of liberal and even radical social science, though firmly committed to a social as opposed to a biological interpretation of race, nevertheless also slips into a kind of objectivism about racial identity and racial meaning" (Winant 2000a:184). Hence, sociologist Stephen Steinberg (1998) aptly critiques social science for its role in legitimating the racial hierarchy. Social scientists' conceptualization of racism in terms of attitudes rather than social conditions led to a focus on White attitudinal change, rather than a focus on changing social conditions. Treatment of racial differences in objective terms without critical attention to the role of racism in creating those differences provides tacit acceptance of the view that race is no longer important, when in actuality its role has been ignored.

This book focuses exclusively on Black Americans to make plain the linkages between the past and the present. It unpacks how race became the basis of inequality historically, and threads together contemporary aspects of inequality. We define Black inclusively (see chapter 2) and explore the contradictions and the heterogeneity of the Black experience in America created by its burgeoning diversity. We engage the prism of differing intersectional social categories, such as ethnicity, gender, and class, which leads to a rich analysis of inequality that exposes how race joins with individuals' privileges and disadvantages to differently shape the life chances of Black people.

Black in America: Revisiting Martin Luther King Jr.'s Dream

The story of Black America is one of struggle and triumph. Black Americans in the twenty-first century are the most educated and financially stable Black generation by far. They have witnessed our nation's first Black President and first Black billionaire. Blacks can be counted among the leadership in almost every industry and profession,

---

[*] Where a term or concept is highlighted in bold in the text, you will find it defined in the Glossary at the end of the book.

from business to education. In the Black community, however, the substantial success of some is juxtaposed with the failure of others. The chasm between the haves and have-nots continues to widen and is redefining what it means to be Black – while race and poverty remain highly correlated, they are no longer synonymous.

The Civil Rights Movement of the 1950s and 1960s transformed American life, changing both the symbolic and material relationships Blacks maintained with the United States through the extension of voting rights and outlawing discrimination. Yet, in many ways, its central promise of true equality remains unfulfilled (Wilson 1978). Dr. Martin Luther King's dream that his "four little children will one day live in a nation where they will not be judged by the color of their skin, but by the content of their character" is interpreted by many as the original call for society to be colorblind. But that was not all Dr. King said. In fact, that was not even the focus of his speech at the March on Washington. The reference to not being judged by the color of your skin was made in the context of addressing the material inequality that was tied to race, specifically Blackness. Far from giving permission to trivialize race and focus on individual behavior, Martin Luther King's now famous "I Have a Dream" speech sought to define the purpose of the march, "to dramatize the shameful condition" of Blacks in America.

It is helpful to revisit Martin Luther King's actual words,[2] because the reality that motivated the March on Washington and inspired King's speech is often overlooked. He opened bemoaning the fact that, despite the signing of the Emancipation Proclamation 100 years prior, in 1963 Blacks were still not free. He continued:

> One hundred years later the life of the Negro is still badly crippled by the manacles of segregation and the chains of discrimination. One hundred years later the Negro lives on a lonely island of poverty in the midst of a vast ocean of material prosperity. One hundred years later the Negro is still languished in the corners of American society and finds himself in exile in his own land.

These powerful words were followed by his assertion that the 250,000 people who came to the nation's capital that day were there "to cash a check."

King described the Constitution and the Declaration of Independence as a "promissory note . . . a promise that all men – yes, Black men as well as White men – would be guaranteed the unalienable rights of life, liberty, and the pursuit of happiness." Yet America, King argued, had failed to honor this "sacred obligation" to Black

Americans. Despite all evidence to the contrary, King still believed in the promise of liberty saying: "But we refuse to believe that the bank of justice is bankrupt. We refuse to believe that there are insufficient funds in the great vaults of opportunity of this nation. So we have come to cash this check, a check that will give us upon demand the riches of freedom and the security of justice." He reminded America of "the fierce urgency of now" and warned that there would not be "rest" while Blacks were less than full citizens. King recounted many social ails from police brutality to the lack of a right to vote, from the ghetto to Jim Crow, and he urged Blacks to conduct civil protest with "dignity and discipline," urging them not to be satisfied "until justice rolls down like waters and righteousness like a mighty stream."

King noted how hard the struggle has been and told Blacks to "not wallow in despair." And only then, four-and-a-half pages into his five-and-a-half-page speech, did he begin to dream, to offer inspiration to the crowd to keep fighting for a promise that had not yet been realized.

> I say to you today, my friends, though, even though we face difficulties of today and tomorrow, I still have a dream . . . I have a dream that one day this nation will rise up, live out the true meaning of its creed: "We hold these truths to be self-evident, that all men are created equal" . . . I have a dream that one day even the state of Mississippi, a state sweltering with the heat of injustice, sweltering with the heat of oppression, will be transformed into an oasis of freedom and justice. I have a dream that my four little children will one day live in a nation where they will not be judged by the color of their skin, but by the content of their character.

The depth of King's dream far exceeds the Black History Month one-liner and ode to colorblindness to which it has been reduced. King aimed for racial justice, for America to be post-racial in the definitive sense, to overcome racism and enable Blacks to be truly free. Yet, just as Mississippi continues to struggle with racial prejudice,[3] Blacks in America are still judged by the color of their skin. In some ways, we are farther away from achieving the dream today than we were in 1963.

We now have a national holiday that recognizes the contributions of Martin Luther King Jr., and laws that prohibit segregation, but racial inequality persists. Blacks in America face the insurmountable struggle of trying to define the discrimination they face without being accused of playing the race card. America embraced **colorblindness** – the racial ideology that suggests the best way to end discrimination is by treating individuals as equally as possible (without regard to race) – while leaving the underlying inequality tied to racial domination untouched. The American Dream itself espouses a post-racial ideal that hard work and effort are all that is required for success, and meritocracy will win out in the end. Yet all of the available evidence suggests we are not there yet. Our racial legacy has left footprints that reinforce the centrality of race and racism in post-civil rights America. Sociologist Adia Harvey Wingfield (2015) argues that insisting on colorblindness comes at a cost:

> By claiming that they do not see race, they also can avert their eyes from the ways in which well-meaning people engage in practices that reproduce neighborhood and school segregation, rely on "soft skills" in ways that disadvantage racial minorities in the job market, and hoard opportunities in ways that reserve access to better jobs for White peers.

The Civil Rights Movement led to a cultural shift in the understanding of racial inequality as inherent (a decline in overt racism), but today many draw on cultural explanations to explain persistent racial inequality alongside widespread belief in the virtue of racial equality. This book documents the role that racism (in shifting forms) has played in structuring the social and economic landscape that Black Americans must navigate.

We orient the reader historically, paying special attention to slavery and its legacy (Jim Crow), to show how the structure of American society, and Blacks' long-time outsider status within it, have lasting contemporary implications. By examining both contemporary and historical facets of the Black experience, through a structural lens grounded disciplinarily in sociology, we aim to illuminate what is easily missed: a comprehensive understanding of the precise ways in which race continues to act as a fundamental organizing principle of American society today. Throughout the book, we integrate spotlights on resistance highlighting how Black Americans grapple with and respond to constraint.

Chapter 1, "How Blacks Became the Problem: American Racism and the Fight for Equality," provides the historical and conceptual foundation for the book, arguing that it is impossible to understand the Black community without also interrogating the role that American racism played in its formation and the continued maintenance of the racial boundaries imposed on it. Education, and the active restriction and constraint on Black education from slavery to the present, is utilized to illustrate the institutional nature of racism and explain that, even though many claim today not to "see" race and therefore believe they cannot be "racist," this logic misses a fundamental truth: one can claim not to be "racist" and yet reproduce a racial hierarchy.

Chapter 2, "Crafting the Racial Frame: Blackness and the Myth of the Monolith" (with Candace S. King and Emmanuel Adero), describes how Black Americans have been framed from without, by the stereotypes that suggest who they are supposed to be and represent. But it also emphasizes how Black Americans have defined and are actively restructuring what it means to be Black from within, resisting all attempts at a simple narrative. This chapter lays the groundwork for understanding the complexity of race, representation, and obstacles to integration. Blackness is often thought of, and projected as, a monolithic experience that includes welfare, poverty, and female-headed households. The ubiquity of these images, and their taken-for-granted associations, force all Blacks to navigate their everyday lives through a lens of deviance, no matter how incongruous the fit. Among Blacks themselves, Black identity and its expression are shaped by a host of intersections, such as gender, ethnicity/ immigrant status, class, sexuality and disability. The *intersection* of identities further marginalizes some Blacks while privileging others. This unevenness in oppression has the ability to create fractures within the Black community, even while it is one of its defining features.

Chapter 3, "Whose Life Matters? Value and Disdain in American Society," reorients the reader away from the – unsettling for some – slogan Black Lives Matter to examine the historical value placed on Black life. We succinctly describe the devaluation of Blacks in the US through a focus on the historical treatment of the Black body and the myriad of ways in which the medical, legal and political system perpetuated it. We then chronicle Black resistance movements from slavery onward, demonstrating that Blacks have always resisted their subjugation, unwilling to accept the disdain for Black life even when racial oppression was violently reasserted. Movements, and the rise of the contemporary social movement Black Lives Matter, have essentially attempted to redefine the problem not as Blackness but as inequality that subjugates Black people.

Chapter 4, "Staying Inside the Red Line: Housing Segregation and the Rise of the Ghetto," emphasizes the role of place in containing the Black body. Racial segregation still defines the life chances and landscape of inequality for Black urban residents, stigmatizing inner-city neighborhoods and rendering its inhabitants vulnerable. While segregation as an official policy, created to protect White citizens and lock in their advantages spatially, was eradicated nearly 50 years ago, other systems continue this protection and perpetuate historically stigmatized spaces such as the ghetto (Lipsitz 2015). Today, not only are we still avoiding "integrated" neighborhoods discursively, but the rationales used to rehabilitate spaces are coded racially. Historically Black neighborhoods are targeted for redevelopment and gentrification, needing "revival" and "resuscitation" through real-estate investment. Yet hegemonic ideas about Blackness, deeply held in the public's imaginary, lock low- and middle-income Blacks out of quality housing that is created. We explore how Black residents make sense of this contradiction and resist.

Chapter 5, "Who Gets to Work? Understanding the Black Labor Market Experience," emphasizes how race structures access to occupational opportunity that marginalizes Blacks in the labor market. In a meritocratic society, access to opportunity should be granted based on how hard a person works, and hard work should lead to economic rewards. This has not been true in America. Occupational opportunities were withheld from Blacks and extended to Whites. Blacks and Whites, men and women, when working alongside one another or in related jobs were compensated unequally because of their race and/or gender. Racism helped manage the dissonance between American ideals of equality and Black exclusion, ideologically and legally justifying the differential treatment of Blacks in the labor market until the Civil Rights Movement. There were some gains afforded by affirmative action, followed by losses as federal interest in enforcement waned. This chapter takes the reader on a journey to understand the context of historically unequal opportunity and the contemporary forces driving socioeconomic inequality today.

Chapter 6, "Is Justice Blind? Race and the Rise of Mass Incarceration" (with Lucius Couloute), examines the historical pathologization of Black bodies, placing it within a larger system of inequality and race-making. It begins first with the state of mass criminalization today, exploring the product of what Michelle Alexander (2010) calls "the new Jim Crow." With millions of Black bodies under criminal justice system control, the chapter asks: How did we get here? The answer lies in the immediate post-emancipation period as social scientists, politicians, wealthy landowners and big business worked to create a system that reinforced racial inequality amid racial flux. We then examine shifting twentieth-century practices and policies grounded in – by then pervasive – racist ideas that governed the growth of our criminal justice system. The chapter then ends where it started, the contemporary period, this time examining the effects of criminalizing Black bodies and the reproduction of racial inequality in newer practices and policies.

Chapter 7, "Reifying the Problem: Racism and the Persistence of the Color Line in American Politics" (with Emmanuel Adero), provides an examination of the role of politics and policy in creating and driving the persistence of racial inequality. It outlines the politics of retrenchment after emancipation, which led to a split between Northern and Southern Democrats and the emergence of the Southern strategy, which appealed to the racism against Blacks held by Southern White voters. We then draw on the similarities between the Democratic and Republican parties and how racial appeals have shaped presidential politics and policies. While Blacks are a base to be catered to and at times courted by one party and antagonized by the other, both have played a definite role in the persistence of Black marginality. Finally, we outline policy as the outcome of racial politics. Though policies are seemingly race-neutral, their disparate impact on the Black community is well documented.

Book Features

We want you to get the most out of this book and have included the features below as additional resources.

- Key terms are bolded throughout and compiled in a glossary.
- Integrated into each chapter is a stand-alone feature called "Spotlight on Resistance" that highlights a contemporary or historical example of Black people asserting themselves and resisting racial oppression.
- At the end of each chapter, there are critical questions to promote engagement and reflection.

1

How Blacks Became the Problem: American Racism and the Fight for Equality

To be Black in America today is to exist among a myriad of contradictions, but there is none more striking and uniquely American than the adherence to the ideal of equality, and its sister meritocracy, alongside pervasive racial inequality. Slavery birthed this contradiction. As slaves, Blacks were the solution to America's labor problem, marked by race for unequal treatment. They were forcibly brought to the United States for the sole purpose of serving as an intergenerationally stable, coercible labor force (Branch 2011). Their racial otherness enabled the brutality that American slavery required (Fredrickson 2002). Black slaves were bought, sold and traded like cattle. "Auctions were government sponsored events taking place on courthouse steps" (Roberts 1997:35). The slave trade was a permanent legal part of the foundation of America.

Slavery normalized the objectification and dehumanization of Blacks, and the Constitution legislated this. The "three-fifths" compromise was the resolution to one of the most contentious issues facing the framers of the Constitution. Supporters of slavery, often slaveholders in Southern states, wanted slaves to be counted as part of the United States population for purposes of taxation and representation. Opponents of slavery, often Northern delegates, only wanted to count the free population, including free Blacks and indentured servants, discounting slaves as property, not people. Historians John Hope Franklin and Evelyn Brooks Higginbotham recount the tensions among delegates at the 1787 Constitutional Convention in Philadelphia, with competing interests as follows:

> Most of the Northern delegates could regard slaves in no light except as property and thus not entitled to any representation. However, del-

egates from Georgia and South Carolina – states where the majority of people were slaves and the free White people a distinct minority – vigorously demanded that slaves be counted equally with Whites when it came to apportioning congressional seats and electoral votes. Gouverneur Morris declared that the people of his state, Pennsylvania, would revolt against being placed on an equal footing with slaves, while Rufus King of Massachusetts flayed slavery in a fiery speech and condemned any proposal that would recognize it in the Constitution. (2011:100)

It was against this backdrop that the now notorious "three-fifths" compromise was forged; it read: "Representatives and direct taxes shall be apportioned among the several States which may be included within this Union, according to their respective Numbers, which shall be determined by adding the whole Number of free Persons, including those bound to Service for a Term of Years, and excluding Indians not taxed, three-fifths of all other persons."[1] Counting slaves equally alongside the free population would have given the South much greater political power due to the size of the enslaved Black population. But how to count slaves for the purpose of taxation and representation was not the only issue pertaining to slavery facing the framers of the Constitution. A pressing question was what to do about the slave trade itself?

In 1787, several Northern states had already banned the importation of new slaves, but the Southern states that allowed it, Georgia as well as South and North Carolina, were adamant in their resistance to outlawing the slave trade. Despite the loud objections to slavery and the rising abolitionist movement, slavery was too important to the fledgling American nation to be abolished or the slave trade prohibited at that time. Instead the framers of the Constitution compromised again, granting Congress the right to ban the slave trade but not for 20 years. American participation in the transatlantic slave trade officially ended on January 1, 1808. Yet slave trading persisted illicitly for many years thereafter.

America grappled with its egalitarian ideals, as belief in them required contortions and racial exceptions. The rise of democracy, in the late eighteenth century, and the associated belief that "all men are created equal" was at odds with American economic dependence on slavery and Black subjugation. While the "three-fifths" compromise solved the dual problems of representation and taxation, it only implicitly addressed the moral conundrum equating Blacks with property not persons. Slavery remained a scourge on the national conscience. Plantation owners, for their part, did not let the questions about the morality of slavery dissuade from their pursuit of economic profit. Wary of reductions in their labor pool, due to the prohibition of importing slaves, slave owners marshalled Black women's reproduction to stabilize their labor force. Legal scholar Adrienne Davis explains the importance of Black women's childbearing to the slave economy, arguing: "[It] created economic value independent of the physical, productive labor they [Black women] performed. Southern legal rules harnessed Black reproductive capacity for market purposes, extracting from it the profits one might expect from a factory or livestock ... In its centrality to the political economy, enslaved women's reproduction was arguably the most valuable labor performed in the entire economy" (2002:109). Black women's designation as property and their reproduction as profit led to particularly cruel forms of exploitation as slave owners desired to extract maximum value from Black women as laborers while ensuring the viability of their progeny (Roberts 1997).

Historian George Fredrickson in his classic book, *Racism: A Short History*, argues that, while Blacks were always perceived as racially other, the ideology of racism as a fulsome defense of slavery did not emerge until later:

> In the United States racism as an ideology of inherent Black inferiority emerged into the clear light of day in reaction to the rise of northern abolitionism in the 1830s – as a response to the radical demands for emancipation at a time when the federal government was committed to the protection of slavery. Defenders of Black servitude needed a justification of the institution that was consistent with the decline of social deference and the extension of suffrage rights to White males, a democratization process that took place in the South as well as the North. They found it in theories that made White domination and Black subservience seem natural and unavoidable. (Fredrickson 2002:79)

Racism played a key role in managing the dissonance between American inalienable rights and Black slavery, ideologically justifying the differential treatment of Black slaves. Indeed, James Henry Hammond, a Democrat from South Carolina, in a speech before the US Senate on March 4, 1858, declared:

> In all social systems there must be a class to do the menial duties, to perform the drudgery of life. That is, a class requiring but a low order of intellect and but little skill. Its requisites are vigor, docility, fidelity. Such a class you must have, or you would not have that other class

which leads progress, civilization, and refinement. . ... Fortunately for the South, she found a race adapted to that purpose to her hand. A race inferior to her own, but eminently qualified in temper, in vigor, in docility, in capacity to stand the climate, to answer all her purposes. We use them for our purpose, and call them slaves. . ... We do not think that Whites should be slaves either by law or necessity. Our slaves are Black, of another and inferior race. The status in which we have placed them is an elevation. They are elevated from the condition in which God first created them, by being made our slaves. (Hammond 1866:318)

The fight for the abolition of slavery in essence birthed the Black problem. As long as Blacks coexisted alongside Whites in a position of dehumanized servitude and did not demand full inclusion into American society, they were not innately a problem. The problem was when they resisted their social conditions, which resulted in the brutal stamping-out of slave rebellions, severe punishment of runaway slaves, and the prohibition of slave literacy. The ideology of racism was intended to quiet the advocates of abolition, justifying slavery as an institution, all in service of maintaining the existing social order of White superiority.

The 1857 *Dred Scott* v. *J-Sanford* case codified what was commonplace at the time: Blacks were not American citizens because "the Black man has no rights that the White man is bound to respect" (Davis 2002:106). Even Abraham Lincoln, the "great" emancipator, said, in September 1858:

There is a physical difference between the White and Black races which I believe forever forbid the two races living together on terms of social and political equality. And in as much as they cannot so live, while they do remain together there must be the position of superior and inferior, and I as such as any other man am in favor of having the superior position assigned to the White race. (Lincoln and Douglas 1894:164)

Sociologist W. E. B. Du Bois (1935) argues in *Black Reconstruction in America 1860–1880* that Black resistance, via increased rebellion and organizing, forced social change. Slaves were unwilling to accept the social order as it was and their upheaval of the Southern establishment through persistent strikes led Lincoln to free them. Most historians argue that slavery was abolished in order to preserve the Union from Southern secession (Fredrickson 2002). In either case, abolition and legal equality for Blacks, guaranteed by the 14th Amendment, required a radical readjustment of the American racial order. Blacks forced this readjustment with increasing resilience during Reconstruction, but racial progress was short-lived. In *Opportunity Denied: Limiting Black Women to Devalued Work*, sociologist Enobong Hannah Branch argues:

> The abolition of slavery freed Blacks from their designation as property, but they remained ideologically and, consequently, socially bound by conceptions of inferiority. Racism, once invoked, became valued in and of itself and it was an inescapable consequence that Whites would insist on maintaining a racist order predicated on denying the equality of Blacks. After the slaves were emancipated, there was no space for Blacks, the racialized Other, to coexist with Whites as equal citizens and competitors in the racialized social structure of the United States. (2011:30)

While racism was initially intended primarily to justify enslavement, after emancipation the pursuit of racial stratification and Black subjugation itself became the goal. Racism played a central role in justifying the unequal treatment of emancipated slaves and led to the rise of Jim Crow, which defined Black life in America for nearly a century.

Racial inequality is maintained by racial ideologies and ideological constructs that normalize racial differences in everyday life. One of the key underpinnings legitimizing American racial inequality is the understanding that Blacks *are* the problem, rather than a group *with* problems reproduced within a racialized social structure. We began this chapter by describing how slavery and its ultimate abolition birthed the Black problem. In the remainder of this chapter, we will review the active resistance to Blacks coexisting in American society as equals, which produced the racial inequality we falsely attribute to Black intrinsic characteristics today. First, we describe how sociologists understand race, racism and racialized social systems to provide a shared understanding of how these intellectual claims manifested in the lives of emancipated slaves.

Defining the Problem: Critical and Conventional Approaches to Race and Racism

Sociologist James Blackwell has argued that "no single theory can explain fully the authentic Black experience in America . . . there is no single authentic Black experience in America except that which developed as a consequence of ubiquitous White racism and color consciousness" (1975:5). Although there is a strong connection between race and racism, they are conceptually and analytically different. In the introduction, we defined *race* as an ideology, a manner of thinking and system of complex ideas about power that justifies who should have it along racial lines. Sociologist Howard Winant goes a step farther, describing race as a "concept that signifies and symbolizes socio-political conflicts and interests in reference to different types of human bodies" (Winant 2004:154). Racism relies on a set of beliefs and practices that make the ideological real and material (Fields 1990). Anthropologist Leith Mullings argues *racism* relies on "a set of practices, structures, beliefs, and representations that transforms certain forms of perceived differences . . . into inequality" (Mullings 2005:684). Racism constitutes a system of oppression that creates ethno-racial others (Fredrickson 2002) and generates a process of *othering*, and normalization of Whiteness as the default racial category (Thomas and Jackson 2019). This othering is legitimized through a system of racial discrimination, exploitation, segregation, stigmatization, exclusion and physical violence against negatively racialized subjects.

There is a fundamental contradiction in the way that conventional and critical scholars approach race and racism. Conventional scholars acknowledge the historicity of race but suggest that its effects are no longer present and any contemporary racism is a remnant of a former time (Alba 1990). Racism in this view is an ideology or a belief and thus lends itself to be studied at the individual level within social psychology (Schuman, Steeh, Bobo and Krysan 1998). Critical race scholars espouse the centrality of race and racism in defining the life chances of racial minorities historically and in the present day (Blauner 2001; Bonilla-Silva 2001). Racism is viewed as being materially based in the structural position of the racial and ethnic groups in the racialized social structure, thus individuals' racist beliefs or lack thereof are not central because they do not affect the structural basis of racism (Bonilla-Silva 1996). Despite the class fracturing along racial lines, all members of the dominant group reap the benefit of dominant group position in a **racialized social system**[2] even if they do not equally share in the material benefits (Bonilla-Silva 1996).

Scholars and activists, such as Cedric Robinson, Keeanga-Yahmatta Taylor, Angela Davis and Tim Wise, argue that there is an intricate relationship between race and capitalism.[3] In this view, racism is a "legitimating ideology used by the bourgeoisie to divide the working class" (Bonilla-Silva 1996:466). Race is not secondary to class, but both are mutually beneficial to one another as the capitalist system exploits the Black community (Robinson 1983; Taylor 2011).[4] Critical approaches to race keep as their central focus "the reality of domination and inequality" in the lives of racialized minorities (Blauner 2001:24). They seek to expose rather than downplay the continuing significance of race in shaping the life outcomes of racialized groups.

It is impossible to understand the Black population in America without interrogating the role that racism played in its formation and the continued maintenance of the racial boundaries imposed on it. Yet this argument that racism is central is debated among sociologists with conventional versus critical approaches to the study of race. Jacques Derrida (in Crenshaw 2000: 550) notes that "Western thought . . . has always been structured in terms of dichotomies or polarities" and that "these polar opposites do not . . . stand as independent and equal entities. The second term in the pair is considered the negative, corrupt, undesirable version of the first." Conventional approaches to race and ethnicity accepted this fact as it was the basis for the rationalization of slavery and "old-fashioned" racism as displayed during the Jim Crow Era. However, with the decline of overt racist behavior and increasing economic divisions within the Black community, conventional race scholars posited that class had replaced race as the most salient determinant of life chances for Black Americans (Wilson 1978).

In contrast, critical race theorists recognized this shift as a transformation of racism from an overt to a covert form expressed as colorblind or cultural racism, rather than an actual decline in racism (Bonilla-Silva 2003a). Critical race scholars argue that the underlying belief in the superiority of the White race was still maintained. It just gained expression through a colorblind belief in egalitarian values while disavowing a "head-start" for the dominant group. Alternatively, in the case of **cultural racism**, subordinated minorities are judged to be culturally deficient and this cultural deficiency/ inferiority is the basis of their demeaned social position, not racism or discrimination (Bonilla-Silva 2003a; Wilson 1973).

This book takes a critical approach to race to unpack the Black experience. Even though many claim today to not "see" race and therefore believe they cannot be "racist," this logic misses a fundamental truth: one can claim not to be "racist" and yet reproduce a racial hierarchy (see Resistance Case Study 1). Sociologist Robert Blauner argues: "prejudiced attitudes are not the essence of racism" (2001:19). While intense prejudice is often expressed via *overt racism* – explicit mistreatment or denigration of a racial minority group – a *racist social structure* does not require individual "bad" actors to maintain racial inequality. Blauner argues that racism in America is *institutionalized*, such that "the processes that maintain domination – control of Whites over non-Whites – are built into the major social institutions" (Blauner 2001:20).

Spotlight on Resistance

Case Study 1 Blacks as the Undesirable Population in San Francisco

In San Francisco, sociologist Christina Jackson conducted an ethnography from 2008 to 2010 in Black neighborhoods in the city: in particular, Bayview – Hunters Point. She joined a diverse community group called Stop Redevelopment Corporations Now (SRCN) that was created to organize against the erasure of Black San Francisco and other groups of color due to redevelopment, gentrification and environmental justice struggles associated with the Hunters Point shipyard. Residents conceptualized redevelopment and delayed environmental clean-up as *implicit racism* within a *social structure* that sought to erase their community. Through interviews and participant observation, Jackson captured the effects of redevelopment on the remaining low-income Black residents in the city. She interviewed Brother Ben, a 41-year-old small-business owner and member of SRCN who grew up in the Fillmore neighborhood and organizes in the Bayview – Hunters Point section. When asked about desirability, redevelopment and the SRCN movement he responded:

> This [redevelopment] is about removing the people and [to] re-people the area with rich white middle-class people, a dog population, children playing, not even children playing in the street but a playground for rich people. And they want to make it this high-class area where most people make $75,000 or more a year, and just completely remove anyone who's not what they call *a desirable population*. And, this is what plays into the depopulation also of Black people in San Francisco, which we say is being done intentionally. . . . So, SRCN is like a conscious movement or body that just allows people to get information, even beyond just the environment . . . but educate the people that they must take back the city government and must become aware of what's happening not just on the hill, but politically aware of what's going on in the city.

The Stop Redevelopment Corporations Now movement sought to educate the community about scientific language, connecting

with trusted scientists to communicate clearly and translate jargon
about levels of contaminants in their neighborhood and to help
put pressures on the Navy team to clean up the area to residential standards. SRCN also sought to shine a light on the racial
and class dynamics of the intended renewal of neighborhoods to
prevent erasure of the Black community.

Racism is not an ideological tool nor a purely historical phenomenon, but it serves as a contemporary basis for the allocation and
receipt of differential rewards that operates not at the level of racial
attitudes but at the level of the social system. Racism in contemporary America can be seen as inherent in the social structure and
manifest in our social institutions such that "old-fashioned racism"
is no longer necessary to perpetuate the existence of the racial order
(Bonilla-Silva 2001).[5] A clear example of this can be found in the
American educational system. While education is commonly thought
to be the great equalizer, and the purpose of public education was to
ensure the formal training of citizens to be literate, permitting their
social and civic engagement, it has structurally defined and maintained racial inequality. This is not accidental or simply a result of
historical or contemporary class dynamics. The educational inequality and achievement gaps we are familiar with today were produced.
In the section that follows, we examine access to and the quality
of education for Blacks and Whites in America as an instance of
institutionalized racism.

Racism in an Institution: Education, Jim Crow and the Racial State

Education is both a predictable measure for analyzing Black progress, and a yardstick of Black failure. It is rife with contradictions
– pervasive and savage inequalities that are at odds with the US
national meritocratic ethos (Kozol 2012). Yet the maintenance of
racial inequality in education today does not require bad actors.
The structural inequality of poor learning outcomes from impoverished schools, unequal access to advanced placement courses and
racially biased selection for gifted and talented programs can be
maintained despite well-meaning people, good intentions and even
policy changes. While obtaining an education has been a core means
of Black resistance, it has also been a venue where the need for

resistance is most obvious. To understand why, we have to begin at the beginning and incorporate a historical view to analyze the generational impact on the Black community of withholding access to a quality education.

Education Denied During Slavery

Withholding access to education was seen in its most extreme form in the South before emancipation, when Blacks were prohibited by law from learning to read and write (Hallihan 2001:50). This legal prohibition was universal, with few exceptions; in some states, free Blacks also had to adhere to this mandate (Lieberson 1980:137),[6] and in others their education was permitted and they established their own schools or conducted them secretly (Du Bois 1901:21). Despite these restrictions, a large number of adult free Blacks, according to the 1850 census, were literate, and many Black abolitionists were self-taught (e.g., Frederick Douglass). However, given that the vast majority of slaves were illiterate, sociologist Stanley Lieberson posits that, after emancipation, "at least 93 percent of all adult Blacks were illiterate at the time of the Civil War" (1980:138).

Sociologist Pamela B. Walters (2001:41) contends that this policy of prohibiting the education of Blacks (as well as poor Whites) served the interest of the plantation elites. Since the South was an agriculture-based economy dependent on unskilled labor, educating Blacks and poor Whites was unnecessary. However, this was not the sole reason that education was withheld. According to Walters (2001:46), "they [Southern plantation elites] thought that providing 'too much' education for either African Americans or poor Whites might empower these subordinated groups to challenge the planter's political hegemony." Education was recognized as a tool of empowerment for the oppressed slaves (and poor Whites) and, in order to maintain their oppression, access to education was withheld.

Education and the Freedmen's Quest for Advancement During Reconstruction

When slavery was abolished, young freedmen and women (emancipated slaves) sought entry into schools. Blacks in the Reconstruction era recognized the importance of an education, and saw it as "one of the few institutions that could lift them from poverty and oppression" (Mickelson 1990:44). Schools were established to serve freed slaves during the Civil War by Union troops occupying Southern territory, and after the war they were established by the Reconstruction government (Walters 2001:40). As schools were established and became increasingly available, their enrollment grew. By 1870, historian John Hope Franklin notes, "there were 247,000 students in more than 4,000 schools" (1956:304–5). Sociologist W. E. B. Du Bois argues that Blacks were not apathetic toward education and pursued it vigorously, "with enrollments reaching 572,000 in 1877; 785,000 in 1880; and slightly more than a million by 1884" (1901:43).

But abolition did not abolish the racial frame that fostered and perpetuated slavery, which held that Blacks were inferior to Whites and less than human. Historian Henry Allen Bullock, in his book *A History of Negro Education in the South*, documents the substantial opposition from Whites against the education of Blacks in the South. Even though a population that was forced to be illiterate by law was now technically able to access education, Bullock writes, "economic pressures were applied against Blacks; Whites opposed mixed schools; and some Whites resented payment of taxes for the education of Blacks" (1967:41–3). Despite this, during the Reconstruction era (1866–77), both groups experienced a period of near-equality (Walters 2001). Navigating the choppy waters of opposition successfully, Bullock (1967) argues, was only possible due to pressure from the federal government and the political power of Blacks demonstrated by their voting strength. Walters notes, "Whites, in general, and White elites in particular, found the equal or relatively equal provision of educational opportunities to White and Black children objectionable" (2001:41).

Yet there was virtually no discrimination in educational funding for Black and White children, during this period (Walters 2001:41). Attempts to distribute taxes by the race of taxpayers (which would have significantly reduced funding for Blacks) were defeated consistently when up for a vote (Newbold 1928:211). Black political strength and representation on local school boards at that time were key to securing this equality in funding. Bullock offers an example drawn from the state of North Carolina in 1873. Blacks comprised 38 percent of public school enrollment, and a near-equivalent amount (33 percent) of state support went to Black schools. Beyond this significant achievement, Lieberson notes, "School terms were the same length and teachers received about the same salary . . . for every dollar spent on Black children for teachers' salaries, most commonly from about $1.10 to $1.20 was spent on the teachers of White children" (Lieberson 1980:138).

During Reconstruction, across Southern states, school expenditures for Black and White students were similar, as was the average school term. The Reconstruction era, however, was short lived, and with the end of federal political control and oversight in the South, schools returned to state control. White elites regained political power and desired to institute their political preferences, one of which was to create inequality in educational spending for Black and White students. In order to do this, however, they had to remove Blacks as a political force, hence the rise of disenfranchisement, which stripped Black people of their right to vote (Walters 2001:41).

Disenfranchisement, a Response to Population and Structural Change

During the Reconstruction era, when both Blacks and Whites possessed a degree of political power, no one group was able to elevate their racial groups' interest over the other, enabling a period of near-equality in educational funding. Sociologist Eduardo Bonilla-Silva defines **power** within a racialized social system as a "racial group's capacity to push for its racial interest in relation to other races" (Bonilla-Silva 1996:470). Thus, Blacks' possession of political power was problematic for the White planter class because they were prevented from unilaterally asserting their interests. Disenfranchisement was a means to an end – it enabled the White planter class to "regain unchallenged political power and subsequently use it to regain their advantage in public educational opportunities" (Walters 2001:41).

The **population and structural change thesis** developed by sociologist Hayward Derrick Horton holds that "changes in the relative sizes of the minority and majority populations interact with changes in the social structure to exacerbate racial and ethnic inequality" (1998:9). Racism, Horton argues, is a multi-dimensional system that reacts to population and structural change (1998:11); it is the means through which majority populations respond to changes in the minority population. Majority and minority here do not refer to the absolute population size but to the relative power associated with each group – dominant and subordinate status, respectively. In this historical instance, the creation of a fundamentally inequitable school system that advantaged Whites and disadvantaged Blacks was a racist response to the freed Black population created by the emancipation of slaves. While there are many reasons why Reconstruction as a political project in pursuit of equality for Blacks failed, Fredrickson points to a fundamental ideological rupture, "emancipation could not be carried to completion because it exceeded the capacity of White Americans – in the North as well as the South – to think of Blacks as genuine equals" (Fredrickson 2002:81).

Once slavery ended and White Southerners lost their right to the automatic control of Black slaves, the size of the population of free Blacks relative to the White population became a problem. The Black population that White slave owners bred for profit now needed to be controlled. Horton argues that the question "How do we continue to maintain control over this large and increasing population?" has plagued Whites since emancipation (1998:11). The answer, he argues, has been to "utilize a racist system of oppression to eliminate Blacks as serious competitors in every aspect of American life" (Horton 1998:11).

Education, Separate and Unequal

Once Blacks were disenfranchised and Whites controlled local school boards, the state subsidy of Black education was drastically decreased while funding of White schools steadily increased. Historian Horace Mann Bond, in *The Education of the Negro in the American Social Order*, notes: "With the passage of legislation giving each county some option in the allocation of funds to the schools of each group, for each dollar spent on Black children the discrepancy moved from $1.18 for each White in 1890 to $5.83 per White child in 1909" (Bond 1934:113).

Within a 20-year period, Whites were able to use their political power to institutionalize their political preference for unequal school funding and regain their advantage; however, they made additional changes to the Black education system during this time, all in keeping with the overriding goal of maintaining White advantage.

Recall that Black and White school terms were approximately equal during the Reconstruction era. Once Whites took control of the school boards, the average school term for Blacks was shortened so that it was "only 80 percent as long as Whites around 1910" (Lieberson 1980:141). The consequence of this shortened school year for Blacks meant that "the average Negro pupil in the South must spend 9.2 years to complete 8 elementary grades with the same amount of schooling afforded for the average White pupil in 8 years" (Wilkerson 1939:12–13). Although the systematic means through which Blacks were disadvantaged in the educational system were seen through school funding and term length, a product of de facto segregation (socially enforced everyday practices), further changes were made that created an educational system for Blacks that was significantly inferior to that provided for Whites (Donato and Hanson 2012).

Teachers of Black students were substantially less qualified than teachers of White students. Lieberson notes that, as of 1940, only 29 percent of Black teachers had at least four years of college education, compared with 53 percent of White teachers (1980:142). Thus, Black students were disadvantaged not only by the shorter length of time they spent in the classroom, but also by the lower quality of education they received due to their teachers' lack of training. Aiding this differential in teacher qualifications was the difference in teacher pay. Recall that, during the Reconstruction era, pay for teachers of Black and White children was fairly equal. However, by 1910, teachers of Black children made only 54 percent of the salary of teachers of White children (Lieberson 1980:143).

Moreover, Black schools were characterized by high student-teacher ratios, and funding for their buildings and equipment was only 20 to 25 percent of that available to White students (Lieberson 1980:145). But the greatest inequality, by far, was withholding access to a high school education from Black children. Although White high school education in the South lagged behind the North, by 1934 "the percentage of Southern White high school aged children enrolled in public schools was close to the national average." For Blacks, "their rate was only a third of the national average" (Lieberson 1980:146).

One could argue that Blacks' inadequate elementary education and supposed propensity to work due to their impoverished status provides an explanation. However, educator and advocate Doxey A. Wilkerson argues that the problem was at its root a structural one. There was an "absence of secondary schools available to Blacks." Despite the growing availability of secondary education in the United States since the late nineteenth century, it "did not begin significantly to affect Negroes in the Southern states until about 1920" (Wilkerson 1939:51). Wilkerson documented that:

> In 1930, there were still some 230 southern counties, with populations that were at least 12.5% Black, that offered no public high schools for members of this group. These counties included 160,000 Blacks of high school age. Another 195 counties in the South failed to provide four-year high schools, and this affected nearly 200,000 more Black children of high school age. Thus, 30 percent of the counties in 15 southern states failed to provide four-year high schools for Blacks in 1930. (data reported in Wilkerson 1939:40–1, cited in Lieberson 1980:146–7)

Gaining access to high school for Blacks was a feat, receiving high school work was a rarity. Sociologists W. E. B. Du Bois and Augustus Granville Dill, in *The Common School and the Negro American*, found that, despite the categorization of public schools as "high schools," the coursework offered was at the grade school level. They note that "Georgia, for instance, is credited with eleven public high schools for Negroes. As a matter of fact there is not in the whole state a single public high school for Negroes with a four years' course above the eighth grade" (1911:129).

The restriction of Black access to education was cumulative and led to compounded disadvantage that prevented Blacks from taking full advantage of their access to post-secondary education. The majority of Blacks in post-secondary institutions were taking primary and secondary school remedial courses. Lieberson concludes that, "compared with the immigrant groups in the North, literally generations of Blacks were prevented from using education as a stepping stone for upward mobility" (1980:147).

Mobility Denied: Education as a Racial Privilege

Education is widely recognized as a means to upward mobility. Slave owners were adamant that slaves should not read, because literacy was perceived as a threat to the institution of slavery. Population control in the postbellum South took the form of restricting the former slave populations' access to quality education. The purpose of classical education was preparation for good citizenship; however, Lieberson argues, this goal was incompatible with the economic and social structure of the South where Blacks were disenfranchised (1980:135). Instead, "special education" was devised for Blacks, notes sociologist Henry Allen Bullock, "that would prepare Negroes for the caste position prescribed for them by White Southerners" (Bullock 1967:89). Access to a higher-quality education by Whites during the post-Reconstruction era in the South was gained by racial privilege. It was a direct result of the disenfranchisement of Blacks, which allowed Whites to institutionalize their political power, exert their economic privilege, and confer educational advantage.

Even in the North, Landry (2000:52) notes, Blacks were "denied access to the educational establishment" and, when they were granted access, obtaining an education did not translate into mobility. In reviewing the occupational distribution of Black women in 1900, Landry finds little difference between their overrepresentation in domestic service and laundress roles in Southern versus Northern cities. He remarks: "In spite of their educational parity with the daughters of immigrant and native-born White working class families, the daughters of Black migrants were generally excluded from clerical and sales employment in all but the small Black enterprises of the growing northern ghettoes" (Landry 2000:48–9). Contrary to the classical goals of education, the express purpose of Black education was to hinder any change in the status of Blacks, in order to restrict their occupational choices to service and laboring roles that did not conflict with the scripted notions of their "proper place."

Education as Destiny: Cementing Blacks as the Problem

This system of separate and unequal schooling of Black and White students persisted until the mid 1950s when the groundbreaking *Brown* v. *Board of Education* case forced integration of all public schools. This ruling technically ended **de jure segregation**, or intentional and government-sanctioned segregation in the public school system (Donato and Hanson 2012). However, once again, as with the abolition of slavery, the ideology behind **de facto segregation**, or that not enforced by the government but socially upheld through private practices in everyday life, was not addressed (Donato and Hanson 2012). Federal troops were called in to integrate schools and protect Black students against violent White protest. Slave ownership was no longer the means of conferring White privilege, access to a quality education was.

Racial retrenchment, the process by which racial progress obtained through policy gains is challenged or undermined by individual and collective actions, could be seen throughout the 1960s and 1970s. Whites fled neighborhoods that were becoming racially integrated and integrating neighborhood schools, creating impoverished urban centers and wealthy suburbs. The end of de jure segregation and efforts to integrate all-White schools was met with much counter-resistance from White communities. For example, school desegregation in Mississippi prompted the rise of private White segregationist academies starting in 1968 in many places, including New Orleans (Andrews 2002). For White parents, their options were to move to another school district, or create their own educational institutions, and many did. This is an example of a subtle attempt to maintain the racial order and promote disinvestment in public schools, hoarding the resources for better, higher-quality schools (Andrews 2002; Lipsitz 2015).

Today, schools are segregated again by race and by class. Those

who did not have the resources to move (Blacks and other minorities) have been forced to stay in public schools despite, in some
instances, deplorable conditions (Kozol 2012). The educational
picture for Whites is mixed: some have entered private schools – in
some instances, state-funded charter schools – and there does exist
the rare integrated school district. The contemporary educational
picture is complex, shaped by a myriad of competing factors from
race to region, charters to the tax base. Yet the impact of Blacks'
historical marginalization within the educational system continues to
profoundly affect their life chances.

William Sewell (1971), in his presidential address to the American
Sociological Association, noted the importance of higher education
in conferring economic rewards and social class mobility. Moreover,
he stated that, "Those who fail to obtain this training, for whatever
reasons, will be *severely disadvantaged* in the competition for jobs and
in many other areas of social life as well" (Sewell 1971:794). Educator
Beverley Anderson, in discussing the permissive and pervasive nature
of inequality in schooling and society between Blacks and Whites,
which builds on the correlation between economic advantage, racial
privilege and schooling, notes:

> Economic exploitation theory also suggests that racial prejudice has
> been helpful in maintaining the economic privilege of White Americans.
> Racial stratification secures better education, occupation, and income
> for Whites, thereby creating a vested interest in the continued existence
> of the economic status quo. It is easier to keep Blacks and other people
> of color who are viewed as inferior in low-status, low paying jobs – and,
> consequently, keep Whites in higher-status, better-paying jobs – if the
> latter are considered more "able" by virtue of the benefits gained from
> racial privilege. (Anderson 1994:445)

Once it was ensured that Blacks did not receive an adequate education, they were effectively locked out of the mainstream job market
due to their lack of skills. While virulent racism severely limited
occupational opportunities in the South and in the North as well
(Landry 2000) prior to the Civil Rights Movement (CRM), after the
passage of the Civil Rights Act and employers' adoption of "egalitarian" labor principles, lack of qualifications became a justification that
did not require malice. The majority of Blacks were not competitive
with their White educated counterparts, effectively preventing them
from posing an economic threat. This, in turn, secured the existence
of an underclass due to the lack of employment/income options for
the advancement of Blacks. Providing Blacks with a poor-quality

"special" education hindered their upward mobility and served to prepare them for the "caste like position" ascribed to them in White society; providing a quality education for Whites served as a road to upward mobility and the means by which to maintain their advantage (Bullock 1967:89; Lieberson 1980:135).

A Critical Race Approach to Blacks in America

In *Still the Big News*, Blauner described the American racial hierarchical structure as having two extremes, "one White, and the other Black" (Blauner 2001:190). James Baldwin reasoned that "the fluidity and insecurity of the American status order required the Negro – so that White people would know where the bottom is, a fixed point in the system to which they could not sink" (Blauner 2001:29). Race as a social construction does not just simply classify and describe differences between groups, its critical function is to characterize social relationships between groups that have unequal access to power (Doane 2003). These power differentials result in a system of racial oppression on the basis of the racial hierarchy.

A major tenet of this approach is the relational nature of racial inequality, the relationship between Black oppression and White domination. Sociologists Melvin L. Oliver and Thomas M. Shapiro note that an intimate connection exists between White wealth accumulation and Black poverty, inasmuch as Blacks have had "cumulative disadvantages," and many Whites have had "cumulative advantages" (1995:5; Lipsitz 2011). Sociologist Joe Feagin further suggests that unjust enrichment of Whites happened as Blacks simultaneously experienced unjust impoverishment (Feagin 2000). Blauner concurs, noting that "White Americans enjoy special privilege in all areas of existence where racial minorities are systematically excluded or disadvantaged: housing and neighborhoods, education, income, and lifestyle" (2001:26).

Yet, in the years since the Civil Rights Movement, there has been no shortage of arguments purporting cultural inferiority as an explanation for the continued subordination of racial minorities despite the removal of formal barriers to their advancement (Glazer and Moynihan 1970). A critical race approach, however, recognizes this as a "reification of culture" in that "culture is treated as a thing unto itself, divorced from the material and social conditions in which it is anchored." Scholars who espouse this position neglect the fact that "the culture of poor and marginalized groups does not exist in

a vacuum." Often it arises as a response to the social conditions with
which they are confronted (Steinberg 1998; Liebow 2003).

For example, the 1968 Kerner Commission Report prepared
in response to the rioting in Black ghettos throughout the country
"identified 'White racism' as a prime reality of American society and
the major underlying cause of ghetto unrest" (Blauner 2001:197).
Yet, for many, that notion is absurd. Slavery was over a long time
ago. The Civil Rights Act of 1964 guaranteed Blacks equality under
the law, and the Voting Rights Act of 1965 reinstated their voting
rights. Some might say White racism can't be blamed for everything.

Motivated in part by this conundrum, Eduardo Bonilla-Silva, in
his book *Racism Without Racists*, sought to answer two questions:
"How is it possible to have such a tremendous degree of racial inequality in a society in which race is no longer relevant? And how did
Whites attempt to explain this difference?" His conceptualization of
racism as taking a new form, which he defined as colorblind racism
that allows Whites to attribute the contemporary status of Blacks to
factors other than race, is critical because it allowed him to notice
subtleties in racial speech and explanations that were not espoused
in explicitly racial terms. To illustrate, let's take one of the tenets of
"old-fashioned racism," a belief in justifiable racial discrimination
in areas such as employment and higher education (Schuman et
al. 1998). A respondent in his study was asked whether "minority
students should be provided unique opportunities to be admitted
into universities." She responded:

> I don't think that they should be provided with unique opportunities.
> I think that they should have the same opportunities as everyone else.
> You know, it's up to them to meet the standards and whatever that's
> required for entrance into universities or whatever. I don't think that
> just because they're a minority that they should, you know, not meet
> the requirements, you know. (Bonilla-Silva 2003a:31)

This response under the conceptualization of racism in its "old-
fashioned" form would have been recognized as anti-racist since it
does not espouse a belief in justifiable racial discrimination in areas
in higher education – rather, it seems committed to egalitarian ideals,
i.e. equal opportunity for both groups.

However, colorblind racist ideology engages in blaming the victim
in an indirect way. It allows Whites to appear to be committed to
equality via the assertion of egalitarian values, while simultaneously
ignoring the social reality / discrimination underlying Blacks' social
position and purporting an equal playing field. Hence, if Bonilla-Silva

had defined racism in old-fashioned terms as being evidenced by (1) a belief in racial superiority, (2) a belief in sanctioned racial segregation, and (3) a belief in justifiable racial discrimination in areas such as employment and higher education, he would have concluded that racism no longer exists and that other factors besides racism must be responsible for students' resistance to leveling the playing field for minorities in college admissions (Schuman et al. 1998).

In the article "'I am Not a Racist but . . .': Mapping White College Students' Racial Ideology in the USA," by Eduardo Bonilla-Silva and Tyrone Forman (2000), the co-authors describe how colorblind rhetoric contributes to the maintenance of a racialized social system that allows notions of "culture" rather than structure to uphold White supremacy in contemporary discourse (Hunter and Robinson 2016):

> Colorblind racism allows Whites to appear not racist ("I believe in equality"), preserve their privileged status ("Discrimination ended in the sixties!"), blame Blacks for their lower status ("If you guys just work hard!"), and criticize any institutional approach – such as affirmative action – that attempts to ameliorate racial inequality ("Reverse discrimination!"). Hence, the task of progressive social analysts is to blow the whistle on colorblind racism. We must unmask colorblind racists by showing how their views, arguments, and lifestyles are (White) color-coded. (Bonilla Silva and Forman 2000:78)

Given the power of metaphors in "shaping how we make sense of the world and what we value and privilege" (Cammett 2014), it is no wonder that, in the wake of civil rights reforms, the definition of racism itself is apparently now open to interpretation and negotiation.

Central to this negotiation is the reduction of racism from the institutional to the individual (Esposito and Murphy 2010). Institutional racism "requires legal policies of structural change, and enforcement of civil rights laws and race-conscious remedies" (Doane 2006), all of which have traditionally run counter to conservative – and, increasingly, liberal – social policy and political interests. Racism as individual behavior, however, "requires only condemnation and perhaps punishment of individual actors," with no cost to those whose broader political interests may comport with the spirit of that individual act, other than a "vague commitment to 'tolerance'" (ibid.). Further, with the role of *power* defined out of racism, it becomes possible to conceive of "reverse racism," with Whites now viewed as victims of intolerant Blacks. This inversion is central to challenges to the remedial policies that resulted from the Civil Rights Movement, including affirmative action (Doane 2006; Mayrl and Saperstein 2013), and

almost necessarily requires an understanding of racial wellbeing as
zero-sum.

A complementary pillar of this negotiation is an open embrace of
colorblindness, a principle rhetorically – and, of course, selectively
– attributed to Martin Luther King Jr. When King is invoked, it
almost complements appeals to "stop looking at race" and focus on
individual effort and merit: a defense of historical White economic
and social advantages wrapped in an acknowledgement of racial
equality. Blacks' complaints of racism or race-conscious appeals for
institutional change are then written off as "playing the race card"
or "oversensitivity." By delegitimizing the claim to pursue equality,
since American society has already ostensibly achieved it, opponents
can argue for the formal elimination of civil rights gains from the past
60 years (Cokorinos 2003).

When and how these racialized frames emerge, and the effect that
they have in shaping debates or stirring national conversations, is
no accident. During and since the enactment of the Civil Rights
Act, well-funded foundations and think-tanks have been central in
shaping public discourse on social and economic policies, both by
advancing colorblind approaches to policies, and by reframing the
concept of racism itself to include *any* racially conscious act. This
neutralizes challenges to the traditional racialized social hierarchy, by
"minimizing the extent of inequality, marginalizing claims of subordinate groups, and moving to make dominant group understandings
normative for the larger society," and, in turn, allows for the framing
of White Americans as victims of post-1960s progressive policies
(Doane 2006).

Conclusion: American Racism and the Black Community

> Nothing handed down from the past could keep race alive if we did not
> constantly reinvent and re-ritualize it to fit our terrain. If race lives on
> today, it can do so only because we continue to create and recreate it in
> our social life, continue to verify it, and thus continue to need a social
> vocabulary that will allow us to make sense, not of what our ancestors
> did then, but what we choose to do now. (Fields, 1990:118)

Resurgence of the post-racial ideal results from a failure to grapple
with the long history of American racism and how it has integrally
shaped the Black community. A majority of Whites acknowledge
that Blacks have a "tough life," but often Whites view this reality as

having little or nothing to do with them or Whiteness. The dominant perspective seems to situate racial problems in Black culture and Black communities, rather than recognizing the role of racism, discrimination, capitalism and White unearned advantages in the current state of Black American life.

Sociologists Tyrone A. Forman and Amanda E. Lewis (2015) point to rising *racial apathy*, and an insensitivity and/or indifference toward racial inequality, among most White college students. Sociologist Margaret A. Haberman (2018), in her book *White Kids: Growing Up with Privilege in a Racially Divided America*, notes the connection between this apathy and attitudes toward affirmative action. Ideals of deservingness, hard work and earning your way dominate our popular narrative. Meritocracy is the American way. This closely held core belief ignores an inconvenient truth: the extent to which the American educational system was and is rigged against Black Americans. Educational achievement has never been a product exclusively of an individual's hard work. It reflects the benefits or hardships of parents' economic and educational achievements, which were impacted by the achievements of their parents. Within two generations, we are approaching a time when Black Americans were structurally marginalized educationally by law, the impact of which reverberates today.

Racism created and maintains the Black problem. By absolving ourselves of responsibility and pointing to cultural deficiencies, we write in red on walls covered in Black blood and claim not to see. In the next chapter, we analyze how the racial frame of Blackness as culturally deficient serves to normalize racial oppression. Stereotypes and controlling images serve to create a monolithic image of Black America, obscuring the intersection of identities further marginalizing some Blacks while privileging others.

Critical Reflection Questions

1 What is the difference between *race* and *racism*?
2 Describe conventional and critical approaches to race.
3 Define the term *racialized social structure*. Using the institution of education as an example, how is racial inequality maintained?

2

Crafting the Racial Frame: Blackness and the Myth of the Monolith

with Candace S. King and Emmanuel Adero

Racialized social structures sustain Black marginality but racial frames normalize and naturalize it. **Racial frames**, or overarching common-sense beliefs that consist of racial stereotypes, ideas, narratives and actions, however, are not created and contested in a vacuum (Doane 2006). The meanings of race, and Blackness, have continuously been shaped throughout American history, in turn shaping the lived realities of Black people and their understandings of themselves. Far from being a "pluralistic process," racial politics and discourse are coupled with power, allowing dominant groups the ability to frame it and disproportionately control the means of its transmission through our society's institutions, including the media, government and education (van Dijk 1997).

Historically, for example, framing Blacks as sub-human was key to the justification of American slavery throughout the seventeenth, eighteenth and nineteenth centuries, putting the burden of proof on Blacks and abolitionists to demonstrate their humanity and the inherent immorality of slavery. The negative framing of Blacks by those in power has obviously outlived the institution of slavery, and it has been manipulated as social and political contexts have required. To best understand how and why frames have shifted, we need to unpack what frames are and how they work. **Frames** are a crucial shorthand for making sense of and navigating the great complexities in our lived realities and interactions, shaping "the mental models, through which individuals interpret social reality" (Doane 2006). Our collective understandings of ourselves, each other, our government and institutions, are shaped either subtly or overtly by the frames that drive our discourse. **Discourse**, sociologist Woody Doane argues, "is an attempt to influence both the rules of the game and others' perceptions of social reality" (Doane 2006:256). Racial frames attempt to normalize racial oppression (e.g. slavery) by making it seem "cultural" or natural to assign blame. Frames can be triggered by imagery, such as those presented in the media, and since there is no interpretation or explicit analysis, they are less likely to be seen as biased. The media as a socializing agent – often subtly – frame Blacks negatively or unsympathetically, and perpetuate **controlling images**, or stereotypes that are both pervasive and persistent which serve to justify and naturalize inequality (Collins 2000).

To illustrate, let's consider media representations of Black single mothers.

Controlling Images and the Caricature of the Black Family in Popular Media

The 1986 CBS News report, "The Vanishing Family: Crisis in Black America,"[1] opens up with a rather simple request from reporter Bill Moyers to a group of Black mothers: "Raise your hand if you're married." When none of the women raised their hand, Moyers asked once more to confirm: "None of you are married?" Tight headshots of the mothers in the room flash consecutively across the frame as they nod negatively. The not-so-distant cousin of the 1965 Moynihan Report, *The Negro Family: The Case for National Action*, which lambastes Black women for the emasculation of Black men, the Peabody-award winning documentary is as much a condemnation as it is an account of the matriarchal Black family structure during the 1980s. Aired during the peak of "The War on Drugs," this documentary contributed to the mounting propaganda attacks against Black women and men. More than this, Moyers' work was received with great support. John Corry, a reporter for the *New York Times* for 31 years, wrote in his review of the documentary: "As close to maturity as we are likely to get. It should be seen; it demands to be seen. It plunges into an enormously important, culturally unpopular topic, and examines it with intelligence and grace."[2] Corry goes even further with his praise, calling it "one of the best television reports in years, redeems television journalism."

The "intelligence" and "grace" Corry applauds is indeed palpable throughout the documentary. Moyers is unabashed in his remarks about the experiences of the single Black mothers featured, characterizing their realities as "a world turned upside down" and a "startling change in values." Not too long after the single Black mothers assure Moyers that they are not married, he puts the question a different way: "But don't you think you might need help in raising that baby, from a man?" LaDawn, one of the Black single mothers in the room, answers that her father was not in the home and, therefore, she does not consider a male figure "substantially important in the family." The scene then cuts without context to Timothy McSeed, a Black father of three children, who tells Moyers that he does not plan to be celibate despite being an unmarried dad. If his partner becomes pregnant, McSeed says, "that's on her." He goes on further: "I'm not gonna stop my pleasures 'cause of another woman." Not only a drastically damaging and reductive framing of Black families, this broadcast dramatizes stunning stereotypical portrayals of Black women like LaDawn as "welfare mothers" with an "uncontrollable sexuality" and Black men like Timothy as "irresponsible" men who are "hypersexualized." All of the Black mothers and fathers in the documentary adhere to both of these scripts to some degree, with Moyers weaving in and out of the narrative as the "objective" moral anchor for the viewers.

As chapter 1 revealed, the history of racism in America left an indelible stain on contemporary meanings of race, and current notions of Blackness in particular. Systems of oppression including slavery and Jim Crow all reinforce the idea of the monolith. The tropes highlighted in this documentary, such as the "poor, single Black mother with too many children for the state to support," or the "lackadaisical and hypersexualized Black man," are emblematic of what sociologist Patricia Hill Collins terms controlling images. They are found not only in productions like CBS' "The Vanishing Family," but also in law, politics and the broader public discourse.

Defined from Without: The Black Immigrant Experience

The denigration of Black women as mothers in poverty offers an illustration of the robust, layered ideological work that characterizes poor Black women as undeserving. However, the maintenance of racial inequality does not require that explicit and pervasive frame. Once it is established and accepted, the racial frame can be just as effective when subtly referenced. The Black immigrant experience highlights the ubiquity of the American racial frame demonstrating how race and skin color persist as obstacles to integration, limiting opportunity. In 1980, the Black immigrant population in the United States stood at 816,000. By 2016, that number rose to 4.2 million, with the majority of immigrants coming from Jamaica, Haiti, Nigeria and Ethiopia. In that same year, Black immigrants and their children comprised one-fifth of the overall Black population.[3]

Sociologists Tamotsua Shibutani and Kian M. Kwan (1965) argue that physical differences serve as status symbols because they clearly become the symbols that identify a group. The authors assert that skin color is more important to us than any other feature in the world and, when a color line develops, the fate of each individual depends on how he/she is classified. Indeed, Blauner notes that the centrality of racism is manifest in one of the key characteristics of our social structure, namely the "division based upon color," which he argues is the single most important split within the society, the body politic and the national psyche (2001:101). However, for most immigrants, it is often only when they arrive in America that race or physical features become defined as a handicap (Portes and Zhou 1993). Bonilla-Silva notes that "neither light-skinned Europeans – nor, for that matter, dark-skinned – immigrants necessarily came to this country as members of race X or race Y" (1996:472). Rather, in America they underwent a **racialization** process, during which their physical characteristics were imbued with racial significance.

> Light-skinned Europeans, after brief periods of being "not-yet White," became "White," but they did not lose their ethnic character. Their struggle for inclusion had specific implications: racial inclusion as members of the White community allowed Americanization and class mobility. On the other hand, among dark-skinned immigrants from Africa, Latin America, and the Caribbean, the struggle was to avoid classification as "Black." These immigrants challenged the reclassification of their identity for a simple reason: *In the United States "Black" signified a subordinate status in society.* (Bonilla-Silva 1996:472, emphasis added)

Sociologists Michael Omi and Howard Winant (1994) note that **racialized minorities** who are defined by and infused with racial meaning can be divided into **racialized ethnic groups** and strictly **racial groups**. For racial groups, the racial dimension is the salient marker, yet for racialized ethnic groups, ethnicity can also be a prominent feature of their identity.

Racialization for White immigrants has resulted in unearned advantages – their racial similarity enabled them to reap the benefits of the dominant position in the social structure (Bonilla-Silva 1996). In American culture, only non-White immigrants are considered "foreigners" (Tuan 1999). Because of racism, White immigrants

often have more rights and privileges (particularly access to opportunities) than most disadvantaged minorities have *ever* experienced
in this country. Sociologist Otis D. Duncan's assertion of the "vital
importance" of choosing parents of "the 'right' skin color" as a future
determinant of socioeconomic status applies equally to immigrants,
in that being of "the 'right' skin color" is of "vital importance"
(1968:108). Sociologist Joe Feagin (2000), in *Racist America*, argues
that Whites are obsessed with delineating Blackness versus Whiteness
and do not draw such distinct lines with other racialized groups such
as Asians and Latinos.

Ongoing immigration is not altering the rigid racial boundary
faced by Blacks in contemporary America. Instead, new immigrants
are being racialized into the existing racial hierarchal structure.
Philosopher George Yancey (2003) argues that the twin processes
of non-Black assimilation and Black separation reinforce the racial
divide in the US. He theorizes that we are heading toward a Black/
non-Black society wherein African Americans remain anchored
to the bottom of the racial hierarchy, because Black immigrants'
ability to become part of the mainstream society has been artificially
limited.

The definitive impact of skin color is further correlated by sociologists Ruben G. Rumbaut and Alejandro Portes (2001), who note that
the social assimilation of Haitian immigrants is limited by their skin
color. As a result, their racialization as Black affects them more than
their individual efforts or characteristics. Sociologists Verna Keith
and Cedric Herring (1991) note that background characteristics such
as parental socioeconomic status were a less consequential predic-
tor of stratification than was skin tone. The authors conclude that
discrimination still persists and it has important effects on darker-
skinned Blacks. Bonilla-Silva predicts that **shade discrimination**,
"preference for people who are light-skinned, will become a more
important factor in all kinds of social transactions" (2003b:278).

Ethnicity does not easily supplant race for Black immigrants.
In *Ethnic Identity: The Transformation of White America*, sociologist
Richard Alba (1990) discusses the decline of ethnic identity amongst
White ethnics and the corresponding rise in a **symbolic ethnicity** as
posited by sociologist Herbert Gans (1979). This form of ethnicity
is voluntary and peripheral in the lives of White ethnics, primarily
because they express their identity in ways that do not conflict with
other facets of their lives. It is defined by a shallow ethnic commitment "confined to a few ethnic symbols that do not intrude on a life
that is otherwise non-ethnic" (Alba 1990:77). The White ethnic shift

to symbolic ethnicity stands in sharp contrast to the involuntary racial identity held by contemporary racialized ethnic immigrants.

Sociologist Mary Waters (1990) notes that for non-White ethnics it is extremely difficult to "turn off" their skin color and blend into dominant White America when it is inconvenient to be a racialized minority. Thus, she notes that the fact that ethnicity is not voluntary and symbolic for non-Whites, as it is for Whites, also means that the social and political consequences are not symbolic and that who your ancestors were or what country you came from, as well as skin color, will affect your life chances. The primacy that American racism places on the maintenance of the color line is key to the continuing significance of racism in the lives of racialized immigrants with dark skin. This was especially evident in January 2017 when President Donald Trump installed a "total and complete shutdown" of Muslims traveling to the United States in an executive order. Xenophobia met Islamophobia and racism in this policy, as immigrants from Sudan, Somalia and Libya experienced discrimination from all sides while trying to enter the country. Nisrin Elamin, a doctoral student at Stanford University and 25-year resident of the United States, had a green card when she was detained in JFK International Airport after the ban. She told *ESSENCE* magazine in an interview:

> I've been in those detention rooms many times since 9/11. Anytime I enter the country, I get questioned. There's a way in which you understand that you're a Black woman and this happens all the time. But this was different. It was just very unpredictable. As the night progressed, I began to feel more and more like a criminal.[4]

Complicating the Racial Frame: Confidence in Blackness

As we see in the experience of Black immigrants, Blackness often serves as a master status marking and differentiating Blacks from non-Blacks. In American political thought and cultural productions, Blackness is presented in digestible scripts, which typically include elements of hip hop culture, poverty, incarceration, degradation and welfare, which paint Blackness not only as a monolithic experience, but also as deviant, and ultimately "other" (Collins 2000; Bogle 2001). Whether for entertainment or in an election cycle, scripts of Blackness are recycled year after year on TV screens, in magazines, in campaign ads and during political debates. The historical interplay between the framing of race and racial groups, and the framing of belonging in the American imagination, continues to situate Black actors just outside of the mainstream, presenting them as interlopers, the opposition, or a problem to be solved for the good of society.

The ubiquity of these images and their taken-for-granted associations forces all Blacks to navigate their everyday lives through a lens of deviance, no matter how incongruous the fit. Take, for example, the admonition President Barack Obama gave in a 2016 commencement speech at Howard University, a historically Black college and university in Washington, DC:

> Be confident in your Blackness. One of the great changes that's occurred in our country since I was your age is the realization there's no one way to be Black. Take it from somebody who's seen both sides of the debate about whether I'm Black enough. (Laughter.) In the past couple of months, I've had lunch with the Queen of England and hosted Kendrick Lamar in the Oval Office. There's no straitjacket, there's no constraints, there's no litmus test for authenticity.[5]

Among Blacks themselves, Black identity and its expression are shaped by a host of intersections, such as gender, ethnicity/immigrant status, class, sexuality and religion. Failure to acknowledge this heterogeneity can lead to mischaracterizations and assumptions of unity or singular perspectives where discord and disagreement abound. The **intersectionality** of identities, interdependent systems of advantage and disadvantage, further marginalizes some Blacks while privileging others. Neither group can escape the consequences of Blackness, but class, heteronormativity, citizenship, Christianity and maleness can provide a buffer that insulates and protects against oppression. This unevenness in oppression fractures the Black community but it is a defining feature of it.

As a result, there is no singular, universal definition of Blackness. In the foreword to *Black Cool: One Thousand Streams of Blackness*, historian Henry Louis Gates proclaimed that "There are 40 million Blacks in America and there are 40 million ways to be Black" (Gates 2012).

Blackness and its Intersections

Before delving into the intersecting identities of Blackness, it is important to first understand how race became the essential ingredient in making the monolith. It began with one of the first defining moments of race, Partus Sequitur Ventrem, "that which is brought forth follows the womb." Established in 1662, this legal principle ensured the perpetual bondage of enslaved Black women and men. Because of this law, any child born to an enslaved African woman inherited her status as a slave, regardless of whether the child's father was free. In this way, Black women's bodies were not only a vehicle for building the country's capital, but also a conduit for birthing and reproducing "Blackness" (Schwartz 2006; Morgan 2011). In other words, "Blackness" was defined and legalized in Black women's wombs, making it easier for race to be determined. Toward this end, both Blackness and Whiteness become relational: A child is White because they do not have a Black mother (hence they are not Black), or vice versa. By the late twentieth century, the United States Office of Management and Budget generated racial categories which divided the nation into five groups: Black; White; Asian; American Indian; or Alaskan Native, Pacific Islander or Native Hawaiian (Pascoe 1996).[6]

As demonstrated earlier in this chapter, race is both fundamental and hypervisible in monolithic perceptions and constructions of Blackness. In this way, moral degradation, poverty, crime and police brutality are a *result of*, rather than society's *response to*, Blackness. Race then becomes the primary, yet permanent, ink used to sketch and depict the monolith. In some cases, the monolith is embraced and accepted by both White and Black communities. Aspirations to ascend to Whiteness become deeply rooted in Black communities, and it manifests in romantic pursuits. Some Blacks purposely seek out lighter-skinned Blacks as life partners because of the pervasive culture that "rewards" Blacks who are "closer" to the phenotypically Eurocentric standards of beauty. In addition to a lighter skin tone, having bright-colored eyes, narrow facial features or fine hair can elevate the status of a Black person both among and outside their community (Keith and Herring 1991).

Though some Blacks may cosign efforts to meet Eurocentric conventions of beauty and lifestyles, there are certain circumstances when "acting White" creates distance and friction among Blacks. Excelling at school or talking in a "proper accent" with an advanced vocabulary are examples of "acting White." However, the origins of "acting White" did not have much to do with Whites at all. In fact, anthropologist John U. Ogbu (2004) argues that "acting White" was a "burden" during enslavement, as most Blacks were prohibited from reading, voting or any other activity that affirmed their humanity, let alone their equality with Whites. Ogbu further notes that this concept shifted after emancipation because most Blacks were required to meet such standards to gain employment and other societal benefits. In the twenty-first century, most Blacks "act White" for similar reasons, which also include maintaining their professional standing or what Ogbu argues is an internalized "linguistic hatred," or rejection of Black dialect (Ogbu 2004).

In addition to "acting White," a repudiation of particular "hallmarks of the culture" – such as lacking rhythm on the dance floor – is another example of in-group policing among Black communities. Such "deficiencies" can "take away" from one's Blackness, thus reinforcing racist stereotypes. For example, the idea that "all Black people can dance" can be traced back to reductive performances and comedic parodies of "Blackness" in minstrelsy (Williams-Witherspoon 2013). As performance artist Kimmika Williams-Witherspoon (2013) observes, such widely held conclusions demonstrate how Blacks "internalize the stereotype and mimic the myth."

Class, sexuality, ethnicity and/or disability can cause Blackness to manifest differently at any given intersection. The following sections explore how each factor shapes the varied lived experiences of Black Americans. As sociologist Kerry Ann Rockquemore (2002) writes, "racial identity construction is an experience that is thoroughly, albeit almost invisibly, gendered." With this in mind, gender is not a separate subsection within this section because it is inextricably linked with race and will be discussed throughout.

Class: Who are the Black 1 Percent?

Numerous studies have indicated that the distribution of wealth reveals a staggering racial divide, with White households having four times the wealth of Black households.[7] According to the American community survey (ACS) from 2012 to 2016, the median household income for Blacks was $39,040, the lowest compared to the averages of other races including White, Asian and Hispanic. A 2016 study from the Institute for Policy Studies reported that it would take until the year 2244 for the average Black family to amass the same amount of wealth White families have today.[8]

In a 2010 interview with *ESQUIRE* magazine, former Illinois Governor Rod Blagojevich unabashedly lamented to journalist Scott Raab:

It's such a cynical business, and most of the people in the business are full of sh** and phonies, but I was real, man – and am real. This guy, he was catapulted in on hope and change, what we *hope* the guy is.

What the f***? Everything he's saying on the teleprompter. I'm Blacker than Barack Obama. I shined shoes. I grew up in a five-room apartment. My father had a little laundromat in a Black community not far from where we lived. I saw it all growing up.[9]

Blagojevich's frame of reference for Blackness is tightly bound with poverty and struggle. The compact family apartment, working-class family business, and the humble occupation of a shoe-shiner literally and metaphorically spoke to Blagojevich's "Blackness." More – in his eyes, it was worthy to "compete" with and ultimately "triumph" over then-President Obama's "Blackness." It appears outlandish, but the idea that poverty is an innate quality of Blackness is not far-fetched. As journalist Eugene Robinson writes, "Our eyes confirm what we 'know,' and ... everybody 'knows' that Black America, on average, has hardly begun to catch up with the rest of society – and since we 'know' this, there is no reason to look more closely" (2010:93). While some Black people certainly live in poor and working-class conditions, as a result of systemic oppression, there are a number of Black people who occupy the wealthier ranks and a full range of others in-between. Let's take a deeper dive into what Robinson calls Transcendent Black America, where other experiences of Blackness emerge to counter the stereotype.

In terms of the upper class, Black people are the 1 percent of the "1 percent," a top tier of Americans who own a majority of wealth in the nation. According to Pew Research Center analysis of data from the Federal Reserve's Survey of Consumer Finances, in 2013, "the wealth of white households was 13 times the median wealth of black households."[10] This reflects a dramatic increase since 2010, when White household wealth was only eight times that of Black households. The disparity among net worth is even more striking. The top median net worth of White households in the "1 percent" is eight times more than the net worth of Black households, even though both groups tend to be older, college educated, married and operating their own businesses.[11]

Wealthy Black Americans tend to experience isolation from both non-affluent Black communities and their White affluent counterparts. This sense of isolation is experienced in two ways: loneliness and discrimination. In a *CNN Money* report, "Unstereotyped: Black 1%," Sheila Johnson, the co-founder of Black Entertainment Television, recounted experiences of racism and bias with banks who refused to lend her money for businesses. She later confessed to Tanzina Vega: "There is a loneliness that very wealthy African-Americans do feel in

their lives. When it all comes down to it, there are very few people in
that category."[12]

The relative rarity of the Black upper class results in Black
Americans who find themselves often misunderstood. This is perhaps
best illustrated in the foreword to *Our Kind of People: Inside America's
Black Upper Class* (2000), a book that paints a portrait of the Black
elite. In it, attorney and author Lawrence Otis Graham writes that
there was a great deal of controversy when the book was released
among wealthy Black people who did not want to threaten their
White and Black counterparts, and from Black people in other economic classes who felt excluded and "looked-down" upon. Graham
argues that the book troubled the stereotype of "the working-class
Black or impoverished Black" as indicative of the complete Black
experience, ultimately concluding:

> Although every racial, ethnic, and religious group in the United States
> claims to want a piece of the American dream, there is no group
> that apologizes more for its success than Black people. The cultural
> identity or integrity of a Black millionaire rap star, basketball player, or
> TV performer will never be questioned. But an equally wealthy Black
> professional with an upper-class background and a good education will
> earn the label of a "sellout" or a "Negro trying to be White." (Graham
> 2000:vii)

As Graham's conclusions unveil, cultural expectations of what it
means to be Black coerce Black elites into a position where they
must straddle their allegiances between their racialized and classed
identities. Nevertheless, a hierarchy persists even among the Black
upper class. The factors that drive wedges between members of
the Black elite are largely dependent on region. For example, in
Washington, DC, it is paramount that Black elites have an established Washingtonian legacy, a lineage that spans at least three or
four generations. One native DC physician told Graham plainly:
"You don't even count unless you're at least third or fourth generation" (Graham 2000:218). In addition, it was imperative that they
secure their place of residence in the "Black gold coast," or the upper
northwest part of the metropolitan area. Generally speaking, it was
not socially acceptable among the Black elite to own a home in a
certain part of Washington, Maryland or Virginia that was deemed
"too White."

Black elites in Atlanta were the "gold standard for [their] counterparts in other cities" (Graham 2000:321). Hailed as the "Black

Mecca," Atlanta is home to six historically Black colleges as well as H. J. Russell and Company, one of the largest Black real-estate companies in the nation. Today, cities such as Memphis, TN, and Montgomery, AL, compete with Atlanta for the top spot for Black business growth.[13] The lives of the Black elite in Atlanta were bound to social rules similar to their counterparts in DC, both being expected to have a lineage spanning at least three or four generations. The preservation of Atlanta's Auburn Avenue, or, as the 1956 edition of *Fortune* magazine put it, "the richest negro street in the world," contributed to this sense of pride.[14] The Auburn district is safeguarded as a city treasure for its history of Black affluence and civil rights. Auburn Avenue was the birthplace of Martin Luther King Jr., and home to the businesses of Alonzo Herndon, a formerly enslaved Black man who became the first Black billionaire and founded the Atlanta Life Insurance Company.

Unlike DC or Atlanta, New York City has a hybrid of Black elites. Black wealth took on a different form as a result of the ethnic diversity present in the area, which included Jamaicans, Haitians and Trinidadians (Graham 2000). In addition to medicine and law practices, Graham observed there were far more pathways to wealth, which included small businesses such as funeral homes. Black elites in Atlanta and DC embraced and sought to preserve the cultural aspects of their racialized identity, whereas Black elites in the North merged their identities with White suburban attitudes and aspirations. As Graham put it, "Be Black, but not too Black."

Sexuality and Gender: What Does It Mean to Be Black and LGBT?

A 2017 Pew Research study revealed that low-income Blacks and Latinos were more likely to identify as lesbian, gay, bisexual or transgender (LGBT) than their White counterparts.[15] According to tracking led by the Gay and Lesbian Alliance against Defamation, of LGBT characters on TV, there are currently no leading characters that identify as gay and Black on any cable or broadcast programming.[16] There are only nine supporting characters that are gay and Black, which include Rutina Wesley, who plays Tara Thornton on HBO's *True Blood*, and Marsha Thomason, who plays Diana Barrigan on USA's *White Collar*. While Black and gay experiences are less visible on screen, the deeply entrenched homophobic attitudes in Black culture are hypervisible.

Spotlight on Resistance

Case Study 2 Black Lives Matter Group Grapples with Sexuality

In Atlantic City, New Jersey, sociologist Christina Jackson conducted an ethnographic study from 2016 to 2019 in which she immersed herself in community struggles within the city to capture the narrative of residents who feel constrained by the casino and entertainment economies of the city. She joined the core team of the local chapter of the Black Lives Matter organization, which is critical of heteronormativity and possesses queer- and trans-affirming principles. This chapter facilitated monthly educational sit-ins over the course of a year about the slow and sudden violence affecting Black communities externally and internally. One month, the local chapter focused on LGBT issues within the Black community in attempts to organize and find solutions for being the "minority within the minority – and the experience of sexuality defining how safe one feels within a movement for Black lives" (Lord and Jackson 2017).

The panelists discussed how, within the Black community, there is an unwritten kind of "don't ask, don't tell policy." Panelists questioned the inclusivity of the name/statement Black Lives Matter, feeling that, many times, queer and gender-nonconforming Blacks are not considered when it is used. Travis Love, Black Aids activist and native of Atlantic City, said: "the more marginalized you are, the less space you have to feel comfortable" (Lord and Jackson 2017). Love and other panelists seek to create spaces within Black communities in which residents can address their own internalized phobias and marginalization to understand their cisgender privileges.

Daily Beast took ABC's *Blackish* to task for "indulging in casual homophobia," after one episode featured Pops, played by Laurence Fishburne, ridiculing his son Dre, played by Anthony Robinson, for stretching in a way that "looks a little gay."[17] Though these sentiments about sexuality are well documented among the Black community, it does not mean that Black lived experiences follow a universal heteronormativity. As Black feminist Audre Lorde argues in one of her pioneering essays, "There is No Hierarchy of Oppressions":

Within the lesbian community I am Black, and within the Black community I am a lesbian. Any attack against Black people is a lesbian and gay issue, because I and thousands of other Black women are part of the lesbian community. Any attack against lesbians and gays is a Black issue, because thousands of lesbians and gay men are Black. There is no hierarchy of oppression. (1983:9)

African studies scholar Tricia Rose (2004) asserts, in *Longing to Tell: Black Women Talk about Sexuality and Intimacy*, that the pillars of race, gender, class and sexual orientation yield complex and layered understandings of Black sexuality. In terms of the monolith, Rose writes that "Black women's sexual lives are pinned between the powerful uses of distorted myths about Black sexuality to fuel racist, demeaning voices about Black men and women and the sexuality myths used to maintain the subordination of women as a whole" (Rose 2004). These myths, which situate Whiteness and maleness as the core, coupled with the deep-seated notions of "sex" and reproductive organs obscure Black sexual life even further, which contributes largely to its invisibility.

In some respects, sociologist Mignon Moore (2011) subverts this social dynamic in her work *Invisible Families: Gay Identities, Relationships, and Motherhood among Black Women*. In studying how Black lesbian women construct families, Moore focuses on how Black women carve their own avenues of autonomy in spite of traditional gender expectations. She centers this study entirely around the lived experiences of Black lesbian women. In doing so, Moore achieves two objectives: (1) showcasing a new "norm" that does not anchor around a "White middle-class lesbian" or "White gay man" subject with his or her family; and (2) rectifying the misconception of a universal Black heteronormativity. As Moore shows, Black lesbian women face unique challenges that are particular to their communities, be they racial or ethnic. She does not shy away from showing how their relationships challenge the narratives of respectability upheld by Black middle-class women or the narratives of Black masculinity upheld by Black men. Whereas Black men are constantly combating the dominant sexual scripts of a predatory hypersexuality which stimulates a violent response from White men, Black men rely on their relationships with Black women to exert sexual dominance and tap into the gender role script. However, as Lex in Moore's study observes, "transgressive women [are] contesting male hegemony by pursuing [a] masculine status at the expense of heterosexual men" (Moore 2011).

Blacks who identify as LGBT are forced to use their agency to create an interconnectedness among themselves as well as in their communities. Resilience and reliance on fictive kinship is a key element of Black LGBT life (Follins, Walker and Lewis 2014; McCune 2014; Hunter, Patillo, Robinson and Taylor 2016). In "Black Placemaking: Celebration, Play and Poetry," sociologists Marcus Hunter, Mary Patillo, Zandria Robinson and Keeanga-Yamahtta Taylor discuss the urban commons of Black gays and lesbians in Chicago, or:

> places to share affinities and resources and to sustain and expand networks in an effort to thrive and survive in the city. Nightlife is a moment to party, unwind, and cope. For Black lesbians and gays in Chicago, nightlife takes on the added importance of facilitating intercommunity connections, bringing together residents of the 'sides' of Chicago and its suburbs to enable a critical mass. (Hunter et al. 2016)

Due to the exclusion Black gays and lesbians are subject to, they create their own social communities, including faith communities, for overcoming life's obstacles with their social identities (McCune 2014). They often organize social events and travel together in an effort to develop relationships and engage openly with their partners within a religious community. Yet, at the same time, Follins et al. also uncover that these same adults displayed higher levels of "internalized homonegativity," or negative attitudes toward their sexual orientation.

While Black gays and lesbians are fighting to create community, Black transwomen are fighting for acceptance and the right to exist, as violent murders have increased. In "Navigating Community Institutions: Black Transgender Women's Experiences in Schools, the Criminal Justice System, and Churches" (2014), public health scholar Louis F. Graham argued that some Black transwomen perpetuated gender dichotomies through "passing" as cis-women to gain respect and eschew social rejection from the broader society. As Jasmine, one of the study's participants, acknowledged: "Blending into society people will respect you. They may even know, but they'll respect you more because they'll say, okay, this person really isn't bothering anybody, you know what I'm sayin'. But like if you out here just looking bad and doin' this and doin' that like people probably will shun you." The "shunning" Jasmine could be referring to is not only in social settings. Black transgender and gender nonconforming individuals experience high levels of discrimination in employment. A 2011 study, "Injustice at Every Turn: A Report of the National Transgender Discrimination Survey," found that the unemployment rate for Black transgender people was twice the rate of the overall transgender sample and four times the rate of the overall population.[18] In that same study, it was also reported that 34 percent of Black transgender individuals experience extreme poverty and had an annual household income that totaled less than $10,000 – specifically, four times the extreme poverty experienced by the general Black population and eight times that experienced by the US population in general. As these data and other studies have revealed, Black transgender people experience double jeopardy resulting from their racial and gender identity, both of which are perceived as deviant.

Blacks across the sexuality spectrum (transgender and LGBT) can face double and triple forms of oppression. Above all, however, Blackness was paramount and at the forefront of their lived experiences. Pam, a 22-year-old Afro-Latina from New York, in *Longing to Tell* said she did not want to date a White partner because of the challenges of racism. In the same breath, however, she admits: "I think we're all racist. I haven't tried very hard to work on my racism towards White people. I think I have a thing for light-skinned women. I probably do, due to the fact that I think they're prettier because they're light. That's internalized racism" (Rose 2004).

Though she rejects the idea of a White partner as a means of denouncing racism, Pam's romantic preferences nevertheless depict a deep-rooted investment in Whiteness. As sociologist Evelyn Nakano Glenn argues, in *Shades of Difference: Why Skin Color Matters*, "Color, like race, situates peoples along the path of history: more white is more European, and more European is more refined; less European is more primitive, and more primitive is more dark" (Glenn 2009:5).

Ethnicity: One Race, Many Cultural Expressions

Black complexity extends beyond class position and sexuality to the very conception of Blackness, creating in-group and out-group dynamics along ethnic lines as individuals throughout the African diaspora come to understand and become situated within American conceptions of Blackness. In an interview with Jstor Daily's Hope Reese, award-winning author and MacArthur "genius" Fellow Chimamanda Ngozi Adichie spoke candidly about her "coming to America" experience.[19] A native Nigerian, she spoke at length about encountering "Blackness" in America and her journey to embracing it:

First of all, I wasn't Black until I came to America. I became Black
in America. Growing up in Nigeria, I didn't think about race because
I didn't need to think about race. Nigeria is a country with many
problems and many identity divisions, but those identity divisions
are mainly religion and ethnicity. So my identity growing up was
Christian, Catholic, and Igbo. And sometimes I felt Nigerian in sort of
a healthy way, especially when Nigeria was playing in the World Cup.
Then I would think about my nationality as a Nigerian. But, when I
came to the U.S., it just changed. I think that America, and obviously
because of its history, it's the one country where, in some ways, identity is forced on you, because you have to check a box. You have to be
something. And, I came here and very quickly realized to Americans
I was just Black. And for a little while, I resisted it, because it didn't
take me very long when I came here to realize how many negative
stereotypes were attached to Blackness.... Looking back, especially my
first year in the U.S., my insistence on being Nigerian, or even African,
was in many ways my way of avoiding Blackness. It's also my acknowledgement of American racism – which is to say that if Blackness were
benign, I would not have been running away from it. And so it took
a decision on my part to learn more. I started, on my own, reading
African-American history. Because I wanted to understand. It was
reading about post-slavery and post-reconstruction, Jim Crow, that
really opened my eyes and made me understand what was going on,
and what it meant.

Adichie's revelations are in fact the subject of common dinner-
table conversations in Black immigrant households. In *Becoming
Black: Creating Identity in the African Diaspora*, African American
studies scholar Michelle M. Wright (2003) posits these tensions as
a "negotiation of two extremes." At one end of the rope is what she
terms the "hypercollective, essentialist identity," and at the other is
the "hyperindividual identity" (Wright 2003). The hypercollective
identity is perhaps best illustrated in Adichie's resistance to the
notion of Blackness when she arrived in the United States. There are
two layers to the "Blackness" Adichie discusses, which encapsulate
the "essentialist" identity: Black as an identity based on race, and
further (even deeper) Blackness as inherently deviant (the negative
stereotypes). Wright writes that hyperindividual identity "grants a
wholly individualized (and somewhat fragmented) self in exchange
for the annihilation of 'Blackness' as a collective term" (Wright
2003:2). Adichie's "hyperindividual" identity is Nigerian, but it is
also influenced by her religious affiliations and her upbringing as an
Igbo woman. As Adichie observed, in America, these aspects of her
identity were later eclipsed by her "Blackness." Her early desires to

discard the label of "Blackness" reveal her staunch commitment to maintaining a "hyperindividual" identity.

Like Adichie, most Black immigrants in America soon concede to the reality that their racial identity will often trump their ethnic identity within the broader society. However, there are certain circumstances in which their ethnic identities have been reimagined to instigate further fracture among Blacks. In "Black Immigrants in the United States and the 'Cultural Narratives' of Ethnicity," anthropologist Jemima Pierre (2004) revisits representations of African American and Black immigrant communities to point out the discursive trends which favor the "ethnic and cultural distinctiveness" of Black/African migrant communities. Perceptions of Black inferiority are repackaged to reaffirm colorblind attitudes and renounce the existence of racism. Moreover, Pierre argues that the negative stereotypes of American-born Blacks are hyperbolized to underscore and commend the cultural value systems of Black immigrants. In doing so, these narratives employ a "model-minority" framework to create and maintain a hierarchy among Black nationalities. These beliefs not only exist in media and scholarship, but, as Pierre later notes, also are embraced by many Black immigrants as well.

Some Black immigrants not only reject the label of "Black," but also believe that many American-born Blacks are "responsible" for their "demise." Pierre found that, while they were willing to admit that racism exists, Black immigrants believed African Americans could combat these circumstances through moral uplift. At the same time, Black immigrants are often ridiculed for their failure to assimilate and cultural degeneracy. Derogatory monikers such as "African booty scratcher" and taunts of "smelling like (insert spice name)" become routine for Black immigrants in schools and places of business (Austin 2004; Boutwell 2015; Imoagene 2015). From the classroom to the workplace, these stereotypes traveled all the way to the Oval Office. In early 2018, Donald Trump referred to Haiti and other African countries as "shithole" countries in a closed meeting about the visa lottery system.[20]

Unlike African/Black immigrants, whose racialization is often conflated with that of native Blacks, the racialization of Afro-Latinos in America is slightly more complex. Individuals who identify as Afro-Latino/a acknowledge their Hispanic and African ancestry. The Pew Research Center conducted a study and observed their patterns of reporting race. The 2016 study found that Afro-Latinos were twice as likely to report their race as "White" than as "Black."[21] In that same study, only 9 percent reported their race as "mixed." These results speak to the discrepancies in the census as well as the crucial role colorism plays in identity.

For Afro-Latinos with darker skin, their Blackness is hypervisible. Dana Danelys de los Santos, better known by her stage name, "Amara La Negra" (Love the Black woman), is a breakout star of the television show *Love and Hip Hop Miami*. The Miami-born musician reopened this debate when she was confronted by a producer for her "Afro." De los Santos is of Dominican descent and she is dark-skinned. After her appearance on the show, some of the cast members and the viewers questioned whether a person could be "Afro-Latino" at all. She spoke about this duality with NPR in an interview: "You're too negra. You're too Black to be Latina. Or you're too Latina to be Black. Or your hair is too nappy. You know, you need to be more petite, more skinny, more slim, long legs. It's your accent. It's everything." [22] Americans were not the only ones who were contemplating this identity. In 2015, the Mexican Census Bureau included an option for Mexicans to identify as "Afro-Mexican." The results showed that nearly 1.4 million Mexicans identified as Black. Mexicans in the United States reclaimed this identity, coining a term of their own: "Blaxican." An Instagram page, Blaxicans of LA, is committed to telling the stories of local women and men who embrace their Black and Latino heritage. One respondent tells her story of being Black and Mexican as a "mystery":

I'm an LA girl through and through. But it's been a mystery that I haven't solved. Because growing up not only did I have a Black mom and Mexican father, but I was also the only deaf person in my family and I've absorbed less of the cultures because of that. I'm left with filling the gaps and asking: What does it mean to be a Black woman? What does it mean to be Latina? And I still find it hard to fit in. And as a deaf person, I have to go above and beyond what is meant for us. Deaf and mute is the common phrase for us and people think we're dumb. I've had to work harder and prove that I am valuable by existing. But there's no sides. And I'm also still learning how to be Mexican because the only grandparent that's alive is my Mexican grandma. Everyone else has died. She's the only one who speaks Spanish but that's a barrier because I have a hard time reading English lips and now, Spanish? But most of the time I guess right. [23]

For this respondent, her Blackness was challenged by not only her Latino heritage, but also her language and disability.

Disability: The Impermissible Vulnerability of Blackness

Many people recognize Harriet Tubman for her courage and fearless dedication to liberating enslaved Black women and men, but few are aware that she suffered from epilepsy as a result of a beating from her master. Fannie Lou Hamer's declaration that she was "sick and tired of being sick and tired" was literal as well as metaphorical. Hamer was blind in one eye, and suffered from kidney damage. The celebrated author Maya Angelou is admired for her poems that moved a nation. Most are aware of the sexual abuse she endured as a child that caused her not to speak for almost five years. Her period of being mute is known as "selective mutism," a disorder stemming from severe anxiety.[24] Tubman, Hamer and Angelou were prominent Black women who also suffered from a disability that was often dismissed altogether in media and scholarship.[25] Though the intersection of Blackness and disability is largely undertheorized, there are a number of Blacks who live within these margins.

From cognitive to physical or mental, there are different kinds of disabilities that require varying accommodations in daily life. The Center for Disease Control and Prevention (CDC) defines disability as "any condition of the body or mind (impairment) that makes it more difficult for the person with the condition to do certain activities (activity limitation) and interact with the world around them (participation restrictions)."[26] According to data from the CDC in 2017, one in four Black people have a disability. The report also found that more than 40 percent of Black people with a disability are obese.[27] As this chapter has discussed, Black people are subjected to a number of negative stereotypes that make outlandish presumptions about their character and vast generalizations about an entire race of people. These stereotypes serve to bolster White supremacy while also reaffirming that Black people are not "human," but "superhuman." Adam Waytz and colleagues (2015) examined White perceptions of Blacks and detected an implicit "superhumanization bias," which included superior athletic abilities as well as mental and physical strength. These characteristics are not to be conflated with talent or resilience. In contrast, Waytz and colleagues argue in their study, this bias was a "subtle" form of dehumanization. Since Black people are not "human," then that means they do not feel pain. Therefore, they are not in need of care and, more tragically, their stories remain largely untold. As a people, they retain a state of "impermissible vulnerability."

Blacks with a disability tend to have the most (in)visibility within the education system, where it coincides with negative biases about Black intellectual capabilities. Disability scholar Amy J. Petersen's (2009) study of four Black women living with disabilities and navigating the education system provides crucial insights. One of the study's participants, Keisha, is a sociology student with attention deficit hyperactivity disorder (ADHD) and an anxiety disorder. Keisha says she faced a lot of resistance from her professors, who refused to grant her accommodations. Like most Blacks – even those without disabilities – Keisha felt she had to be twice as good:

> I was constantly working to prove everyone wrong. I knew my professors were not only unwilling to accommodate me, but they believed I shouldn't even be in their class. So I had to work twice as hard as the White girl sitting next to me. I had to prove myself deserving of even being in their class. I had to prove that I was smart! (Petersen 2009:434)

In Keisha's case, having a disability did not ease the pressures of academic performance, but instead increased them. Yet, for Keisha, the source of the discrimination is at times unclear. She tells Petersen: "If it's not my race, it is other things, like being a woman, or my disability. . . . It's as if they [professors and peers] are intent on keeping me guessing. If I don't know, exactly, then I can't counter whatever they think they may know about me" (2009:435). Keisha's experience is perhaps why many scholars have begun to conceptualize "Blackness" itself as a disability. In "The 'Other' Side of the Dialectic: Toward a Materialist Ethic of Care," cultural studies scholar Nirmala Erevelles argues that disability is not a matter of deviant difference, but rather a materialist manifestation of transnational capitalism that produces disability as a lack. Biology's role in this regard is inconsequential. To further assert this point, she writes: "if social problems were assumed to have their roots in human biology, then it is only natural that social policy be inspired by clinical knowledge to seek solutions to these problems" (Erevelles 2011).

Legal scholar Kimani Paul-Emile (2018) advances these ideas and further contends that Blackness should be recognized in disability law. To be clear, Paul-Emile is not suggesting that Blackness in and of itself is a biological disability, however she is acknowledging the racial undertones in policies and practices that disproportionately target Blacks.

Conclusion: The Black Community Pulling Apart

In this chapter, we have examined the rich diversity that is Black America. While they are often simplistically framed and certainly misunderstood, Blacks in America are absolutely not a monolithic group. In fact, *Washington Post* columnist and MSNBC analyst Eugene Robinson (2010) argues in *Disintegration: The Splintering of Black America* that, over decades of desegregation, affirmative action and immigration, the concept of a singular Black America is no more. He identifies four distinct Black Americas: Mainstream, Abandoned, Transcendent and Emergent. Each type cuts across rather deep cultural, political and economic lines. Robinson's four "Black Americas" yield crucial insights about Blackness which deviate from the aforementioned mass-produced monolithic scripts. First, he hones in economically with an exploration of the Black middle class, which he conceptualizes as the "Mainstream." For Robinson, this group not only is "invisible" to American consciousness, but also lives in a duality. Although they have advanced financially and amassed a catalogue of professional achievements, there is still "a nagging sense of being looked down upon, of being judged, of being disrespected" (Robinson 2010:81). From separate church congregations to exclusive gated communities and unequal education opportunities, these are some of the "de facto" aspects of middle-class American life that plague the Black mainstream experience. This reality, Robinson observes, compels middle-class Black Americans to isolate themselves, seeking "safety, acceptance, and solidarity in numbers" (Robinson 2010:81).

It is important to emphasize that the social mores in the Black Mainstream deviate from conventional White middle-class standards. For example, Robinson notes that it is common and socially acceptable to have a matriarchal familial structure. Contrary to the narrative of the "welfare queen" discussed earlier in this chapter, Black women in the Mainstream have charted their own paths of fulfillment in womanhood and motherhood. They are not in a constant pursuit to find a life partner, and, if they have children, they are content raising them on their own. In fact, Robinson points out, many accomplished Black women play crucial roles in establishing fictive kinship ties, as they take on the children of relatives who cannot afford to care for them, or even adopt children of their own (Robinson 2010).

Like the Mainstream, Blacks in the Abandoned tier, who are of lower economic status, are also "invisible." Whereas Mainstream

Blacks are invisible because of America's palpable discomfort with Blackness being regarded as a universal experience, Robinson further argues that Abandoned Blacks are invisible because they are forgotten altogether. They have been pushed out of neighborhoods, out of businesses, and, more tragically, out of society's psyche. To locate Abandoned Blacks, according to Robinson, requires venturing into the depths of downtown cities and "shabby little pockets of the inner suburbs, where refugees from gentrification have found precarious sanctuary" (Robinson 2010:124).

Robinson insists that the plight of Abandoned Blacks is predetermined in poor Black women's wombs. A combination of the disparities in prenatal care and the exposure to drugs and alcohol during pregnancy give poor Black children a false-start – not to mention that poor Black children have an increased likelihood of being obese or having diabetes, compared to White children. Robinson points out that these factors perpetuate a pernicious life cycle for poor Blacks. To church leaders and policymakers who admonish Black women for their reproductive choices and offer unsolicited recommendations for marriage, Robinson retorts: "'Too bad your father's not around' is not a policy prescription; it's a cruel taunt directed at children who are already being victimized by forces beyond their control" (Robinson 2010:133).

After exploring the intricacies of Mainstream and Abandoned Black America, Robinson enters elite Black America, or the Transcendent. In what he deems a palpable and vital "direct consequence of the successes of the 1960s – civil rights, desegregation, affirmative action, Black political empowerment" – Transcendent Blacks possess wealth and a level of power that affords them an incredible slice of influence (Robinson 2010:148). The Transcendent tier is a composite of Blacks who once existed in Mainstream, but managed (read: strived) to surpass the hard-pressed gates of middle-classdom. Not only is this a national trend, but, as Robinson observes, it is global.

There is a schism between Transcendent Blacks who lived during Jim Crow and Transcendent Blacks who did not. Having experienced firsthand what it means to be "left out," Robinson notes that many Transcendents can become either paralyzed or motivated. Blacks who managed to break free from lower economic circumstances in search of better horizons are fully aware of the harsh realities of race. For some, this triumph steels their resolve to assist more Mainstream and even Abandoned Blacks to achieve such status. Therefore, Robinson remarks that Transcendents who lived during Jim Crow "cling" to their experiences. In some ways, this posture reaffirms their Blackness despite claims that they are not "Black enough" due to their elevated economic standing.

Transcendents who did not live during Jim Crow have knowledge of that period, but they still feel as if they have something to prove. Robinson observes that the post-Jim Crow generation of Transcendents want to assert themselves on their own terms, separate from the Transcendents who grew up during Jim Crow. As Robinson puts it, they feel "new strategies and tactics are required for a new era" (Robinson 2010:160). Nevertheless, whether they lived during Jim Crow or not, Robinson indicates that, like Mainstream Blacks, Transcendents never truly feel like "insiders." They have a hard time reconciling what it means to no longer be on the "outside" financially. Despite the figure in their bank accounts, the name on their second or third degree, or the property in their name, they are "imposters" within their own class.

Robinson concludes in a two-part section about Emergent Black America, where he accounts for ethnic difference, particularly in communities of Black immigrants and individuals of mixed-race (Black and White) heritage. In this portion of the book, Robinson demonstrates the elasticity of race and class. A prime example Robinson provides is the overrepresentation of Black Emergents (children of African/Black immigrants) in certain affirmative-action initiatives. Though all Black students are academically disadvantaged in schools, Robinson indicated that poor African/Black immigrants received more assistance. Class played a huge role in how this dynamic played out. Many native Blacks came from Mainstream-level or affluent backgrounds, whereas most Emergent Blacks came from low-income households. He later acknowledges, "It would not make sense to offer help to the Black daughter of a corporate vice president, but withhold it from the Black son of two parking-lot attendants, no matter where their parents or grandparents were born" (Robinson 2010:169). In other words, in these instances, class comes into focus.

Cultural values and upbringing also played a significant role in student performance. Robinson references a 2009 study conducted by sociologists Pamela Bennett and Amy Lutz, which reported that children of African/Black immigrants were more likely to attend private secondary education institutions and come from two-parent households. Each factor individually gives Blacks a higher chance of admission into an elite college (Bennett and Lutz 2009; Robinson 2010). Moreover, their parents were more likely to be educated, having studied law or medicine in their native country. If they were working odd jobs in America, they were probably working up to something better. Having a household of two educated, working parents set the tone of stability for their children.

America may include more than these four "Black Americas"; this concept, however, provides a useful shorthand to review emerging distinctions among Black Americans that are obscured by the monolithic frame. The challenge to the simplistic view of Blackness lies not in the quantity of "Black Americas," but in the driving forces that create them. As this chapter demonstrates, efforts to capture one universal definition of Blackness yield futile and inconclusive results. However, one detail remains certain: Black people will always remain the architects of their identities and destinies, evolving in spite of mainstream tropes that attempt to define and confine them.

While the Black community is increasingly seeking internal coherence, in the next chapter we explore one defining commonality – the historical and contemporary devaluation of Black life – that necessitates resistance in pursuit of full inclusion within American culture and society.

Critical Reflection Questions

1 What are *controlling images* and how have they been used against Black Americans?
2 Can Black immigrants pursue symbolic ethnicity? Why, or why not?
3 What does a monolithic view of Black identity obscure?

3
Whose Life Matters? Value and Disdain in American Society

The slogan Black Lives Matter has been a powerful reminder of the structural violence against Black Americans. Unsettling to some Americans, it would seem obvious to state that Black lives indeed mattered. The rebuttal may sound something like this: "All lives matter, despite a few tragedies, horrible misunderstandings between police and Black men/women. We can agree that all lives matter not just Black lives." This point of view is not uncommon. It is a point of discussion in many dining rooms, college classrooms and, especially, police stations. Perhaps a simpler question is: Whose life has mattered historically? *For whom has America signaled value and/or tolerated disdain?* In the historical frame, most would agree Blacks were not valued, but many would argue any issues today are an aberration on a road of racial equality. To make the issue less Black and White, let's first examine a seemingly less charged issue – medical care.

"First, Do No Harm": Eugenics, Medicine and Devaluing Black Life

The devaluation of Blacks in the US is exemplified in the historical treatment of Black bodies. As the twentieth century dawned, so did a fledgling eugenics movement in the US, a movement aimed at mitigating societal ills (crime, poverty and immoral acts like promiscuity) through selective breeding. Foundational to eugenics is the supposition that the aforementioned ills are genetic in nature, and can be bred in or out of a population in the same way that eye or hair color can (McDaniel 1996). In practice, eugenics has promoted births from the most "fit" groups (Whites, in the Western context), and the suppression or elimination of births from "unfit" groups (in the US, Blacks) (McDaniel 1996). Leading US figures, including President Theodore Roosevelt, warned that, unless White families did their patriotic duty and bore children at rates sufficient to outpace non-Whites, the US would lose its distinctly American culture. Numerous states enacted policies allowing state or local governments the discretion to surgically sterilize any resident who was deemed unfit to reproduce, with these policies predictably targeting Black populations. The Supreme Court upheld the constitutionality of these policies in the 1927 *Buck* v. *Bell* decision, thus Black bodies – current and future – were now at the mercy of local and state officials, with supposed moral infractions often being sufficient grounds for sterilization.[1]

The early twentieth century also saw the emergence of the birth control movement, with pioneer and Planned Parenthood founder Margaret Sanger initially framing contraception as a means of women's control over their own fertility, and, for poor women, a means of controlling the size of their families. There was initially great opposition to birth control among early twentieth-century conservatives, and Sanger often found herself the target of federal obscenity laws. Whether calculated or not, Sanger was able to neutralize much of conservatives' antipathy toward her birth-control programs when she allied herself with the aforementioned eugenics movement. While her presentation of birth control to Black populations was ostensibly aimed at financial security through family planning, the wider discourse framed birth control as a means of controlling Black women's fertility, whether its use was voluntary or compulsory (Davis 1981; McDaniel 1996; Roberts 1997).

As the twentieth century continued, so did these efforts to control Black women's fertility. The massive assault on Black women's bodies has been described as the "New Jane Crow" to highlight the lack of discourse and historical trajectory of the oppression of Black women in particular (Jones and Seabrook 2017). There were many reasons for sterilizations, including population control as connected to stereotypes of Black motherhood, US welfare discourse, as well as practice for medical students at local universities (Thomas 1998).[2] US doctors routinely refused to deliver the babies of Black women and Medicaid recipients who had already borne two or more children unless they consented to sterilization, whereas, under a concurrent practice, White and middle-class mothers who had not had "enough" children by a given age were *refused* sterilization (Davis 1981).[3]

Black women only received legal protection from coercive sterilization after the fallout resulting from the notorious 1973 sterilization of Minnie Lee Relf, a 14-year-old Black girl in Mississippi who was first administered Depo Provera, and was subsequently surgically sterilized, after social workers noticed that boys were hanging around her house and feared Minnie might become pregnant while her family received benefits (Dorr 2011). Because these procedures – which Relf and her impoverished and illiterate parents were not fully informed of – had been paid for with federal funds, President Nixon hurriedly banned the use of such funds for the sterilization of minors, and the informed consent guidelines that we consider standard today were established. While Blacks' intrinsic worth as citizens was denied, their utility as subjects in medical experimentation has long been exploited. Yet, for Black Americans, protection has not historically applied, and they have been subject to extensive unethical treatment within the medical industry. There are some notorious examples.

The Tuskegee Study of Untreated Syphilis in the Negro Male, or the Tuskegee Experiment as it is commonly known, began in 1932. The US Public Health Service recruited 662 poor rural Black sharecroppers in Macon County, Alabama, for the benefit of exploring the untreated course of syphilis, which at the time was referred to as "bad blood" (Brandt 1978; Brown 2017). Black sharecroppers were recruited under the guise that they would receive treatment for "bad blood" and free healthcare if they consented to the study; instead, they received only placebos as their condition worsened. To the medical establishment, they were expendable; as of 1955, it was recorded that 30 percent of the participants had died (Brandt 1978). When penicillin was made available as an option for treating syphilis, it was denied to participants in the study (Brandt 1978). This study shockingly went on until 1972 and spanned the Jim Crow period into the Civil Rights Movement.

Around 18 years after the start of the Tuskegee Experiment, Johns Hopkins University used the cells of Henrietta Lacks, a Black rural tobacco farmer from Virginia, to create the polio vaccine, making advancements in disease research that led to the expansion of the biomedical industry (Skloot 2010). Henrietta Lacks' human cell line, referred to as HELA, was the world's first immortal cell line to live indefinitely outside of the body and it is now bought and sold to laboratories across the nation. Cells from the cancerous tumor within her cervix were cut out months before she died from cervical cancer in 1951, without her knowledge or consent (Skloot 2010). As a Black woman, Lacks' cells were looked at as remarkable and prolific, but consent was not considered necessary for their exploitation.

In short, Black bodies and their body parts were repeatedly used indiscriminately to find cures for diseases and vaccinations, which led to the success of the biomedical industry (McDaniel 1996; Thomas and Jackson 2019). Just as in slavery, when denying Blacks full humanity enabled their harsh and brutal treatment, racism justified this intentional harm of Black life. Blacks were viewed as expendable, explicitly devalued and deemed not worthy of being consulted for consent, informed of risk, and more. While value and disdain are subjective, the treatment of Black patients is an objective indicator of the value placed on Black life. Doctors and related professionals reflect the society in which they live and, despite the oath to not do harm, did so intentionally and lied about it. Deep suspicion still characterizes the engagement of Blacks with the medical establishment today.

The universality of Black devaluation and subjugation gave rise to resistance. Blacks have never been complicit in their marginalization. Black resistance has a long history, from slavery to the present, that rejects racism and the broad disdain for Black life in American society. Resistance has always had a necessary relationship with oppressed groups and, in particular, Black Americans, because they have represented the bottom of the racial caste system globally. "Faces at the bottom of the well" have always found ways to revolt and claim their humanity despite the effect of America's institutions enforcing a second-class status (Bell 1992).

The remainder of this chapter traces the history of Black resistance and radicalism from slavery, to the Black Freedom movement, to Black Lives Matter, highlighting the prominent role that the political system, the criminal justice system and the church have had in influencing their organization and strategy.

Understanding Black Resistance

The killing and devaluation of Black life and humanity remain part of the social fabric of America and have taken different forms depending on the decade. Despite the organizing attempts and advances made climbing America's social ladder, particularly after the 1960s gains, the public imaginary of Blackness and its embodiment remains the same: that of a problem (Ioanide 2015). Just as there are many ways to be "Black," Black people have devised many ways to resist. Black movements have essentially attempted to redefine the problem – with mixed success – not as Blackness, but as inequality that subjugates

Black people. Resistance has historically attempted to work within the system, create new systems, use micro and macro forms of protest, assert and reassert humanity and Black value, and/or call attention to systematic racism in America. Movements have had different asks, from large to small, large being illustrated in more revolutionary social movements, while others may focus on smaller or more place-specific concerns.

Several national and local movements have demanded change or reform from American institutions that produced inequalities and second-class citizenship status (Dennis 2016). Some movements have sought the total restructuring of American society, i.e. abolition of slavery and the fight for civil rights. Some movements have asked for better conditions, justice for a particular form of inequality within a case or event, more representation, different kinds of power or a radically different relationship to American institutions, e.g. police. The growth of White counter-resistance to Black movements illustrates the transformative potential of resistance efforts by drawing attention to injustice, institutional oppression and racism. As a result, Black resistance has been met with legislation, violence, surveillance, criminalization, dismissal and distortion, often framed as inappropriate and/or excessive (Dennis 2016).

Although our contemporary frame of reference for Black resistance is of large-scale, collective movements, we must expand our scope. Prior to the official beginning of the Abolition Movement, in the 1830s, which aimed to abolish slavery and eradicate the transatlantic slave trade, slaves resisted daily through individual and collective efforts (Dennis 2016). As Dorothy Roberts explains in *Killing the Black Body: Race, Representation and the Meaning of Liberty*, slaves banded together to maintain their health and wellbeing, replacing the two-parent household with a larger kinship network that could withstand the sudden departure of any single member at a slave owner's whim (1997). At times, resistance came in the form of slaves having abortions or killing their own children in order for them not to be born into a life of slavery. It was one way of ensuring the non-exploitation of their loved ones (Davis 1981).

In "Oppression, Freedom and the Education of Frederick Douglass," social scientist Brian Warnick notes that the effect of slavery is not just seen in the physical confinement of Black bodies but also in the "pedagogical tactics" used to keep the minds of slaves oppressed (2008). The *Narrative of the Life of Frederick Douglass* illustrates these tactics, which were intended to "1) decrease the slaves' confidence in their abilities to act freely, 2) deny the skills of painful literacy, 3) rob the slaves of liberating silence, 4) increase slaves' sense of 'gratitude,' and 5) dismantle any relationships of family and community" (Warnick 2008). Hence, our understanding of resistance should be broadened to consider any actions that countered these slave owners' tactics. Within their confinement, slaves used a variety of different methods to resist, including building community, learning to read, singing spirituals, launching rebellions and plotting escapes.

In 1831, in Southampton County, Virginia, Nat Turner, a 31-year-old Black slave, led one of the largest slave rebellions and uprisings in American history. In August of that year, he and five other slaves set out early in the morning to kill their owners, the Travis family, and then proceeded to move from house to house killing White inhabitants. The rebellion grew to more than 40 slaves, and 55 Whites were killed in total. Years later, in 1849, the iconic Harriet Tubman from Maryland led the Underground Railroad, leading around 70 slaves 90 miles north to freedom in Pennsylvania. In 1863, Tubman led the Union Army in a surprise attack, known as the Combahee River raid, rescuing more than 750 slaves in South Carolina (Taylor 2017). This raid later gave rise to the formation of the Black feminist organization called the Combahee River Collective in 1974 (Taylor 2017).

Slave spirituals utilized Christianity as a tool to resist. Spirituals, which were mainly used as a way to communicate with other slaves and promote endurance and strength, sent a clear message of restlessness and resistance (Warnick 2008). Slaves used songs to claim their humanity and view their lives beyond the present servitude, exploitation and inhumanity. Songs were also used to send messages about covert actions to other slaves (Warnick 2008). When we think of mainstream resistance, we think of protests and sit-ins. Both are important examples of Black resistance and organizing, but what is often left out are the daily forms of resistance by oppressed or subordinated groups that are often hidden from view (Camp 2004).

This is problematic because it sets a standard for what "resistance" must look like. Depending on the situation, context and positionality of Black people, resistance has manifested in different ways. In his book *Domination and the Art of Resistance*, James Scott discusses lower-profile forms of resistance that have been used by the oppressed and the enslaved to protest against their subjugation (Scott 1990; Ransby 2003; Camp 2004). He coined the term *infrapolitics* to describe these forms of resistance, including an individual's gaze, speeches and gestures that take place off-stage during interactions and situations in which power is being negotiated (Scott 1990). Slaves used subversive forms of resistance every day, Scott argues, as they challenged oppression in less overt, or even hidden, ways, including breaking or misplacing tools and learning how to read (Scott 1990).

Blacks had to possess a "fighting spirit" that couldn't always be expressed in overt ways. Their actions, both overt and subtle, were part of a large reservoir of resistance needed to help galvanize collective action over a long period of time (Ransby 2003). Slavery officially ended in 1865 with the end of the Civil War, but the need for resistance did not. Instead, the target and the means of resistance grew.

Resistance at the Ballot Box: Pursuing the Party of Equality

Black political engagement not only predated the end of slavery, but was a significant driver of the abolitionist movement. The post-war extension of citizenship and political rights to Blacks – and the 15th Amendment's guarantee of Blacks' right to vote – ushered in a brief era of vigorous engagement with the political system. This engagement included not only the first time that Black citizens sought widespread involvement in selecting representatives, but, in the South, the region of the country with the most significant Black population, it also led to the first widespread election of Blacks to local and state offices.[4] This made the South the most diverse and progressive political region in the history of the country, before or since.

In the years immediately after the Civil War, Black Americans had every reason to enthusiastically support the Republican Party. Republican reforms ostensibly ended slavery in the United States, and the party was the first to allow Blacks to run for office (Hoffman 2015). In contrast, Democrats in the South resisted post-war reforms and impeded Blacks' full incorporation into US society. Both political parties put equality on the back burner in the 1870s, and conservative Democrats launched a vigorous campaign of pushback, introducing extralegal and – often dubiously – legal measures of selective regulation and intimidation to bypass the 15th Amendment and keep Blacks from voting.

Hence, despite being guaranteed the right to vote by the 15th Amendment in 1869, Black Americans have only briefly enjoyed full and unimpeded enfranchisement, facing obstacles to voting throughout the entirety of the twentieth century. Post-reconstruction, numerous measures were enacted at polling places, largely in the South, to limit Blacks' voting without the outright appearance of singling them out by their race. These measures included poll taxes, complicated literacy tests[5] and Grandfather clauses, each of which theoretically applied to White voters as well, but understandably – and quite intentionally – disproportionately affected Black voters with limited income or education, or whose own grandfathers had not voted. And when these measures were insufficient, outright extralegal force – such as intimidation by the Ku Klux Klan (KKK) and death at the hands of lynch mobs – were employed (Rodriguez, Geronimus, Bound and Doring 2015).

The presidency of Franklin Delano Roosevelt, from 1933 to 1945, marked the beginning of the electoral shift among Blacks. In addition to the promise of New Deal policies and proposals, Roosevelt's nomination of Harold Ickes – a Republican and proponent of civil rights – as Secretary of the Interior, signaled that he himself was far more committed to civil rights than previous Democrats had been. As a result, Roosevelt would receive 71 percent of the Black vote in 1936 (Hoffman 2015). Blacks continued to vote Democratic in overwhelming numbers throughout the mid twentieth century, while remaining open to whoever had the inclination and capacity to address their concerns (McFayden 2013). Indeed, Dwight Eisenhower's avowed commitment to enforcing the civil rights laws that preceded him garnered him 39 percent of the Black vote, though he would be the last – to date – Republican nominee to receive that level of support.

The Black Freedom Movement and the Civil Rights Movement

Black political engagement is an act of agency and resistance, a means to shape society through voting for candidates who plan to pursue equity. Due to the political marginalization of the Black vote, more public and disruptive acts of resistance were needed to draw attention to the plight of the Black community. During the early Civil Rights Movement, while Blacks were still governed by Jim Crow, there was a series of events that garnered national attention, projecting the often-hidden plight of Blacks in the South to the world, and drawing attention to the fight for civil rights.

Most Americans have been taught about the 1955 incident of Rosa Parks not giving up her seat to a White man on a city bus in Montgomery, Alabama; this was the most successful of the challenges by the National Association for the Advancement of Colored People (NAACP) to bus segregation in the state. Prior to that, there were other individuals and groups that resisted and challenged Jim Crow legislation. In 1943, before the Montgomery Bus Boycott, civil rights activist Ella Baker, while adhering to Jim Crow law regarding the separation of dining services on trains, was *still* hassled because she was too close to Whites who were eating at the time. On more than one occasion, Ella Baker sat in the designated "colored" section to eat. In the first incident, White soldiers were sitting in the colored section and she asked them to move over into the Whites-only section. The soldiers did move, but the steward as well as others claimed that Baker's behavior was "insulting and abusive" (Ransby 2003). In this case, there was not a confrontation.

Weeks later, in the second incident, Baker again sat in the colored-only dining section, but the curtain between the colored and Whites section was not down. Baker was asked to leave until the Whites were finished eating, and declined (Ransby 2003). The steward then called two White military policemen traveling on the train to remove her from the dining car. Baker claimed that, while they were forcibly removing her, they snatched her up by her arm and bruised her leg in two places (Ransby 2003). These individual moments of resistance were significant in creating change, and both Parks and Baker should be honored as heroines, but it is important to note that much was done before these moments to build collective relationships and organize protest (Hunter 2015). Individual acts took place within the context of a large system of intentional organizing and organizational networks which served as collective resistance to propel the personal into the political.

In Ella Baker's biography, historian Barbara Ransby describes the period from the turn of the twentieth century, during segregation, into and beyond the Civil Rights Movement as the Black Freedom Movement, a time in which Blacks collectively fought to obtain full civil rights (Ransby 2003). In *Freedom is a Constant Struggle: Ferguson, Palestine and the Foundations of a Movement*, Angela Davis said the goal of the Civil Rights Movement was to eradicate racism legally and to abolish the legal system of segregation; yet racism was not eradicated completely (Davis 2016). The abolishment of legal segregation did aid in slowly integrating America's institutions, including the government and the education system. Official integration brought about small increases in the number of Blacks in higher education and governmental positions, but also battles for White protection appealing to the Constitution. In this sense, the actions of the state prompted social movement action – resistance and counter-resistance (Tilly 1978; McAdam 1982; Andrews 2002).

On the national scale, the growth of the Black Freedom Movement and the Civil Rights Movement was solidified through the Civil Rights Act of 1964 signed by Lyndon B. Johnson and initiated by John F. Kennedy before his death in 1968. There were many factions included in the Black Freedom Movement, including left/progressive and more militant/nationalist strategies for ensuring civil and human rights for Black people. The 1960s gave birth to many movements – in particular, the women's movement, the anti-war (Vietnam) movement and the gay rights movement. Given the intersectionality of Black people, the Civil Rights Movement was an umbrella for many movements, and many involved in it were active in other movements as well.

Brought to the forefront first by the Combahee River Collective was the centering of Black women's voices that gave rise to the Black feminist movement, which acted as an alternative both to the National Black Feminist Organization and the National Women's Movement (Taylor 2017). Founded by Barbara Smith, Beverly Smith and Demita Frazier, the Combahee River Collective brought identity politics and the interlocking oppression of Black women to the forefront (Taylor 2017). White feminist organizations were too limited in their conceptualization of the feminist political agenda and lacked the nuance Black women embodied of being othered for not only their gender, but also their race (Taylor 2017). Black women advocated new entry points to the conceptualization of the relationship between identity, oppression and movement organizing, as exemplified within Black feminist theory (Taylor 2017).

Despite the role grassroots groups played in the Civil Rights Movement, large civil rights organizations such as the NAACP, the Student Nonviolent Coordinating Committee (SNCC), the Black Panther Party (BPP) and The Nation of Islam received much of the national press coverage. The NAACP is one of the longest-standing civil rights organizations for Blacks in the United States, and was founded by W. E. B. Du Bois, Ida B. Wells, Mary White Ovington, Archibald Grimke and Mary Church Terrell in 1909, with goals of ensuring civil rights for the racially oppressed and abolishing racial discrimination. Not long after, in the 1930s, the Nation of Islam, a Black Nationalist religious organization, was founded by Elijah Mohammed. Malcolm X would become their spokesman. In 1954, the Reverend Dr. Martin Luther King Jr., rose as a symbol and leader of the Civil Rights Movement, leading the Montgomery Bus Boycott as the first President of the Southern Christian Leadership Conference (SCLC).

During this time, public awareness around local struggles came together with the national cause for civil rights, not based solely on protests and marches, but also due to its connection to the personal transformation of Blacks. This transformation is evident in Ella Baker's understanding of the purpose of resistance: to her the protest for radical change was more of a means to an end rather than having a single end. Her understanding characterizes the long trajectory of Black resistance in America, and Barbara Ransby describes it in her biography: "Ella Baker understood that laws, structures, and institutions had to change in order to correct injustice and oppression, but part of the process had to involve oppressed people, ordinary people, infusing new meanings into the concept of democracy and finding their own individual and collective power to determine their lives and shape the direction of history" (2003:1). Radical change was turning everyday Black citizens into freedom fighters, making the personal political, ensuring their protection under the Constitution of the United States. Baker and others advocated for the continued tradition of Black people being the makers of their own fates and creating and sustaining organizations to cultivate Black agency and mobilize resistance.

Racializing Religion, Piety and Resistance

Religion, particularly Christianity, heavily influenced Black political thought and Black protest against the racially restrictive status quo, even when religion and politics may otherwise have appeared incompatible (Blum 2011). Jesus, as a symbol and a person, serves as a counterpoint to anti-Black racism, historian Edward J. Blum argues, even while Christianity was used by some Whites to justify that racism. Abolitionists used religion in their moral assault on the institution of slavery, and, a century later, Martin Luther King Jr.'s Southern Christian Leadership Conference was able to find much cross-racial sympathy and support by emphasizing the relevance of Jesus' principles to civil rights.

Black political and social resistance has also been fueled by religion. Introduced by Wallace Fard Mohammed and popularized by Elijah Mohammed and Malcolm X, the doctrines of the Nation of Islam provided Blacks with a form of separatism that was both religiously based and distinctly Black, allowing adherents to reject Christianity, the "religion of those who enslaved and discriminated against them," without compromising the centrality of religion to the lives of many

Black families. The lifestyle proposed by this particular brand of Islam was one that also rejected mainstream American – namely White – society, calling instead for the creation and maintenance of Blacks' own cultural, economic and political institutions, similar to Marcus Garvey's early twentieth-century movement.

Due to these disparate models, many conservatives see Black religion as synonymous with Black resistance, and even fueling anti-White racism. The rhetorical tying of President Obama to his former Reverend, Jeremiah Wright, served the same purpose as the accusations that Obama is a Muslim: Wright's doctrine is critical of America's perpetuation of inequality, and traditional Islam is widely misunderstood as being antithetical to America itself. While Obama is unlikely to be both radical Christian *and* Muslim, either would make him an enemy of the narrowly defined American tradition.

Social and political minorities' agenda cannot achieve mainstream legitimacy until they are accepted by those in the majority, and until the majority – in part or in whole – no longer sees them as a threat (Davis 2016). Religion was key to the cross-racial coalitions that helped fuel the Civil Rights Movement. The brand of Christianity that King espoused was similar to the Protestantism that abounded in the mid twentieth century, and the values he derived from it, non-violent and peaceful methods of resistance, were palatable to White moderates and liberals (Burden-Stelly 2018).

The Rise of Black Radicalism

In the 1960s, a much-needed wave of Black student activism heavily influenced the Civil Rights Movement. On February 1, 1960, four Black college students sat down at a Whites-only lunch counter at Woolworth's in Greensboro, North Carolina, and refused to move. After a few days, the restaurant finally served the college students, but this ignited a series of sit-ins across the country, and within several months these demonstrations had spread to more than 100 cities (Ransby 2003). This sit-in was the driving force behind the creation of the SNCC, founded by Stokely Carmichael, now known as Kwame Ture. From there, young Black college students used their power to put their bodies on the front lines with more sit-ins to challenge the caste-like system of segregation in North Carolina, South Carolina, Virginia and Tennessee. Students attending historically Black colleges and universities, such as Hampton University, Shaw University, Fisk University and North Carolina A&T State

University, to name a few, participated actively. Sit-ins gave rise to forms of resistance that were unlike those that had previously taken place in the Civil Rights Movement due to their militant and confrontational style.

As the movement for civil rights gave way to Black radicalism and Afrocentrism, Blacks in the latter movements enjoyed less support and collaboration from White institutions, resulting in an often intentional insularity. However, post-civil rights Black activism was oriented toward addressing and ameliorating institutionalized racism, as opposed to solely seeking integration as the key means of advancement. A combination of that racism and Blacks' own reluctance to assimilate into the system that perpetuated that racism has historically complicated Blacks' path to inclusion (Davis 2016).

To this end, many Black post-civil rights groups sought only those coalitions in which Blacks could be accepted as equal to Whites, and in which their interests were politically and economically similar (Ture and Hamilton 1992). They resisted, in part, the default presumption that Black interests were identical to those of liberal, labor or reform groups, and viewed appeals to conscience as insufficient to sustain coalitions. In the 1960s and 1970s, when groups weren't entirely aligned in their experiences of inequity, either in terms of social class or intersectionally, as in the case of White and Black feminists, coalitions failed.

The BPP was considered one of the most antiracist and confrontational Black radical organizations, but, according to Barbara Ransby, the BPP didn't "invent the confrontational tactics they embraced; rather they inherited and reconfigured them" (2003:216). Confrontation has often been a part of Black resiliency. Founded in 1966 in Oakland, California, the BPP must be understood within the context from which it emerged. The organization was founded by Huey P. Newton and Bobby Seale as a way to end police brutality, and they organized neighborhood patrols to accomplish this goal. As a group, they believed in self-defense and the right to bear arms, often in direct opposition to Martin Luther King Jr.'s philosophies of nonviolence.

The public conception of the BPP is divorced from the myriad of ways in which this organization took care of the Black community. The BPP began a free breakfast program, while they were vilified in the media for their approach.[6] Not only did the BPP serve free breakfast, but it was part of their Ten Point Program in which they called for "land, bread, housing, education, clothing, justice and peace,"[7] creating opportunities for health clinics and legal services, among other efforts to improve Black life. Ideals of resiliency were used to promote the liberation of the Black community in urban spaces.

Much BPP activism centered on freeing political prisoners as well as fighting for humanity and better conditions within prisons. Prison activists including George Jackson founded the Black Guerrilla Family inside prison walls, mixing both Marxist and Maoist political thought. Jackson and the "Soledad brothers" were charged with the killing of a White prison guard in 1970. In 1971, Jackson tried to escape the San Quentin prison but was shot and killed. Renowned civil rights and human rights activist Angela Davis, an ally of the BPP, was said to have helped Jackson's attempted escape. She was charged with murder for allegedly helping with an escape that resulted in the death of a prison guard, and spent 18 months in jail. Two weeks after Jackson's death, one of the largest prison uprisings, known as the Attica prison rebellion, involving over 1,000 inmates, occurred at a correctional facility in Attica, New York.[8] Prisoners were angered by poor conditions in the prison and racial mistreatment of prisoners, and by Jackson's death.

Police brutality has always been a major source of organizing in the Black community – it was one of the founding issues of the BPP. Resistance to police brutality did not just begin with the contemporary Black Lives Matter movement. In his 2014 article "Between the World and Ferguson," journalist Jelani Cobb relates the social context of Richard Wright's poem entitled "Between the World and Me" to the shooting of Michael Brown in Ferguson, Missouri. He complicates the notion of terrorism, claiming that, in this view, Black Americans have never felt safe on their own soil due to state violence (Cobb 2014). One of the most extreme examples of state violence against Blacks was the bombing of the MOVE organization.

In 1972, a year after the death of George Jackson and 346 miles away in Philadelphia, Pennsylvania, John Africa started a movement family of Black revolutionaries that promoted the connections between life, self-government, the environment and liberation not only of animals but of those oppressed under the American system. Liberation, in the eyes of MOVE family members, also included freedom from police abuse and violence. The history of state violence against MOVE is primarily based around two incidents. On August 8, 1978, in the Powelton Village section of West Philadelphia, there was a police-led attack on the MOVE family that left one police officer, James J. Ramp, dead, and nine MOVE members in jail for life. MOVE family members claim that the shot did not come from their home, and yet all were convicted of third-degree murder.[9] After

39 years in prison, one member, Debbie Africa, was recently released in July, 2018; she is the first political prisoner of the MOVE 9 to be freed, while one died in prison.[10]

Years later, on May 13, 1985, MOVE had their second confrontation with the Philadelphia Police Department on the 6200 block of Osage Avenue, but this time it was deadlier. Under the tenure of Philadelphia's first Black Mayor, Wilson Goode, the police shot 10,000 rounds into the MOVE compound and used a Pennsylvania State Police helicopter to drop high-powered C4 explosives onto the roof of the house.[11] The bombing killed 11 people in the house – 6 children and 5 adults – damaged 65 homes, and left 250 people homeless. This incident remains the worst fire in Philadelphia history and one of the most egregious acts of state violence in recorded history.

The Era of Black Lives Matter

The extreme use of force that characterized MOVE encounters with police will seem for many an aberration, a failure of restraint by the state. Yet, for others, especially poor Black Americans who live in a near-constant state of police surveillance, the fear of an encounter is familiar, as is the absence of restraint.[12] A 2017 study, by public health scholar James Buehler found that Black men were nearly three times as likely to be killed by police using force as White men were. Social psychologist Jack Glaser, author of *Suspect Race: Causes and Consequences of Racial Profiling* (2015), argues that stereotyping and racial bias lead to these discriminatory outcomes. In many ways, the oppression and subjugation of Blacks remains unchanged. Michelle Alexander, author of *The New Jim Crow: Mass Incarceration in the Age of Colorblindness*, argued publicly that "we have not ended racial caste in America; we have merely redesigned it" (2010:2). Not only have the structures of Jim Crow been redesigned, sociologist Eduardo Bonilla-Silva would argue, they have been replaced by a *new racism*, complete with subtle and institutional practices that seek to oppress and subjugate within a period characterized as post-racial (Bonilla-Silva 2015). Movements like Black Lives Matter are particularly vocal in their disdain for this *new racism* by pushing for more overt discussions of racial justice issues whose manifestations have become subtler.

Black Lives Matter started in 2013 through a Twitter hashtag created by Opal Tometi, Patrisse Cullors and Alicia Garza after the acquittal of 27-year-old George Zimmerman, who shot Trayvon Martin, a 17-year-old Black youth in Sanford, Florida. Today, The Black Lives Matter Global network (BLM) is a chapter-based, member-led organization with chapters in major cities that uses social media to spur direct action protests around the nation, which have taken on both national and local issues of anti-Black violence, police brutality and racial oppression. BLM may have been prompted by the inhumanity of the increasing number of African American lives lost at the hands of the police, but to Keeanga-Yamahtta Taylor, BLM has "created a feeling of pride and combativeness among a generation that this country has tried to kill, imprison and simply disappear" (2016:190). It is a movement that seeks to validate and bring to the forefront, yet again, the inhumanity of anti-Black racism that is evident worldwide.

The national visibility and sense of urgency of the movement were triggered by three culminating events. The February 26, 2012 civilian shooting of Trayvon Martin in Sanford, Florida; the July 17, 2014 police chokehold-induced death of Eric Garner in Staten Island, NY; and the August 9, 2014 police shooting of 18-year-old Michael Brown in Ferguson, Missouri. These seemingly disparate events galvanized the Black community nationwide. After Michael Brown's death, a Freedom Ride was organized and more than 500 Black protesters converged on Ferguson, Missouri. Other protests sprang up in major cities across the nation. During 2014 and into 2015, shootings of other African Americans by law enforcement and vigilantes gained national and international coverage – due in part to the Black Lives Matter movement – including Los Angeles' 25-year-old Ezell Ford; Dearborn Heights, Michigan's 19-year-old Renisha McBride; Cleveland's 12-year-old Tamir Rice; Beavercreek, Ohio's 22-year-old John Crawford III; Waller County, Texas' 28-year-old Sandra Bland; Baltimore's 25-year-old Freddie Gray; and countless others.

Most of the outrage in these cases was driven by the perception that their untimely deaths resulted from the targeting and disparate treatment of young Black people who were seen as a threat, but, secondarily, the lack of prosecution and preponderance of acquittals of police officers and vigilantes who shot and killed them. In 2015, two years after the conception of Black Lives Matter, a new subsection of the movement was formed, called "Say Her Name," which focused on the Black female victims of both anti-Black violence and police brutality that largely went unnoticed by mainstream media (Taylor 2016). This movement resurrected the interlocking oppressions and intersectionality focus of the Combahee River Collective as a lens to understand violence against Black women through the combination of other identity markers such as class, race or sexuality (Taylor 2017). These intersectional movements brought accompanying and other marginal experiences to center stage, including the lives of Black queer and trans people who are doubly and triply oppressed and targeted by structural violence (Hill II 2017; Taylor 2017).

Spotlight on Resistance

Case Study 3 Defining Black Lives Matter Locally in Atlantic City

Local Black Lives Matter chapters operate to galvanize residents and neighborhoods to contribute to national initiatives, but also to educate and organize around issues that affect their community every day. In Atlantic City, the residents articulated several local concerns: affordable city living in a casino economy, the impending official state takeover of the city usurping local power, and the privatization of their water system, among other concerns. Residents felt that Black, Brown and poor communities were disproportionately affected by these realities.

Community residents find chapter membership empowering. It serves as a tool to build awareness and a common language for local concerns. For example, one member described it as "A way to let local residents know that Black lives *do* matter [despite] built in racism [in our justice system] . . . it is a way for local residents to come together and try to figure out how to do better at taking back the issues of Black Americans and [grow] an awareness to everybody of the issues facing Black Americans" (Interview 3, November 19, 2016). Monthly forums encourage regular attendance of residents across Atlantic City and the surrounding Atlantic County, which are increasingly distinct from one another. Atlantic City is urban, largely composed of people of color alongside tourists, whereas the surrounding Atlantic County, with the exception of a few towns, is mostly White and suburban. One member said:

It's about building a community beyond Atlantic City. . . .. It's helped me come out of my shell and bubble, so that gives the chance to really have a sense of what is happening. I still don't know enough, but I know more now than I did before. The awareness building is important. We don't have the police tensions as much as other cities, but the racial tensions in the county are unique. The county and city are so segregated . . . The ability to be able to build connections across segregated communities is the benefit to me and [to] reduce ignorance (Interview 9, November 19, 2016)

Another member valued that the chapter intentionally brought people together across differences including color, sexuality, religion and gender expression. Local Black Lives Matter chapters also have the potential to build place-specific language to point to oppressive structures and policies in their own backyard. One member said: "It's setting a base for people to come together to learn about common issues and to learn so that there begins to be a common language when you talk about issues of race and gender, that people begin to have a way to talk about those things" (Interview 10, November 19, 2016). Collective language, pre-established relationships and empowerment of local residents to identify issues of concern to them intergenerationally are important to building a sustainable movement (Hunter 2015).

Although the Atlantic City BLM chapter struggled to attract youth and teens, a few did participate. Older residents remarked on how powerful and empowering it was to hear young people talk about how race impacted their daily lives. The chapter provided a platform to bring together younger and older segments of the community to discuss issues that more mature members struggled with in the past and that younger residents continue to struggle with today. One member said, "there is a level of trust that is there to lay the groundwork to begin that work" (Interview 10, November 19, 2016). Three years after the eruption of the Black Lives Matter global network, local chapter gatherings in Atlantic City, New Jersey, continue to allow members to come together, get to know one another and build trust, which is foundational to movement growth.

As a movement, Black Lives Matter is not about feelings and tears. It aims to be a public intervention into a system that centralizes Whiteness. It makes statements about how our nation's institutions value Whiteness and the consequences of this in our legal system, education system and political system. The aim is to disrupt what we know, challenging America's sense of right and wrong. Du Bois' now century-old proclamation that the problem of the twentieth century is the problem of the color line, rings true to the Black Lives Matter agenda in the twenty-first century. The problem of Blacks as the "Other" remains. Black Lives Matter is about more than individual Black, White or Brown faces – it is an alert to the fact that we all participate in a system that devalues Blackness and Black bodies on American soil, and across the world.

The Black Lives Matter Global network is often compared to the Civil Rights Movement, considered an "updated" version, but this really minimizes both movements, due to their differences in context and impetus. It is true that both movements and those existing during the 1970s, 1980s and 1990s, were always fighting for the recognition of Black humanity and equality worldwide. While the fight for fuller equality, and the eradication of second-class citizenship and structural violence may be similar, BLM also has more explicit desires to be non-hierarchal, gender/queer/trans-affirming, not heteronormative, and connected to the international community looking at anti-Blackness structurally beyond the American frame. Official chapters have a revolving leadership and Black-led structure to each official core team. Movement principles include:

- Every day, we recommit to *healing ourselves* and each other, and to co-creating alongside comrades, allies, and family a culture where each person feels seen, heard, and supported.
- We acknowledge, respect, and celebrate *differences* and commonalities.
- We work vigorously for freedom and justice for Black people and, by extension, all people.
- We intentionally build and nurture a beloved community that is bonded together through a beautiful struggle that is *restorative*, not depleting.
- We are unapologetically Black in our positioning. In affirming that Black Lives Matter, we need not qualify our position. To love and desire freedom and justice for ourselves is a prerequisite for wanting the same for others.
- We see ourselves as part of the *global Black family*, and we are aware of the different ways we are impacted or privileged as Black people who exist in different parts of the world.
- We are guided by the fact that *all* Black lives matter, regardless of actual or perceived sexual identity, gender identity, gender expression, economic status, ability, disability, religious beliefs or disbeliefs, immigration status, or location.
- We make space for transgender brothers and sisters to participate and lead.
- We are self-reflexive and do the work required to *dismantle cisgender privilege* and uplift Black trans folk, especially Black trans

women who continue to be disproportionately impacted by trans-antagonistic violence.
- We build a space that affirms Black women and is free from sexism, misogyny, and environments in which men are centered.
- We practice empathy. We engage comrades with the intent to learn about and connect with their contexts.
- We make our spaces *family-friendly* and enable parents to fully participate with their children. We dismantle the patriarchal practice that requires mothers to work "double shifts" so that they can mother in private even as they participate in public justice work.
- We disrupt the Western-prescribed *nuclear family structure* requirement by supporting each other as extended families and "villages" that collectively care for one another, especially our children, to the degree that mothers, parents, and children are comfortable.
- We foster a *queer-affirming network*. When we gather, we do so with the intention of freeing ourselves from the tight grip of heteronormative thinking, or rather, the belief that all in the world are heterosexual (unless s/he or they disclose otherwise).
- We cultivate an *intergenerational and communal network* free from ageism. We believe that all people, regardless of age, show up with the capacity to lead and learn.
- We embody and practice justice, liberation, and peace in our engagements with one another.

As a network, Black Lives Matter attempts to reform patriarchy, family structure and the silencing of queer and trans Black people. Celebrating difference for BLM is about creating a platform to acknowledge the intersectionality of Black lives, while promoting healing and restoration in the process, given the historical legacy of American racism and inequality.

Black Lives Matter, Pan-African movements and aspects of the Black Freedom Movement have sought to make broader connections with Africans, beyond America, building a broader global identity. Black internationalists centralize the global structure of racism and oppression enforced by power, violence and militarism, enabled often by histories of colonization (Umoren 2018). This transnational focus is not new; leaders within the American Civil Rights Movement and the South African anti-apartheid movement engaged and supported one another. As the acclaimed book *Winning Our Freedoms Together: African Americans & Apartheid, 1945–1960* documents, they saw their fates as linked. In both instances, Black activism was focused on the role of the state in perpetuating racial politics and suppressing Black resistance (Grant 2017).

Recently, Angela Davis and Mark Lamont Hill have been modern-day Black voices who draw connections between Black Lives Matter and other domestic/international movements, such as the Boycott, Divestment, Sanctions Movement (BDS) for Palestinian rights. Davis and Hill have both made direct connections between rather than comparisons of the global system of racial oppression identified by the BLM Global network and the use of force to occupy territories in both Black and Palestinian communities (Davis 2016; Scott 2017). The prison and military-industrial complex supports this larger system of oppression and keeps the most racially and economically vulnerable as its target (Davis 2016). To Davis, Black struggle includes gender struggles, immigrant struggles, and the fight against homophobia as well, and is related to the Black radical tradition of how race and capitalism work together to create a larger apparatus for oppression (Davis 2016).

Conclusion: The Media and the Future of Black Resistance

One of the largest differences between the Black Lives Matter movement and historical movements of Black resistance is the role of the media and technology, not only in capturing misconduct, but in permitting the wide sharing of it in the Twitter universe. Twitter has emerged as a new source of sociological study for learning about our social world, especially among Black youth (Carney 2016; Cox 2017). The ability to share and reshare pictures and videos with honest short captions within minutes has transformed the way our society disseminates information. Twitter has provided a new forum for sharing information and news, enabling the original poster to frame their reading of the item, if they choose, with a choice of hashtags. It has surfaced as a new form of social and political engagement that is attractive to youth and middle-aged adults.

According to the Pew Research Center, the #Blacklivesmatter hashtag has been used on Twitter 13.3 million times between 2013 (the first publicized shooting) and 2018.[13] During and after controversial shootings or other related events, Twitter saw increased use of #Blacklivesmatter hashtags, showing engagement among Americans to spread information around injustice. Since the explosion of BLM, we have seen the growth of Black Twitter as well as a response to it, with hashtags including #bluelivesmatter or #alllivesmatter. In particular, the creation of #Blacktwitter has surfaced as a way for young Black Americans to participate in adding to Black Digital Commons (Hunter and Robinson 2016). It has provided a platform for young

African Americans to share information and frame it in a way that relates to their experiences and perspectives on topics beyond police brutality to broadly being Black in America (Hunter and Robinson 2016).[14] According to Pew, African Americans use Twitter at a higher rate than other racial and ethnic groups, and 30 percent of all Twitter users are between the ages of 18 and 29. Black Twitter has served as a platform to connect young Black people across the nation.

Black Twitter has also become a way, like local BLM chapters, to provide place-based language to frame issues happening in the cities and neighborhoods of young Black residents. In "Black Placemaking," sociologists Marcus Anthony Hunter and Zandria Robinson, in particular, describe Black Chicago as being an epicenter of Black Twitter in 2013. From Drake and Cayton's systematic analysis of Black Chicago (1945), to today as it is now discursively described through Black youth tales of sexual harassment, its murder rate and ongoing police brutality, Black Chicago remains central to national Black life.

Blacks in Chicago tweeted about rhythm-and-blues singer R. Kelly and how he preys on young girls, in ways that reflected honesty and realism from those who could be potential victims. In another instance, residents framed Chicago's murder rate and the prevalence of police brutality in their own voices using the hashtags #savechicago or #wechargegenocide (Hunter and Robinson 2016). Twitter has enabled these Black voices to be heard, providing a platform to frame the importance of these issues to their community on their own terms for a national and international audience.

In the next chapter, we will take a closer look at Chicago, underscoring how Black urban spaces were purposefully created through policies and attitudes that sought to keep the Black problem spatially contained.

Critical Reflection Questions

1 What does the medical treatment of the Black body suggest about the value of Black life?
2 What are *infrapolitics* and why were they an important form of resistance during slavery?
3 How does the Black Lives Matter movement compare to the Civil Rights Movement? What has changed or persisted with time?

4
Staying Inside the Red Line: Housing Segregation and the Rise of the Ghetto

In *Killing the Black Body: Race, Representation and the Meaning of Liberty*, legal scholar Dorothy Roberts reminds us of the connection between eugenics and the segregation of urban neighborhoods dating back to the influence of Thomas Jefferson, who insisted biological racial inferiority made Blacks incapable of being independent, making rational decisions or having the self-control needed for self-governance (Roberts 1997). Segregation as a national policy was introduced as a *fix*, to isolate the deviant from the pure, in areas such as housing, marriage and economic development, and was accompanied by other national policies that upheld its principle (Roberts 1997).

The systematic and intentional creation of Black urban spaces in the United States through governmental policy, racism and racial attitudes reflected the desire to separate the deviant and problem-ridden from the pure, through the creation of White-only spaces (Lipsitz 2011). Blackness and Black people were the *problem* in need of physical containment. Foundational to early urban policies, and arguably still true today, is the idea that people who have problems are, in fact, the problem, and the dilapidated places they inhabit reflect and reaffirm that fact. In this vein, the Black poor in urban spaces are viewed as being responsible for their living conditions (Du Bois 1898; Zuberi 2004; Lipsitz 2011). This circular thinking informs policy and is an American cultural product in itself, framing "rational" contemporary theories around urban redevelopment, gentrification and the "cosmopolitan" thinly disguised whitening processes used today to displace Blacks in neighborhoods and public spaces (Hill 1998; Anderson 2011).

Segregation and the displacement of the poor from recently revalued "blighted" neighborhoods contribute to their racialization as

deviant. These processes also contribute to the socialization of targeted residents in urban neighborhoods, making visible the racialized
and classed processes that drive the renewal of urban spaces. This
raises questions for existing Black residents about who has the power
to define their neighborhood, and for whom? The answers to these
questions are self-evident to many existing residents in gentrifying
spaces, as their neighborhoods change. They understand that new
investment and businesses are not catering to them, but to an incoming middle-class, and often largely White, population.

   While the invisible yet sticky red lines defining suitable boundaries
for Black people and enforcing their containment no longer exist, the
remnants of this past linger. In order to make the invisible visible,
we need to understand better how urban Black communities were
formed.

Urban Black Settlement Patterns and the Negro Problem

Most Northern Black communities were created by migration from
the South to the North, and this shift changed the landscape of the
city dramatically (Massey and Denton 1993). The urban North was
imagined by many Southern Blacks to be the Promised Land – or one
that was free from racism (Scott 2018). Lottie Scott in her autobi-
ography, *Deep South, Deep North: A Family's Journey*, describes how
she learned very quickly that the North was not the Promised Land.
Scott talks about her experience of moving from South Carolina to
Norwich, Connecticut, and her preconceived thoughts.

> [I thought] there was an opportunity for jobs and that there was no
> racism. I believed that people were free to eat and work where they
> chose, and I was ready to enjoy the freedoms and equality of living
> in the North. It was not long before I discovered I had not arrived at
> the Promised Land. Norwich was not a place free from prejudice and
> discrimination. The Westside was where newly arrived Blacks lived. It
> was hard for Blacks to find housing outside of the Westside. Attempts
> to move to other areas were met with resistance. When you showed up
> to see an apartment, you were told it was taken, while Whites who came
> later were told it was still available. (Scott 2018: 174)

Ms. Scott learned very quickly that racism did in fact exist in the
North and was not vastly different from that in the South. She learned
that the Westside was the place where Black people lived and there
were few places they could live outside of that. She learned that the

development and sustainability of Black urban neighborhoods were underhanded, hidden and subtler than in the South, but very much still alive in shaping boundaries and borders with adjacent White neighborhoods. Urban Black settlement patterns were created by a mix of both overt institutional practices that enforced isolation and segregation of Blacks, and racial attitudes, which reflected the fears and stigmas around what Blackness and Black people represented. The result was agreement on, and singular pursuit of, Black containment.

Generally ignored from a typical urban sociology course unless you are lucky, W. E. B. Du Bois' 1899 study *The Philadelphia Negro* was iconic in being the first non-racist study of the urban Black population. Coming from Great Barrington, Massachusetts, Du Bois earned two Bachelors' degrees, from Fisk University and Harvard University; studied at the University of Berlin; and eventually became the first African American to earn a Ph.D. from Harvard University (Morris 2017). Du Bois paved the way for an emerging approach of conducting mixed-method social scientific research on non-White populations that did not rest on the racist ideas of those who lived behind a veil or on the receiving side of the color line (Morris 2017). Du Bois promoted community engagement through ethnographic methods before it became trendy in sociology, by advocating against what others referred to as "arm chair" sociology, but he described as "car window sociology." To him, at the heart of "car window" sociology is the tendency of sociologists to make inferences on urban populations without ever becoming part of them and talking to urban residents themselves (Morris 2017).

Setting the stage for *The Philadelphia Negro*, Du Bois put forth the idea, in his 1898 article "The Study of Negro Problems" in the *Annals of the American Academy of Political and Social Science*, that Negroes are not the problem although they do face a complex nexus of problems brought about by racial oppression, similar to other groups in the same condition (Du Bois 1898; Zuberi 2004). Du Bois' *Philadelphia Negro* was a study of racialized social patterns, settlement and stratification that made the connection between the problems groups have and the structure that creates them, preceding Chicago School White urban sociologists including Robert Park, Louis Wirth and Ernest Burgess (Loughran 2015). Hired by the College Settlement Association, W. E. B. Du Bois was tasked with identifying why the Black population living in the 7th ward of Philadelphia did not participate civically and socially, as their White counterparts did – essentially, what was the Black population's problem with properly integrating into American society?

Profoundly, Du Bois concluded the opposite, stating that Negroes are not the problem, but they are afflicted with enslavement, capitalism, discrimination and prejudice that have stopped them from functioning fully in society (Hunter 2013; Zuberi 2004). Du Bois' study used advanced research methods to study Philadelphia's Black urban population and the development of its own institutions, while meticulously documenting the condition of the population through surveys, maps and interviews, for occupations, ages, household size and housing conditions. Du Bois differentiated four different kinds of residents in the 7th ward. By documenting nuance in the Black community, he set the stage for a more intersectional rendering of how class and race were shaped by relations of power (Morris 2017). A few years later, he published the foundational text *The Souls of Black Folk* in which he continued to dig deeper into the racial inequality of Black Americans, asking the fundamental question, "How does it feel to be a problem?" (1903).

Du Bois set the stage for more studies and understandings of "the Negro problem" in other urban spaces, including but not limited to St. Clair Drake and Horace Cayton's 1945 *Black Metropolis: A Study of Negro Life in a Northern City*, about the Black Belt of Chicago, and Arthur Hippler's 1974 book *Hunter's Point: A Black Ghetto* about San Francisco. Drake and Cayton took *The Philadelphia Negro* further to study the urban settlement and community created in Chicago's Black Belt, and the racial stratification and inequality in the Bronzeville section of the city (Hunter and Robinson 2016). When describing Chicago's Black metropolis, Drake and Cayton say: "but beneath the surface are patterns of life and thought, attitudes and customs, which make Black metropolis a unique and distinctive city within a city. Understand Chicago's Black Belt and you will understand the Black belts of a dozen large American cities" (1945:12).

Chicago historically remains one of the most studied Black urban settlements in the Midwest United States, and is a model because of the great lengths used to contain and isolate its Black population. When comparing Irish and German settlements with Negro settlements, Drake and Cayton claimed that the latter were not "fully absorbed" into the population and that their communities occupy the "least desirable" neighborhoods. As the Black population grew, Drake and Cayton claimed that "its population grows larger and larger, unable either to expand freely or to scatter. It becomes a persisting *city within a city*, reflecting in itself the cross-currents of life in Midwest Metropolis, but isolated from the mainstream" (1945:17; Hunter and Robinson 2016). Black urban settlements such as Philadelphia and Chicago historically have persisted as a city within a city, created in isolation and stigma during the first wave of the Great Migration.

The second wave of migration from 1940–70 brought more Black Southerners to places in the West, including California (Daniels 1980; Broussard 1993; Banks et al. 2012; Jackson 2014). Prior to World War II, in San Francisco, a small Black community of "pioneer urbanites" lived in the Fillmore neighborhood, and even smaller Black communities could be found in other sections of the city (Daniels 1980). In 1940, there were only 4,846 Blacks living in San Francisco. These Blacks encountered some violence, but were not considered a threat as long as they remained "spatially and socially subordinated," ensuring that they were not a danger to White property and wealth (Pulido 2006:43; Jackson 2010). After 1943, the Fillmore and Bayview – Hunters Point neighborhoods housed the city's largest in-migration of Black workers, which was seen as a "severe aggravation to White sensibilities" (Fullilove 2005). The Black population grew to over 43,000 by the 1950s, a nearly ten-fold increase in a roughly ten-year period (Jackson 2010).

For established residents and Navy representatives, the burgeoning Black population was a social problem that required an unwelcome adjustment, since interactions with Blacks were no longer intermittent and infringed on Whites' daily life. Further, the growth of the Hunters Point Black community after the end of the war was also considered a civic problem as it confounded expectations that Black migrants would return to the South once the war ended (Hippler 1974; Jackson 2014). They were to be a temporary nuisance, not a permanent fixture of the community. San Francisco, like many cities before it, embarked on a quest to contain the Black community, defining and maintaining Black urban space.

Urban Segregation and the Creation of the Ghetto

The same hands that drew red lines around Prince Jones drew red lines around the ghetto. (Ta-Nehisi Coates in *Between the World and Me*)

In *Between the World and Me*, Ta-Nehisi Coates illustrates the historical continuity of killing, policing, excluding and controlling Black bodies, showing the relationship between this and the structurally defined urban spaces that Blacks inhabit. Prince Jones was a young Black college student killed by a Black police officer in Washington,

DC, in 2000. Coates describes the murder of Jones as politicizing his life in the same way that the Michael Brown verdict politicized his son's life. The red lines Coates spoke of viewed Blacks, both individually and collectively, as a threat in need of being contained. The murder of Prince Jones provides nuance to Blackness, structural violence and containment. Jones' killer was a Black police officer, and he was not shot in an environment understood to be a ghetto, or even in the inner city.

The threat and boundaries of Blackness create a structural problem that can be manifested on an individual level within the places we identify as "impoverished," or as a cloak associated with Black bodies that have never stepped foot inside of a ghetto (Anderson 2012). Many times, the words "urban," "ghetto" and "inner city" are used interchangeably, but they are distinct. **Ghettos** or "inner cities" are areas that are usually subsections of larger urban metropolitan areas, which are characterized by cumulative disadvantage. Not all urban spaces are cumulatively racially and economically disadvantaged in the same ways, and most consist of varying levels of isolation, poverty, racial mixture economic status.

To contain the "problem" of the growing Black population, the federal government and independent locales explicitly enforced legal segregation, which was the primary cause of the creation of low-income Black disadvantaged and ghetto environments because it constrained the choice of housing for Blacks to overcrowded urban spaces (Rothstein 2017). Housing segregation was part of a much larger orchestrated segregation between Blacks and Whites in many spheres, including jobs, stores, post offices, lunch counters, churches, etc. The purpose was to create two worlds – on paper, separate but equal, but, in practice, separate and very much unequal, according to the 1968 Kerner Commission (Hunter and Robinson 2016).

As egregious as official residential segregation was in its heyday, its social effect solidified a caste-like racial order and a fatal coupling of race and space that still unequally defines and constrains Black life today. It also heavily affected White Americans, as it secured advantages in White neighborhoods that are too alive and well in the present (Lipsitz 2011; Rothstein 2017). Segregation was not and is not an isolated experience. Due to the coupling of race, space and value, segregated housing leads, in White areas, to segregated schools with better facilities and teachers, leading to better school and neighborhood networks, increasing job prospects and wealth growth, and affecting the eventual earnings of the children, which ultimately maintains a system of racial subordination

(Massey and Denton 1993; Lipsitz 2001; Sharkey 2013; Rothstein 2017).

In *American Apartheid*, sociologists Douglass Massey and Nancy Denton (1993) argue that one of the main drivers behind the creation of the walls of the ghetto through segregation is White prejudice. Tied to this, though, was a fear of the growing population of Blacks in White spaces. While other ethnic groups faced intense segregation and discrimination, the Black population remains one of the most isolated groups in America, and their segregation levels are not comparable to any other group (Massey and Denton 1993). The extreme segregation of Blacks is not the product of happenstance – it was intentional and actively enforced (Rothstein 2017). To date, there has been little change in the size of the Black middle and upper classes since the Civil Rights Movement. "72 percent of Black adults living in today's urban ghettos were raised by parents who also lived in the ghetto a generation earlier" (Sharkey 2013:45). The Black middle and upper classes are still physically and socially closer to cumulatively disadvantaged neighborhoods than their White counterparts (Patillo-McCoy 2000).

Today, Black Americans are also subject to a segregation tax, which is the entanglement of historic practices of segregation to significantly lower property values for Black homeowners, compared to Whites. Neighborhoods that are over 50 percent Black, on average, have a 23 percent lower home value compared to other neighborhoods with similar characteristics (Perry, Rothwell and Harshbarger 2018).

Hence, although many Blacks believe and have pursued the American Dream of homeownership, they continue to be blocked from reaping its full economic rewards due to the relative low values of their homes and their proximity to the Black poor (Patillo-McCoy 2000; Perry et al. 2018). This is the long-term impact of a century of racial residential segregation.

In particular, because residential segregation is place-based, it acts as a foundation enabling other forms of oppression, which can have a kind of domino effect on Black urban neighborhoods. Urban ghetto neighborhoods vary in size, location and history of discriminatory practices that have sought to act as social and physical boundaries between Black residents and proximate neighborhoods. Racial residential segregation occurred in several ways including racial zoning, restrictive covenants, redlining and violence.

Forms of Residential Segregation

As cities became more urbanized toward the end of the nineteenth century and the beginning of the twentieth, residential segregation by race began to define the landscape of American cities. The start of the first wave of Black migration outside of the South, from 1910 to 1920, spurred the desire for separation from the increasing Black population. In this wave, segregation was accomplished largely through mild overtures, such as racial harassment to reinforce that Blacks weren't welcome in certain neighborhoods. As middle-class Blacks moved farther out from the inner-city core, residents would receive threatening letters and elevated personal harassment, and Neighborhood Improvement Associations would attempt to buy out Black families who recently bought homes in White neighborhoods, as illustrated in Lorraine Hansberry's *A Raisin in the Sun*. In addition, businesses who supported Blacks would be boycotted.

The earliest recorded use of a *racial zoning law* was in 1910 in Baltimore, Maryland, mandating separate Black and White living spaces (Rothstein 2017). Following Baltimore, Atlanta (GA), Birmingham (AL), Miami (FL), New Orleans (LA), Richmond (VA) and several other states adopted racial zoning laws that prohibited Black residents from buying homes on majority White blocks. In 1922, in Atlanta, the City Planning Commission published a zone plan that claimed that racial zoning was essential for keeping the peace, and it benefitted both Black and White Americans. It went on to divide the city into an R 1 White district and R 2 colored district (Rothstein 2017). In other cases, for example St. Louis, the zoning ordinance would change as it was needed. If Black families were moving into areas, they would rezone residential land to industrial to prevent their migration (Rothstein 2017).

During the second wave of migration, more sophisticated and institutionalized forms of segregation were enforced, including redlining and restrictive covenants. These practices were upheld by the Federal Housing Act of 1949 which allotted federal funds to metropolitan cities, but lacked a clause forbidding racial discrimination. **Restrictive (racial) covenants** were agreements among property owners that stated they would not permit Blacks to own, occupy or lease their property for a period of time (Massey and Denton 1993:36; Rothstein 2017). Despite the fact that restrictive covenants were outlawed by 1948, real-estate agencies still found ways to not rent or sell to Black families. According to Massey and Denton, a 1950s Chicago survey of real-estate agencies revealed that 80 percent of realtors still refused to sell, and 68 percent refused to rent, to Blacks.

If Black families did succeed in escaping these artificial racial restrictions, owners and real-estate companies found ways to prevent them from moving in: from outright refusal to lying – saying the place was already rented – to the addition of a more careful screening than required of White residents, or financial barriers, such as an added security deposit (Massey and Denton 1993:50). Black residents resisted, whenever and wherever they could. Some would have White allies put their name on the house in order to purchase property. Others would apply for mortgages in areas that were not officially redlined yet, but many were met with social stigma and violence.

Redlining, which was born through the Housing Act of 1934, provides another example of how segregation was purposefully enforced. Redlining associated Black people, Blackness and other communities of color with being a financial risk and encouraged *disinvestment* in those areas. In the 1930s, the Homeowners Lenders Corporation (HOLC) created residential security maps for 239 cities and evaluated neighborhoods by four grades: green and blue as best and still desirable, and yellow and red as declining and hazardous. Neighborhoods that were outlined with red were considered the riskiest places to invest; these were neighborhoods with predominantly Black residents. Within redlined zones, banks would deny loans for residents to move out or rehabilitate their homes. Redlining not only kept Black families from living outside of the ghetto and constrained their movement, but also prevented them from rehabilitating their own homes to increase their property value. Once an address was determined to be in a redlined zone, the application was routinely denied. Redlining contributed to the long-term systematic disinvestment of spaces by the government, private citizens and the private sector. It effectively curtailed the building of intergenerational wealth for Black families and other minorities as it contributed to further disinvestment and isolation of the ghetto.

Spotlight on Resistance

Case Study 4 Memories of Living within the Redline

In Atlantic City, New Jersey, sociologist Christina Jackson conducted an ethnographic study from 2016 to 2019 in which she immersed herself in the community. She asked a 68-year-old Black resident, Richard, who grew up in the redlined neighborhood called the Northside, to describe the process of redlining in the city. He responded:

> Now, I'm gonna show you how the redlining goes ... There is a street Arctic, there is a street Baltic ... in the Black neighborhood it's called Baltic. You get to that same street, still in Atlantic City, when you cross over Missouri Ave, it becomes Fairmount, same street. You go a little further, when it goes into Margate and Ventnor, that same street becomes Winchester. *Same street, hasn't changed, but the neighborhoods changed.* So, you go in to get a loan, and you say you are on Fairmount, obviously the provisions that you have under that loan are different, than if I say Baltic, but I'm on the same street.

Richard illuminates the arbitrariness of the redlined boundaries, giving the example of a street that has different names at different points. Your address determined the freedom and the conditions in which you lived within the city. Following the caste-like status of racial oppression, the conditions of redlined neighborhoods were poor. Mr. Johnson, an 80-year-old resident, described how redlining associated Black families with lowering values and having a deleterious effect on a community; this perception had consequences that followed Blacks even when they moved.

> Number 1, you couldn't live where you wanted to live. You had to live where you were told to live, which was where it was open to Black people. Often times, the housing was substandard. Unfortunately, people had to live there, they had no choice. . ... When the laws were changed and Black people started moving into what was at one time a White neighborhood, then White people started leaving the area and the neighborhood generally became all Black.

Mr. Johnson outlines a common pattern. Even when redlining was outlawed, and African Americans would move into previously denied areas, White residents would move out, contributing to White flight to the suburbs or the surrounding county. As a result, the impact of redlining was pervasive in the decades to follow.

Despite this reality, Blacks actively resisted the debilitating perceptions of their environments and worked hard to turn their neighborhoods into places of congregation and community. Many Black residents who grew up in the redlined Northside of Atlantic City spoke of it positively. One resident said, "You saw your teachers and your principals in your churches. You saw them in the neighborhood stores. You saw them everywhere you went, so it built a tighter relationship between the people in your community because you saw them in every facet of your life."

Similarly, in San Francisco's Harlem of the West in the 1940s, Black residents recalled the experience of living in the all-Black Fillmore neighborhood positively. In "Remember the Fillmore: The Lingering History of Urban Renewal in Black San Francisco," by sociologists Christina Jackson and Nikki Jones (2012), Jackson interviews a long-time Black resident of the Fillmore neighborhood, named Shirley, about how life was in the space. She described a time when the neighborhood was home to clubs and restaurants and other Black-owned businesses that Black people could afford and where they were welcomed.

> In the Fillmore, right there on Fillmore Street, there was a [dry-] cleaners there. My family would drop their coats and whatever was dry-clean-able there, and I could go back in a couple days and pick it up and say [to the owner], "Mom says she'll take care of you whenever." The owner would say, "Sure, just go, your mom said she wanted this right back." You know what we do . . . we were a community . . . everybody. He didn't worry about getting paid, because he knew it was gonna get paid. And mom would be here Friday or Dad would be here Friday and pay you, whatever.

Shirley described a sense of community and trust that was created among the Black residents that still exists today, despite the different waves of change affecting it. While previously redlined neighborhoods like the Northside in Atlantic City and the Fillmore in San Francisco have seen declines in homeownership, valuations of property and credit scores, Black residents still made these spaces affirming. Redlined neighborhoods created tightly knit communities who together faced institutional racism.

The Institution of the Ghetto

Today's American ghetto institutionalizes not only the racial attitudes, fears and stigmas White residents project onto low-income Black and Brown people, but also the government's historic hand in creating and sustaining its boundaries. Since our cities are intentionally valued according to race and class due to exclusionary housing practices, today, if real-estate agencies and residents are not explicit and thoughtful, they can contribute to the maintenance of racially segregated neighborhoods. The design of the ghetto, a place of cumulative racial and economic disadvantage without locked-in advantages, is a permanent idea in our society, although the boundaries and understandings of that space change (Blauner 2001). What once were dilapidated ghettos that middle-class Americans feared to live in are now sought after due to their proximity to downtown cosmopolitan centers and affordable property values enabled by the processes of ghettoization and disinvestment.

The creation of the ghetto is also associated with the population size and threat of those being ghettoized. Recall, in San Francisco prior to the 1940s and during the wartime period, Blacks lived among Whites relatively peacefully, due to their low non-threatening numbers. This is consistent with attitudes after the Civil Rights Movement as well. In *American Apartheid*, Massey and Denton found that, in Detroit as of 1976, once a neighborhood was one-third Black, the limits of racial tolerance were reached for the majority of Whites (1993:93). At that point, "73 percent would be unwilling to enter, 57 percent would feel uncomfortable, and 41 percent would try to leave" (1994:93). Whites' discomfort with proximity to Black residents is due to stereotypes and the legacy of redlining that connects their presence in increasing numbers to negative effects on property values in a neighborhood.

Once the Black population increased and appeared to be "taking over," attitudes shifted, raising fears that triggered the government and real-estate agencies to redefine racial boundaries in more systematic ways, or renew and strengthen their emphasis, as Arnold Hirsch describes the 1940s period in *Making of the Second Ghetto: Race and Housing in Chicago* (1983:5–9). The creation of the ghetto has also been analyzed as an expression of domestic colonialism. Scholars such as Harold Cruise, Kenneth Clark and Robert Blauner have put forth the idea that ghettos are the institutionalization of powerlessness created from cumulative racial and economic disadvantage, and poverty. Blacks do not own the ghetto, and are controlled by those who live outside of it rather than within it (Blauner 2001). "The dark ghettos are social, political, educational, and – above all – economic colonies. Their inhabitants are subject peoples, victims of greed, cruelty, insensitivity, guilt, and fear of their masters" (Clark 1965:3). Cruise and Blauner contend that American capitalism has blocked the development and sustainability of major Black institutions and economic mobility, making it difficult for Blacks to own property even within the ghetto (Blauner 2001; Cruise 1968).

The Origins, Meaning and Usage of the Ghetto

In *The Color of Law: A Forgotten History of How Our Government Segregated America*, economist Richard Rothstein details the government's intentional and unconstitutional role in the creation of residential segregation and the persistence of contemporary ghettos in America (Rothstein 2017). While most Americans are generally embarrassed to use the word "ghetto," because it is a loaded and complicated term that is used in different ways, the avoidance of it also reminds us of the systematic process of isolation.

> Over the past few decades, we have developed euphemisms to help us forget how we, as a nation, have segregated African American citizens. We have become embarrassed about saying *ghetto*, a word that accurately describes a neighborhood where government has not only concentrated a minority but established barriers to its exit. We don't hesitate to acknowledge that Jews in Eastern Europe were forced to live in ghettos where opportunity was limited and leaving was difficult or impossible. Yet when we encounter similar neighborhoods in this country, we now delicately refer to them as the *inner city*, yet everyone knows what we mean … We've developed other euphemisms, too, so that polite company doesn't have to confront our history of racial exclusion. (2017:XVI)

Rothstein goes on to discuss the word and how it has been adopted by the general public and Blacks living in ghettos. We also have other euphemisms, such as "slum clearance," which is associated with disinvestment and displacing poor neighborhoods of color that are seen as in need of saving and repair, oftentimes in the context of redevelopment and gentrification.

The "ghetto" can be considered as a space to live in or avoid, or as an idea, an adjective and identity (Jones and Jackson 2012). For many middle-class White Americans, who might avoid the word "ghetto" out of embarrassment, the term "inner city" might be used instead – but it does not have the same structural foundation as the word "ghetto." For those who grew up in the ghetto, but may or may not live in it now, "ghetto" can be used as a term of endearment, reminding them of a space which they have developed social and familial networks in, have "worked their way out of" or have survived (Jones 2008). It's a word that is associated with middle- to upper-class Blacks who have never lived in the ghetto and find the need to adjust their presentations and *facework* in order to avoid social repercussions linked with the space (Anderson 2012; Goffman

1955). It has become a word that is associated with Blackness and Black people, but overshadows much of the positivity, congregation and resistance created within these spaces (Hunter and Robinson 2016). The word "ghetto" exists beyond its walls, but was not originally associated with Blacks.

The term was first used to describe Jews in Venice, Italy, in 1516, who were stigmatized and excluded from the rest of the population, considered morally different due to their religion (Haynes and Hutchinson 2011). The term was used to describe Black people primarily after the 1940s, and, in some places, earlier. Because Black people were equated with low market value, their containment and segregation contributed to the ghettoization of neighborhoods nationally. **Ghettoization** refers to the othering process of a space becoming a ghetto, or becoming disinvested in due to racial and classed attitudes, coupled with the withdrawal of jobs, industries, public offices and other forms of investment, creating more isolation (Wilson 1987; Gans 2008; Bennett 2018). When these ghettoized neighborhoods suffer from severe disadvantage and isolation, or possess high percentages of poverty given the institutional processes that created them, they are referred to as advanced marginal spaces or hyperghettos (Wacquant 2007). Hyperghettos are increasingly being targeted for urban renewal – however, developer interest and government funding often signal the erasure of the existing, often Black, community.

Urban Renewal as Black Removal and Displacement

Starting in the 1950s, urban renewal had a tremendously negative impact on Black communities across the United States, effectively eradicating and destabilizing them. In *Root Shock: How Tearing Up City Neighborhoods Hurts America, and What We Can Do About It* (2005), psychiatrist Mindy Thompson Fullilove analyzed the effect urban renewal has had on community identity, and the root shock that residents are forced to endure. *Root shock* is defined as the destruction of an area's emotional ecosystem through the serial displacements of urban renewal (Fullilove 2005; Jackson 2018). Urban renewal produced profound root shock and instability. Residents often turned these segregated neighborhoods into hubs of culture and congregation prior to renewal, but land clearance eroded the stability they tried to create and intensified class divisions, as those with means fled while others without means were forced to stay in dispersed yet confined sections of the city (Jackson 2014).

Urban renewal funding was initially derived from 1930s New Deal Era programming led by the federal government to promote economic recovery from the Great Depression, and to federally assist distressed urban cores (Mollenkopf 1983; Jackson 2014). After World War II, the 1949 Federal Housing Act that created the financial resources to rebuild the urban infrastructure created redevelopment agencies nationwide, and urban renewal programming to aid distressed urban centers (Jackson 2014). "In 1950s America, urban renewal was a synonym for 'progress,'" but what is progress and who was this progress for? (Fullilove 2005:57). Progress was looked at as bringing in new jobs, new technologies and new ways to use existing dilapidated land. Those who occupied the land slated for progress simply stood in the way of the transformation and renewal.

In San Francisco, the Fillmore neighborhood was decimated by urban renewal. In the same year that the 1949 Housing Act provided the financial resources, the city's redevelopment agency was created. The San Francisco Redevelopment Agency operated as a superagency, with powers that rose above city legislation, with the ability to use **eminent domain**, a legal practice used by the government to obtain private land for public use. Eminent domain was mostly used when land was identified as blighted or a slum (Fainstein and Fainstein 1985; Judd and Swanstrom 1998; Hartman 2002; Jackson 2014). According to the rhetoric, in order for cities like San Francisco to remain financially competitive in an industrial economy, they had to focus their efforts on the physical redevelopment of city centers and adjacent neighborhoods (Mollenkopf 1983; McGovern 1998; Jackson 2014). These adjacent neighborhoods were previously redlined and overcrowded because they held excluded poor communities of color. The Fillmore neighborhood was classified as an inner-city slum due to symptoms of exclusionary practices such as overcrowding, dilapidated housing and high rates of unemployment (Jackson and Jones 2012; Jones and Jackson 2011). Redevelopment logic placed new exchange values on slated neighborhoods by determining how much capital could be made from these spaces, while Black and other poor communities of color were disproportionately left out of the decision-making (Logan and Molotch 1987; Mah 1999; Jackson 2014).

In her dissertation, "Black San Francisco: The Politics of Race and Space in the City," sociologist Christina Jackson (2014) described how urban renewal affected the Fillmore neighborhood; writing in 1963, the writer James Baldwin visited San Francisco's Black Fillmore neighborhood and termed the city's efforts "Negro removal" rather

than urban renewal (Standley and Pratt 1989; Jackson 2014). Similar
to the labels given to 1910 racial zoning in Atlanta, Georgia, the two
urban redevelopment plans implemented were called the "Western
Addition A-1" in 1953 and "Western Addition A-2" in 1963 (Mah
1999). The redevelopment agency used eminent domain to take
control of land in the Fillmore neighborhood, leading to the displacement of thousands of Black families (Jackson 2014). In an interview,
one of the city's well-known Black religious leaders, 67-year old
Reverend White, described to Jackson his church's historic position
as an advocate for the Black community in the city, and, in particular,
the Fillmore. Reverend White vividly shares the effect that redevelopment in the city had on the African American community:

> The Redevelopment Agency, 40 years ago, said to the African American
> community: "We're gonna tear down these old houses, these old
> Victorians, y'all can rebuild the community.. . . Those of you who have
> businesses and have homes, we're going to give you a certificate, once
> things that need to be rebuilt are rebuilt, [then] you can come back."
> That's what that whole Fillmore area is supposed to have been, but
> the Redevelopment Agency did not keep faith – it did not deliver on its
> promises to Black folk. It was not urban renewal, it was Black removal!
> And even the study that the Redevelopment Agency did indicates that if
> they were to do it again, they would not do it the way they did it because
> it was a disservice to Black people. . .. After 40 years, lives have been
> destroyed, families torn apart and broken apart, people end up giving
> away everything they had when they declared eminent domain. . .. took
> homes from people and through redlining, others were forced out of
> Victorian homes that would be worth millions today. You know who
> own the ones that they didn't tear down, who gets the millions of
> dollars out of those now by and large? White folk. (July 29, 2008)

Reverend White explains the economic consequences of these broken
promises for Blacks in the city. To him and others, urban renewal
tore apart the community's unity and stunted opportunities to build
wealth for future generations (Jackson 2014).

From the perspective of Black residents, it is White people who
have profited most from redevelopment and the displacement of
Blacks within cities, and it has led to a decline in their engagement with the city's power structure (Jackson 2014, 2018). Most
importantly, a sense of trust and community, along with a sense of
"rootedness," was lost (Fullilove 2005; Jackson 2014, 2018). As
time progressed and these neighborhoods began to transition, Black
neighbors created spaces of resilience and community. Sociologists

Marcus Anthony Hunter and Zandria Robinson coined the term **Black placemaking** to refer to the creation of sites of resistance in urban Black neighborhoods by residents who use joy and culture to reframe what their spaces mean to them (2016). As we have learned, Black urban neighborhoods are usually characterized as violent, poor, drug infested and dilapidated; these negative perceptions are often extended wholly to the people who live within these spaces. Using Black placemaking as a frame for Black neighborhoods allows scholars to focus on the resistance and endurance of the Black creative imagination in making what they can out of a situation of institutional confinement. Residents may have nuanced feelings about gentrification because more investment in their neighborhood could be positive, yet more resources only come when White residents start moving in. Given this, residents hold on to particular sites or events of cultural importance as they remind them of what the neighborhood "used" to be.

Racial Attitudes and Gentrification

Much of this chapter has focused on the historical problem of containing Blackness. Despite the fact that segregation is no longer the law of the land, our cities remain incredibly segregated socially due to racial attitudes, but also the persistence of institutional structures that enable a passive segregation free from government interference. Segregation is a large-scale structural process that exceeds any individual's capacity for change. While individuals may integrate certain neighborhoods, the social process remains intact. Black segregation is one of the most extreme forms of racial residential segregation; its effect trumps individual achievement or financial means. Blacks remain segregated despite having higher incomes and education (Massey and Denton 1993).

The purpose of segregation historically was to ensure White spaces as a vehicle for the maintenance of privilege, and the containment of Blacks in smaller more dilapidated neighborhoods to concentrate disadvantage. States would begin to outlaw segregation in the 1950s, and the 1964 Civil Rights Act forbade segregation of cities that still upheld these laws. The 1968 Civil Rights Act, also known as the Fair Housing Act, outlawed legal discrimination of any form being used in obtaining housing, and it is still enforced by the Department of Housing and Urban Development (HUD). Yet high rates of segregation remain, even today. Rezoning and redistricting are still ways to keep neighborhoods racially pure, and marginalized individuals out.

The urban landscape has changed and is still changing, but much remains the same. Previously redlined neighborhoods that contained Black populations are still harmed from historical processes. On average, homes in Black neighborhoods are $48,000 dollars lower in value compared to similar neighborhoods that are not predominantly Black (Perry et al. 2018). Despite this, there is still power and collectivity in once predominantly Black neighborhoods, as some local organizations, cultural events and small businesses are forced to cater to new and old tastes.

Urban cities now face many changes due to redevelopment and accompanying gentrification. While redevelopment and gentrification are different processes, many times they are inextricably linked. **Redevelopment**, the rehabilitation of, or building of new, physical structures in a place, is usually accompanied by **gentrification**, a process in which urban neighborhoods inhabited by the poor and/or people of color are repopulated by wealthier and/or White people, changing the culture of the neighborhood. Blacks can also gentrify a neighborhood if they are middle to upper class moving into a poorer community.

Gentrification preys on vulnerable communities that have been disinvested in historically, and promotes further alienation of existing residents (Prince 2014). Gentrifying neighborhoods *feel* different to existing poor and/or Black and Brown residents. With gentrification come trendy shops, art galleries, hipper styles and expensive lattes. Residents in San Francisco, for example, say that they see newer White residents walking their dogs or jogging down the street. They begin to know fewer and fewer people on the block. Local incoming businesses such as cafes or organic grocery stores are more expensive, with a design and feel more attractive to a younger crowd. After the 1990s, demographically, gentrification is evidenced by a sizable increase in middle- to upper-income people and/or White residents in urban spaces.

Whites fled cities in the 1950s and, with mildly changed racial attitudes and an interest in the centrality of downtown, they started to move back primarily in the 1990s. Investment follows White middle-class families. Their racial and classed presence has prompted reinvestment in and the displacement of older communities of color – in particular, Black communities. While many community residents in the Bayview – Hunters Point neighborhood of San Francisco are vilified as anti-gentrification, many are vocal that they want change and renewal, but dislike the type and amount of change being brought to the area. When White families move in, residents observe their neighborhoods are invested in again. Many wish that gentrification in its most common form, displacement of Black and Brown communities by Whites, was not the only way to bring much-needed investment into their neighborhood (Freeman 2006).

Racial integration in gentrifying neighborhoods can be superficial, and many utilize colorblind logics to justify and legitimize continued inequality. In integrated neighborhoods, Blacks and other minorities still suffer from hate crimes, violence or racial harassment (Bell 2017). People who live next to each other on a block can still have vastly different experiences, preferences and choices, created by their family exercising the social and cultural capital they may or may not have (Shapiro 2004). They can still live within a block of poor and/or Black and Brown folks and avoid them, contributing to more stigma. White Americans have reported that many are most comfortable in neighborhoods identified as up to 30 percent minority (Timberlake 2000). Neighborhoods *still* need to be majority White for White residents to feel safe and comfortable within them. As gentrified neighborhoods still possess racial tensions, stigma and a steeper ladder for Blacks, even those in the middle class must be creative when attempting to buy a home.

For advantaged Blacks, sociologists Jacob S. Rugh, Len Albright and Douglass Massey argue, race remains a cumulative disadvantage "because of its direct and indirect effects on socioeconomic status at the individual and neighborhood levels," with consequences that accumulate for borrowers across generations (Rugh, Albright and Massey 2015:186). In their Baltimore, Maryland case study, Rugh, Albright and Massey find that Black disadvantage in lending and foreclosures, that persisted after accounting for occupancy status, credit scores and income, could be explained by race and neighborhood segregation. This cumulative disadvantage is one reason that Blacks are at a much higher risk of moving into renter status than White homeowners, which has led to a widening racial gap in homeownership (Sharp and Hall 2014).

Blackness can still be contained on a block-to-block level, or avoided on neighborhood websites like Nextdoor or Yelp. Today, since it is not politically correct to discursively exclude and marginalize existing residents by race and class, we use **racetalk,** or racially coded words, in a more sanitized way on online platforms when discussing gentrified neighborhoods to identify those who are Black, Brown and poor (Bonilla-Silva and Forman 2000). Words like "ghetto" or "urban looking" isolate others and link their value with having deleterious effects on the neighborhood (Massey and Denton 1993; Bonilla-Silva and Forman 2000; Shapiro 2004; Jones and Jackson 2011).

In "You Just Don't Go Down There: Learning to Avoid the Ghetto in San Francisco," sociologist Nikki Jones and Christina Jackson discuss the interactions between existing residents and new White and more well-off residents who are moving back into the city in the Fillmore / Western Addition neighborhood of San Francisco, which was historically redlined. As new residents enter these neighborhoods, many navigate it through the avoidance of particular parts or "types of people" they view as "ghetto," "rough" or "sketchy" (Jones and Jackson 2011; Shapiro 2004). Words like these are racially coded with colorblind logic that contributes to discursive redlining (Jones and Jackson 2011). White residents possess fears and anxieties about property values both when Whites are moving into Black environments and the reverse, when Black families are moving into areas that are predominantly White (Jones and Jackson 2011; Shapiro 2004). Of concern is not just whom you live around, but whom your kids are going to school with (Shapiro 2014). This kind of preference-driven decision-making enforces a new kind of segregation (Goldberg 1998). In *The Hidden Cost of Being African American: How Wealth Perpetuates Inequality*, sociologist Thomas Shapiro interviewed Black and White families in both Boston and St. Louis about their housing and neighborhood choices in 2002. He interviewed a White family, the Quinlins, who live in a working-class part of Boston where some Black families started to move in. They expressed some of their concerns:

> "There's a lot of Blacks that moved in. That I was starting to worry about, because I was afraid it was going to go down. I'm not prejudiced, but it's just that once a certain type comes in, that's it! My concern when a lot of Blacks started moving in was with the drugs, the pushing of drugs on your kids. Maybe getting stabbed or something. Or shot." (Shapiro 2004:124)

In this passage, the Quinlins use colorblind logic to describe the kinds of people they don't want to live around. Quick to say they are not prejudiced, the couple succinctly associates Black people and Blackness with a neighborhood spiraling downwards, violence and drugs. This racetalk contributes to the semantics we use to avoid neighborhoods or parts of neighborhoods, leading to further disinvestment.

Many times, information about the neighborhood or part of the neighborhood in question is not gained from personal experience but through secondhand accounts or newspaper articles that perpetuate discursive redlining (Jones and Jackson 2011). Jones and Jackson define *discursive redlining* as "informal, talk-based declarations or warnings that discourage newcomers and outsiders from making interpersonal investments in certain parts of the city" (Jones and Jackson 2011). Even though White and Black families may live closer to each other in an "integrated" or gentrified neighborhood, anti-Black racism still simmers beneath the surface, due, in part, to the government's hand in equating Blackness with decreasing housing values, but also colorblind and laissez-faire racial attitudes (Bonilla-Silva and Forman 2000; Shapiro 2004). Instances like the ones described above contribute to a new racism in urban redeveloped and gentrified neighborhoods that still excludes and disinvests socially and economically in Black communities and in relationships with Black residents (Bonilla-Silva 2015: Bonilla-Silva and Forman 2000). This new racism employs racetalk that produces **discursive redlining**, or ways of expressing racial attitudes with language that might be sanitized and subtle but still affects how we think about the redevelopment and gentrification of Black neighborhoods (Jones and Jackson 2011).

Conclusion: Toward a Revitalization of the Ghetto

The ghetto as an institution was created to protect Whites' lives outside of it and to marginalize Black and Brown lives within it. Not only are the walls of the ghetto still alive and well, but, according to Ta-nehisi Coates' life in Baltimore, the ghetto creates a whole other world for Black inhabitants, excluding them from factors that can positively integrate them into the nation's class hierarchy. Despite the institutional control of urban spaces inhabited by Black Americans through segregation, restrictive (racial) covenants, redlining, urban renewal and the other processes discussed, residents have historically resisted. Many times, when urban scholars study Black spaces, they focus solely on the institutional racism that created these spaces due to racial attitudes. While it is important to chronicle that particular history, it lacks the more nuanced discussion of the structure and agency used by Black urban inhabitants to make and shape their community spaces, as we see today in Atlantic City.

Gentrification arose as a trendy and popular word to describe changes in urban neighborhoods inhabited by the poor and/or people of color. Many once predominantly Black neighborhoods are currently, or will soon be, undergoing the processes of gentrification. All kinds of neighborhoods go through transitions, but for predominantly Black ones the process tends to strike a bittersweet and cautious chord due to the methods that have brought about the change. In theory, neighborhood residents do not want to contribute to increasing gentrification. It happens as a kind of side-effect for some, and as a direct cleansing of the neighborhood for others. Either way, making progress in transitioning neighborhoods requires healing, acknowledgment, redefining neighborhood values and correcting the wrongs of the past.

Neighborhood transitions should not, ideally, be built upon the disadvantages associated with institutional redlining. Black 'culture' should not be a reason for the condition of these urban neighborhoods. White racial attitudes, policies and local ordinances need to change in order to break the cycle of assuming Blackness equals low property values, enabling the creation of more integrated communities, and reducing Black isolation. Gentrifying communities must adopt practices and policies that ask for more renter and eviction protection, the promotion of low-income housing, and community-inclusive decision-making processes to lessen the deleterious effects of gentrification and reduce the displacement of long-term low-income Black residents from their neighborhoods.

Today, unless real-estate agencies, community development corporations and individuals work toward the creation of healthy revitalized neighborhoods, mixed with racial and economic diversity and interpersonal investments, we will continue to move toward the growth of segregated, gentrified neighborhoods. Lower-class and middle-class Black Americans still stand to be the most isolated; even when they possess some financial stability, education and social and cultural capital, since they are subject to the realities of racial inequality that differentially shape homeownership. The purposeful segregation of Blacks found in the ghetto is also evident in the world of work, as we will explore in the next chapter, race has historically structured access to occupational opportunity, marginalizing Blacks in the labor market.

Critical Reflection Questions

1 Why was *The Philadelphia Negro* a significant study of Black urban life?
2 What is the segregation tax and how does it affect the ability of Black families to accumulate wealth through homeownership?
3 Describe three historical ways that the segregation of Black people in urban neighborhoods was accomplished.
4 What is discursive redlining? Compare and contrast it with historical redlining.

5
Who Gets to Work? Understanding the Black Labor Market Experience

Hard work is foundational to the American collective sense of self. As a people, Americans are now and have always been defined by an adherence to the Protestant work ethic, in which hard work is the means to secure present and future rewards (Weber 1930). Former President Bill Clinton summarized it aptly: "If you work hard and play by the rules you should be given the chance to go as far as your God-given ability will take you" (Hochshild 1995:18). In a meritocratic society, **occupational achievement** – the occupation and compensation an individual attains – should reflect one's hard work. The economic status of a worker should reflect their effort and exertion. Two people working alongside one another should not be compensated unequally because of their race or gender. Opportunity should not be withheld from some and extended to others; access should be granted based on how hard a person works. These ideals have never been achieved in America.

Race structures the world of work. Occupational segregation is a fundamental feature of the American labor market. In their classic book *The American Occupational Structure*, sociologists Peter Blau and Otis Duncan concluded, "the American occupational structure is largely governed by universalistic criteria of performance and achievement, with the notable exception of the influence of race" (1967:241). The authors reached this conclusion after making three sets of comparisons: first, between the basic inequalities in Black and White occupational chances; second, the effect of region of birth – North or South separately for Whites and Blacks; and third, a comparison of three broad White ethnic groups with native-born Whites (1967:207).

Not surprisingly, Blacks were disadvantaged in the characteristics that would positively impact occupational achievement (educational attainment, early career experiences, and parent income or social origin). However, even after statistically giving Blacks the same desirable characteristics (same education, first jobs and social origin) as Whites, Black occupational achievement was still consistently inferior. Blau and Duncan concluded "being a Negro in the United States has independent disadvantageous consequences for several of the factors that directly affect occupational success" (1967:209).

In contrast, they found that "the occupational opportunities of White ethnic minorities, on the whole, differ little from those of Whites of native parentage" (Blau and Duncan 1967:233). Further, their inferior position could be explained away by, and was largely due to, lower rates of educational achievement. When the relevant factors were taken into account (social origin, education and first job), the differences between White ethnic minorities and native-born Whites were slight. After systematically studying the American occupational structure, Blau and Duncan concluded: "Equality of opportunity is an ideal in the United States, not an accomplished fact" (1967:207).

This quantitative assessment documents the success of a hundred-year-long struggle for what historian David R. Roedinger (2007) describes as the wages of Whiteness. Sociologist Robert Blauner argues, "racial privilege . . . is expressed most strategically in the labor market and the structure of occupations. If there is any one key to the systematic privilege that undergirds a racial capitalist society, it is the special advantage of the White population in the labor market" (2001:26). Racism and the devaluation of Black labor produced this systematic privilege. However, in order to understand the origins and persistence of this privilege in a meritocratic society, we need to explore how race and the societal malignment of Blackness made it possible to reconcile the dissonance justifying unequal treatment.

Labor and Race-Making in a Historical Perspective

While understanding the experience of emancipated Black slaves in the South is critical to understanding the Black labor market experience, it is much more illuminating to start in the North before emancipation and explore the perceptions and restrictions of free Blacks in the perceived land of opportunity. It clarifies the oversimplified picture of the North as benevolent and exposes the denigration of Blacks nationwide. In *The Wages of Whiteness: Race and the Making of the American Working Class*, Roedinger (2007) documents the evolution of the relationship between Blacks and Irish immigrants from friendship to hostility, showing how the subsequent fight for a clear line of demarcation drove Irish vilification and hatred of Blacks far beyond that of White Southerners at the time. Recall that in the South, Blacks were slaves, legally considered property of their owners. The significant power differential between slave and master led to a paternalistic relationship, as long as Black slaves stayed in their place. However, historian George Fredrickson argues, "if they [Blacks] seek to rise out of their place and demand equal rights with members of the dominant group, they are likely to be exposed to a furious and violent form of racist reprisal" (2002:93). This is the context under which we must consider the treatment of free Blacks in the North.

The Battle to Define and Protect White Jobs

The North, in the mid 1800s, was defined by limited labor market opportunity. Race was a gatekeeper to even low-skilled jobs, nativism ruled the day and the Irish were viewed with disdain. They were called "low browed and savage, groveling and bestial, lazy and wild." These derogatory references likened them to Blacks during the ante-bellum period (Roedinger 2007:133). The Irish were not recognized as White and were referred to as the "Celtic Race." These were the racial dynamics of the urban North encountered by free Blacks seeking opportunity not available in the plantation South. The Irish were cast with Blacks due to their proximity and circumstances – occupying the same neighborhoods and performing the same kinds of work. Both groups were poor, and not "native" Americans. As such they were joint victims of the Boston "race riot" in 1829. For some time, Irish Americans seemed to intermingle with Blacks without conflict. In native Ireland, prominent leaders held strong anti-slavery stances and encouraged their Irish American brothers to do the same. They drew similarities between the need for Black and for Irish freedom, from slavery and colonialism, respectively. Frederick Douglass, the great abolitionist, even visited Ireland during the "Great Famine" (1845).

However, it was about this time that the Irish American view of Blacks began to change, and they rejected the call to support aboli-tion. New Irish immigrants arriving after 1845 desired to draw sharp lines between themselves and Blacks. The relative availability and restriction of occupational opportunity was a certain driver of this sea change. Some Irish Americans who immigrated prior to the famine had greater choice in employment, becoming farmers, but this was not the norm. Those who immigrated after the famine were all low-paid unskilled or skilled workers. They lived in poverty and occupied the slums and shantytowns of the cities.

Irish immigrants sought certain status as true Americans, "full citizens of this great and glorious republic," and embraced their Whiteness and its entitlements, distancing themselves violently from Blacks (Roedinger 2007:136). Although the Whiteness of Irish Americans was not firmly established, they treasured it because they believed it entitled them to political rights and jobs. They became the enforcers of the racial order and rioted against Black hiring in "their" jobs and general Black association in order to strengthen their claim to Whiteness. As a result, "Even before taking a leading role in the unprecedentedly murderous attacks on Blacks during the 1863 Draft Riot in New York City, Irishmen had developed a terrible record of mobbing free Blacks on and off the job" (ibid.). Black suffering at the hands of the Irish increased, so much so that newspapers of the time described poor Irish men as one of the greatest threats to the Black population. Roedinger describes the making of the Irish worker into a White worker as a two-step process: "Irish immigrants won acceptance of the larger White population . . . and they came to insist on their own Whiteness and on White supremacy" (2007:137).

Unlike English, Scandinavian and German immigrants who had access to more desirable occupational opportunity that was solidly closed to Blacks, Irish immigrants, due to their lack of skills, were largely confined to hard labor. They resented their association with Blacks, and their joint performance of "America's hard work." Irish women, for example, dominated domestic service in 1850, representing three out of four women in household service jobs, the primary occupation available to Black women outside of the South (Branch and Wooten 2012). While securing jobs has long been argued as the cause of Irish American racism, this view minimizes the perceived challenge that their association with Blackness posed to achieving the Irish goal of becoming White (Roedinger 2007).

The Irish asserted their right to work because they were White but found it difficult to separate their performance of unskilled labor from the stigma associated with such work since it was widely defined as "Black" work. For Blacks, who could be found in large settlements in the North from 1880 onward, experiencing competition for undesirable work was a significant departure from in the South, where Whites were loath to enter occupations that were associated with Blacks since slavery (Sernett 1997). The solution Irishmen devised was to "drive all Blacks, and if possible their memories, from the

places were the Irish labored," resulting in severely restricted occupational opportunity for Blacks – men and women alike – in Northern
states (Roedinger 2007:150).

The rise of manufacturing in the late nineteenth and early twentieth centuries created new occupational opportunities for unskilled
workers that were free from the "hard work" stigma and Black racial
association. Union membership became the gateway to opportunity,
as it was often a prerequisite to employment, and racial exclusion was
explicit and unwavering. Indeed, sociologist Stanley Lieberson found,
the exclusion of Blacks "served to enhance the bargaining power of
the unions," especially at the local level (1980:339).[1] Although craft
unions were hostile to some White immigrants as well, the smaller
gaps in their representation in desirable industrial occupations suggests union hostility was not nearly as great or persistent toward
White immigrants as it was to Blacks (Lieberson 1980). Sociologist
W. E. B. Du Bois argues that the radical inequality observed between
White immigrants and Blacks early in the twentieth century was
due to strongly entrenched public opinion that quietly, and at times
publicly, supported the economic restriction of Blacks:

> [If there were not] ... an active prejudice or at least passive acqui-
> escence in this effort to deprive Negroes of a decent livelihood, both
> trade unions and arbitrary bosses would be powerless to do the harm
> they now do; where, however, a large section of the public more or
> less openly applaud the stamina of a man who refuses to work with a
> "Negro," the results are inevitable. (1967:332–3, cited in Lieberson
> 1980:346)

The innovation and industrialization of the late nineteenth and early
twentieth centuries provided an employment alternative to hard labor
for unskilled and semi-skilled laborers, transforming the landscape of
occupational opportunity. However, the new jobs were defined as
White jobs and the zero-sum battle for access to Whiteness and the
relative economic perks it secured made White ethnic immigrants
agents of racial oppression prohibiting Black advancement.

Restricting Black Labor in the South

While the North possessed certain challenges for Black laborers, it
enabled Blacks to escape the suffocating racial oppression that typified the South. Slavery was an economic, social and political system
predicated on racial inferiority and exploitation that dictated every

aspect of Black life in the South. Emancipation, a consequence of the South losing the Civil War, freed Blacks from their designation as property but did not disrupt or challenge the social order of the South that believed deeply in the appropriateness of Black subordination and economic exploitation. In *Opportunity Denied: Limiting Black Women to Devalued Work*, sociologist Enobong Hannah Branch argues:

> Emancipation presented a monumental challenge: How would Blacks be treated in a society that valued "free labor" but historically saw them as exempt from this ideal and fit for "unfree labor"? Would they be allowed to labor voluntarily and be accorded respect and civil treatment by their employers and society? Or, would the duality of the U.S. labor system that was predicated on divisions between free and coerced labor, Black and White workers, reinvent itself? (2011:31)

There was not much time to debate these ideological issues. The Civil War threatened the economic stability of the South and therefore the nation (Foner 1988). Many plantations lay in ruins and the Union Army, immediately following emancipation, was in charge of restoring order. That meant restoring the labor of former slaves (Branch 2011).

Spotlight on Resistance

Case Study 5 Black Women's Labor Withdrawal after Emancipation

Black families sought to test their new found freedom, slavery coerced the labor of the entire Black family, freedom enabled them to decide whom they wanted to work for, and many chose to withdraw women and children from the fields. By some estimates, Black labor declined by nearly one-third as a result. (Foner 1988:139–40).

Historian Herbert Gutman reported on the Watson plantation in late 1865 that the freedwomen said they "never mean to do any more outdoor work that white men support their wives, and they mean that their husbands shall support them" (1976:167). Planters complained to the Freedmen's Bureau stating "some of the women on the place are lazy and doing nothing but causing disturbance" (1976:168). The choice to withdraw from the labor force was a family decision as the case of Pete illustrates – his plantation mistress complained, "Pete is still in the notion of

remaining but chooses to feed his wife out of his wages rather than
to get her fed for her services" (ibid.).·

Black men desired to protect their wives and daughters from
exploitation in the fields and homes of other men, and Black
women desired to care for their own households and assume a
more traditional woman's role (Branch 2011). Neither of these
desires could be realized during slavery: emancipation offered
Blacks a chance to define themselves and their families anew, and
they seized it.

Many Blacks sought to leave plantations, entering Southern cities
in droves. However, army officials issued directives restricting their
movements. In Virginia, historian Eric Foner documents, General
Ord "barred rural freedmen from seeking employment [in the city]. . ..
In early June, soldiers and local Richmond police arrested several
hundred Blacks and shipped them to the countryside" (1988:154).
While Blacks were free to labor, they were not free to choose where
to labor or even what type of labor to perform. **Black Codes**, or laws
which were enacted to specify the rights of former slaves, were often
framed with the express goal of attempting to stabilize and control
Black labor (Branch 2011). In South Carolina, historian Jacqueline
Jones notes, Black Codes enacted in 1865 prohibited Blacks from
employment in "any occupation other than farmer or servant except
by paying an annual tax ranging from ten to one hundred dollars."
The law further specified expected behavior: "labor from sunup to
sundown and a ban on leaving the plantation" (1986:52).

The Freedmen's Bureau was founded in the summer and fall of
1865. Its goal was to establish a free labor system in which "Blacks
labored voluntarily, having internalized the values of the market-
place, while planters and civil authorities accorded them the rights
and treatment enjoyed by Northern workers" (Foner 1988:143–4).
Initially, Blacks and plantation owners (called planters) embraced the
Freedmen's Bureau role in orchestrating labor arrangements, but for
very different reasons that were tied to their self-interests. Planters
saw the Bureau's role as getting emancipated slaves back to work on
plantations, while former slaves saw the Bureau's role as protecting
them from unfair treatment, including coercion. These goals were
not necessarily incompatible, but they were entirely incongruent
within the Southern racial order that did not accord autonomy and
discretion to Blacks. Northerners who toured the South remarked
that White Southerners "do not know what free labor is"; Southern

planters replied that Northerners "do not understand the character of the negro" (Foner 1988:132).

Despite this ideological fissure, during Reconstruction (1865–77) Blacks did make some strides in the Southern states (Hahn 2003; Franklin and Brooks Higginbotham 2011). However, with the withdrawal of Northern troops, Southern leaders sought to limit the newfound freedoms acquired by Blacks. Planters sought to secure compliant Black labor, and the only way to guarantee this, they surmised, was to ensure that Blacks were prohibited from owning land of their own (Foner 1988). Planters closed ranks, agreeing never to rent or sell land to Blacks; they maintained a steady labor force by creating detailed and exploitive labor contracts that effectively reinstated master–slave relationships, ensuring Blacks were perpetually in debt and bound to the plantation (Foner 1988; Branch 2011; Rothstein 2017).

Beyond the plantation gates, the political system of the South enforced a racial caste system. From Black Codes to **convict leasing**, which forced prisoners to perform uncompensated labor, the laws were manipulative and meant to keep Blacks in servitude in a "slavery-like" system in America (Blackmon 2008). Vagrancy laws, for example, stipulated that "officials could apprehend an 'idler' who had no visible means of subsistence and then hire him or her out at the available wage rate, usually as a servant or common laborer" (Glenn 2002:103). Although these laws were race-neutral, sociologist Evelyn Nakano Glenn documents, "Blacks were overwhelmingly those arrested and ordered to work" (ibid.).

The racial climate of the South worsened as Jim Crow settled in as early as the 1870s. What was once a fear of Blacks turned into a hatred of Blacks, and Jim Crow was reinforced with violence and brutality (Rothstein 2017). The oppressed and subjugated position of Blacks was solidified legally by the 1896 Supreme Court case, *Plessy* v. *Ferguson*, which sealed a separate but equal doctrine that allowed for state-sanctioned segregation (Whitman 2017). Black life and labor in the South were hard. Many Blacks became disillusioned and sought refuge in other regions. Despite the limitations the North posed, there was not the unanimity of racial oppression.

War and Black Labor

The US racial labor hierarchy and its debilitating consequences for Black employment persisted, largely unchallenged, until World War

I. Prior to the war, the need for an ever-expanding workforce due to booming industrialization was met by large-scale immigration from European countries (Katzman 1978). However, with the beginning of World War I in 1914, emigration from European countries was severely restricted, thus limiting the available labor pool and forcing employers to be less selective and to hire laborers from groups that they would not have otherwise considered. Black laborers were granted access to jobs from which they had formerly been excluded (Branch 2007). The easing of racial occupational restrictions impacted Black men and women differently due to the sex segregation of jobs at the time.

Domestic service, for example, was one of the few occupations available to Black women in the South, but they were largely excluded from this work in the North as it was dominated by White immigrants (Katzman 1978). The stoppage of immigration transformed Black women from a regional domestic labor force to a national one, because they remained blocked from accessing most other occupational opportunities (Branch 2011). As manufacturing, professional, trade and clerical occupations were increasingly dominated by women, Black women were excluded on the basis of their race. War, however, created labor shortages and opportunities for Black women, yet efforts to control their labor intensified. If they sought opportunities beyond what society deemed racially appropriate labor, such as domestic service work, Black women's attempts at self-betterment were actively blocked (Branch and Wooten 2012). For example, "work or fight" laws that were originally crafted to draft unemployed men into the war effort were used to punish Black women who left domestic service (Branch 2011). Southerners argued that Black women's work was critical to the war effort in that it freed White women "from the routine of housework in order that they may do the work which Negro women cannot do" (Hunter 1995:350). Black women who were employed outside of domestic service, such as hairdressers, were subject to arrest as a result.

Even during World War II, Black women's labor options were actively constrained. For example, in July 1942 – a year after President Franklin Roosevelt signed the Fair Employment Act, which barred racial discrimination in defense industries and the federal government – a Black woman named Altha Sims sent a letter to the President describing a visit to the US Employment Service office. She had been rudely treated and informed "there was not defense work for a Negro woman." She asked President Roosevelt for confirmation of this fact and an explanation as to "why there is no work for us."

This news was particularly hard to believe, in her opinion, since it was coming from a local authority (Green 2006:96). Altha Sims also wrote to the Mayor of Memphis pursuing employment alternatives, saying, "I want a Job but I don't [want] no cook job." Reporting that she had been told there was "no job for you but a skillet an pan," she asked, "Where would the Negro woman apply for work?" (Green 2006:97). The Mayor replied, "I know of no positions for unskilled colored women other than domestic work . . . and I imagine that is why [the welfare director] told you that he could not give you a place" (Green 2006:97).

War, though, had direct – albeit short-term – consequences on the labor market options for Blacks in periods of severe labor shortages. Yet, even then, historian Karen Tucker Anderson describes, during World War II, employers engaged in discriminatory practices and "established a complex hierarchy of hiring preferences based on the composition of the local labor force and the nature of the work to be done," before incorporating Blacks and women into their workforce (1982:83–4). In industries that were manual labor-intensive, Black men were preferred, and women were utilized only if there were not sufficient men to meet the labor demand – whereas, in industries that required minimal manual labor, White women were preferred. Black women, however, were never preferred. "Even some employers," she writes, "willing to hire white women and black men in large numbers balked at including Black women in their work forces" (Anderson 1982:84). The intensity of discrimination against Black women is particularly noteworthy since Black women made up 60 percent of Blacks who entered paid employment during the war years (Branch 2011).

While both World War I and World War II had transformative impacts on the American economy, creating new occupational opportunities and ushering in an economic boom, Black women's labor market opportunities were largely unchanged (Branch 2011). Black men, however, fared somewhat better. Sex segregation of the labor market tied the economic fates of Black men and women to the anxieties and hostilities of White men and women, respectively. The hostility of White men focused on issues of promotion, reflecting their desire to "safeguard economic prerogatives," while the hostility of White women focused on their "desire to maintain social distance" (Anderson 1982:86). As a result, Black men could be found in entry-level industrial positions but rarely advanced, but Black women were rarely hired unless a separate shift or physical separation could be arranged (Branch 2011).

Blacks were widely used as replacement workers while the soldiers were away, and after the war, the vast majority of Blacks, particularly Black women, were forced out of these positions and encouraged to return to their "place" (Milkman 1987). Blacks, however, pressed hard for social change. Upon returning from the war, many Black servicemen were unwilling to return to their "place" in the American racial hierarchy. After fighting for the freedom of Americans abroad, they demanded freedom at home. The conditions were finally present for social change in America. In 1948, President Truman signed an executive order reinforcing an end to discrimination in hiring in the federal government – civil service – and barred segregation in the military (Mayer 2002). While this change was a significant milestone, its impact was limited and Blacks still did not gain access to equal opportunity under the law.

Equal Opportunity Under the Law, Almost a New Day for Black Labor

As we see in the case of Altha Sims, the issuing of executive orders did not universally translate into change in the practice of actively discriminating against Black workers. Prior to the passage of the Civil Rights Act of 1964, it was legally permissible to deny Blacks equitable access to employment opportunity. When Blacks did gain access to work, it was often poorly paid, performed in undesirable surroundings, and had little opportunity for advancement (Branch 2011). The relegation of Blacks to secondary labor roles meant that they were perpetually under- or un-employed and created a large reserve labor pool from which employers could draw during periods of labor shortage, and that was otherwise expendable (Anderson 1982).

Race and gender led to the dual exploitation of Black women as workers, and conceptions of the proper "place" for Blacks and women provided justification for their extraordinarily low wages (Branch and Wooten 2012). As Jacqueline Jones' depiction of wage inequality in the middle of the twentieth century illustrates, "Nationally, women workers as a whole received less than two-thirds the pay of their male counterparts, but Black women took home yearly paychecks amounting to less than half of White women's" (Jones 1986:261). Occupational segregation by race and gender enabled the perpetuation of racial economic inequality despite persistent hard work.

The passage of the Civil Rights Act legally transformed access to occupational opportunity for Black labor, outlawing for the first time employment discrimination on the basis of race or gender. This required a radical change in the way employers conducted business, since racial discrimination in the labor market was rampant. Initially, enforcement was weak. A 1975 report by the General Accounting Office found that enforcement of affirmative action policy by the contract compliance program was "almost nonexistent" (Branch 2011:137). Despite this, measurable progress in Black occupational achievement was made, due in large part to employment growth. Economist Jonathan S. Leonard argues that representation of minorities and women significantly increased "in establishments that were growing and so had many job openings, irrespective of affirmative action" (Leonard 1990:50).

Yet affirmative action did matter and its impact is seen most clearly in the uneven distribution of Blacks in the public and private sector by 1980. Increased enforcement of affirmative action began in the mid to late 1970s. All organizations were supposed to follow its guidance, but for federal contractors there was an enforceable obligation tied to their bottom line. Executive Order 11246 issued by President Lyndon B. Johnson on September 24, 1965, required federal contractors to take affirmative action to ensure equal opportunity for employment. Section 202, which outlines the contractors' agreement states:

> The contractor will not discriminate against any employee or applicant for employment because of race, color, religion, sex, or national origin. The contractor will take affirmative action to ensure that applicants are employed, and that employees are treated during employment, without regard to their race, color, religion, sex or national origin. Such action shall include, but not be limited to the following: employment, upgrading, demotion, or transfer; recruitment or recruitment advertising; layoff or termination; rates of pay or other forms of compensation; and selection for training, including apprenticeship.

The most severe penalty for non-compliance was prohibition from participation in future federal contracts. Between 1974 and 1980, Leonard found the share of Black men and women "increased significantly faster in contractor establishments than in noncontractor establishments," and this pattern persisted even after taking establishment size, growth region, industry, as well as occupational and corporate structure into account (1990:50).

Affirmative action, however, only formally applied to the public sector and to private companies that received federal contracts, leading to the overrepresentation of Blacks in the public sector and their incremental integration into the private sector. But continued enforcement of affirmative action to sustain progress required political will, and by most accounts it was short-lived. Sociologists Kevin Stainback, Corre L. Robinson and Donald Tomaskovic-Devey examined the role of shifting political tides regarding enforcing affirmative action on trends in workplace racial desegregation, and concluded, "Racial desegregation is an ongoing politically mediated process, not a natural or inevitable outcome of early civil rights movement victories" (2005:1200). The failure to continue after 1980 the trend toward racial desegregation that began in 1966 signaled that the political will had died. The Reagan administration changed affirmative action from an active program to a symbolic one since there was virtually no enforcement after 1980 (Branch 2011). Blacks did not have a generation fully reap the benefits of civil rights and affirmative action. Instead, their progress was interrupted almost as soon as it began.

The consequences were swiftly seen. Leonard found that, "between 1980 and 1984, both Black male and female employment grew more slowly among contractors than non-contractors," a sharp reversal of the late 1970 trend (1990:58). In 1985, the Equal Employment Opportunity Commission (EEOC) substantially narrowed its scope and influence by deciding to move away from taking legal actions to help minority groups broadly and focused instead on individual instances of discrimination. Again, the impact on Black workers was decisive and harmful. Sociologists A. Silvia Cancio, David T. Evans and David Maume Jr. found that the wage penalty for Black workers increased when comparing cohorts of young workers in 1976 and 1985 and were not explained away by industrial change, educational attainment or differences in soft skills. Instead, they argue, the failure of the EEOC to enforce anti-discrimination laws "affected the hiring, pay, and promotion practices of organizations," and firms "discriminated against Black workers because the penalty for doing so was reduced or eliminated" (1996:548).

The threat of affirmative action enforcement mattered, as much as action being taken, because it incentivized employers to overcome the tendency toward racial-typing. Once that incentive, coercive pressure and threat was gone, employers returned to old habits, using racial identity as shorthand for a desirable or undesirable employee. As late as 1986, sociologist Robert Kaufman found a "systematic patterning of the allocation of Blacks and Whites to labor-market positions," after taking into account differences in their individual work-related characteristics (1986:310). He concluded racial-typing of jobs was evident, such that "low-skill work has been labeled as appropriate and high-skill work has been labeled as inappropriate for Blacks by this society in the past" (Kaufman 1986:321).

Despite formal prohibitions against prejudice and discrimination, racism expressed through the racial preferences of employers in allocating workers to jobs remains a stubborn obstacle for Black workers. Employers often use race and gender as proxies for productivity, such that "individuals are stereotyped as qualified or not, with more attention given to their membership in a race or sex group and less attention paid to their personal qualifications" (Kaufman 2002:550). Yet the rise of credentialization, since the 1970s, has tempered the use of ascriptive characteristics (such as race and gender) in job placement, limiting discrimination among credentialed (educated) workers. However, in the absence of a skill constraint, "employers [still] meet employment needs by hiring their preferred group, White men" (Kaufman 2002:565; Moss and Tilly 2001). Sociologist Donald Tomaskovic-Devey similarly argues that "[r]acial and gender segregation are intertwined with the very fabric of work," such that race and gender shape the allocation of workers to positions as well as the rewards associated with the position, even for workers performing the same role in the same workplace (1993:4).

The pervasiveness of racial discrimination in the private sector led Black workers to seek work in the public sector, where affirmative action formally applied. Between 1950 and 1970, the percentage of government workers compared to all workers grew by 44 percent; however, the percentage of Black women who were government workers grew by 140 percent (Burbridge 1994:104). Between 1970 and 1990, the percentage of government workers declined relative to all workers by 6 percent; but the percentage of Black women who were government workers grew by 7 percent despite the overall decline (Burbridge 1994:105). Public-sector employment fueled the growth of the Black middle class, but it left Blacks vulnerable to economic swings, policy shifts and budget cuts as public-sector work declined. From 1980 to 1990, sociologists Yvonne D. Newsome and F. Nii-Amoo Dodoo (2002) found that the percentage of Black women employed in public-sector jobs declined from nearly 32 percent to roughly 28 percent. Similarly, sociologists George Wilson, Vincent J. Roscigno and Matt Huffman (2013) found that privatization in the public sector leads to downward mobility among Black men who work full-time.

Trouble for Black workers arose due to decreasing affirmative-action enforcement, a declining public sector *and* changes in the

nature of work itself. America's industrialized sector, which once supported low-skill workers with a living wage, has eroded since 1970.
The rapid growth of the technological and service sector did not make
up for the job losses since it demanded well-compensated high-skill
workers and poorly compensated low-skill workers. Manufacturing
decline had a clear impact on Black workers as union jobs at a
manufacturing plant were what many aspired to (Honey 1999). Once
they gained access to these semiskilled and unskilled jobs, serving as
operatives and laborers, they were at the end of the seniority line. The
last workers hired and the first to go, Black workers bore the weight
of involuntary job loss due to plant closures between 1979 and 1986
(Kletzer 1991).

Moreover, low-skilled Black workers were unable to find comparable jobs to the ones they had lost. The emergent post-industrial labor
market rewarded highly skilled workers, but the majority of Blacks
were overrepresented in and reliant on older and declining segments of the economy (manufacturing, construction, etc.) (Fischer
and Hout 2007; Kalleberg 2011). Low-skilled Black women were
absorbed by the burgeoning service economy, sociologists Becky
Pettit and Stephanie Ewert found in their study of the erosion of
Black women's relative wages since 1980, noting that Black women
"are overrepresented in occupations that are more likely to be both
part-time and poorly paid," reflecting their lack of occupational
choices (2009:474).

As it did in the past, occupational segregation plays a key role in
the maintenance of inequality. When examining the cause of the
wage differential of Blacks employed in predominantly Black jobs
versus predominantly White jobs, sociologists Irene Browne, Cynthia
Hewitt, Leann Tigges and Gary Green found that "Predominantly
Black jobs are overrepresented within the positions that experienced
falling returns to wages with the restructuring of the US economy –
service industries and occupations that require few skills" (2001:473).
The proliferation of the service sector, decline of manufacturing,
and increase in the returns to education have significantly altered, if
not erased, the path for semi- and unskilled workers to exit poverty
(Morris and Western, 1999).

Working Poverty, Welfare and the Racial Frame

Thus far, we have seen how race structured access to work in
America, legally discriminating against Blacks until 1964 and lim-

iting opportunity through racial-typing and occupational/industrial change thereafter. The consistent Black American reality has been of unequal opportunity and depressed economic rewards. Persistent Black poverty must be understood as a direct consequence of historical deliberate Black labor market restriction. In the middle of the nineteenth century, the vast majority of American workers could be considered working poor. But the make-up of the working poor has always been circumscribed by identity, and racial identity was the dividing line in this historical context. Even the challenges of immigrants were defined in racial terms and overcoming these challenges became tied to the adoption and recognition of White racial identity, as described in the case of Irish immigrants above.

Sociologists Hayward Derrick Horton, Verna Allen, Cedric Herring and Melvin Thomas in their 2000 study, "Lost in the Storm: The Sociology of the Black Working Class, 1850–1990," found that the majority of Blacks were represented in the working poor until 1940, whereas the majority of Whites were represented in the working poor only until 1870. These differences were even more exaggerated when they considered the impact of gender on working poverty. The majority of White women were represented in the working poor through 1910; whereas the majority of White men were represented therein only through 1870.

For Blacks, the gender story is even more striking and prolonged. The majority of Black men were represented in the working poor through 1910, but by 1920 their numbers in the working poor and working class were equal, and by 1940 the majority were in the working class. In 1920, which represented a major period of transition in labor market opportunity for Black men, the vast majority of Black women (86 percent) were still represented in the working poor (Branch 2018). Moreover, the majority of Black women did not exit the working poor until 1960, amid a time of industrial shifts and occupational uncertainty. For those with low skills, options were few and barriers were high. These trends reflect the pervasiveness of race- and gender-based occupational segregation. A growing and diversifying economy presented expanding opportunities that enabled the occupational and economic mobility of Black men and White women, while strict adherence to racial and gender hierarchies artificially constrained Black women (Branch 2007). They were overrepresented in poorly paid occupations and nearly absent among lucrative occupations.

Employers were explicit in their preference for White workers, and hosts of stereotypes typified their view of Black women. Social scientists Edward William Noland and Edward Wight Bakke, in their 1977 book *Workers Wanted: A Study of Employers' Hiring Policies, Preferences, and Practices in New Haven and Charlotte*, document the prevailing views. White women were assumed to be superior to Black women as workers. In production, employers excluded Blacks because they believed them to be of lower intelligence and insufficiently trained. Beyond job-related characteristics, employers frequently extended their musings to the personality and character of potential employees. Black workers were described as "unreliable, irresponsible, lazy, overbearing, unambitious," by Northern employers, but Southern employers, Noland and Bakke argue, "found little necessity for applying such terms since they did not feel under obligation to justify any discrimination in preferences" (1977:32). The stereotypes about Blacks as undesirable workers persisted because Blacks were essentially excluded from occupational opportunities where they would have had the "chance" to discredit the stereotype. It is through this lens of artificially constrained occupational opportunity and the resultant working poverty that we want to consider anew stereotypes about Black women, welfare and dependency.

Welfare and the Consequences of Unequal Opportunity

Black women have traditionally occupied the lowest rung on the American economic ladder. Even today, the general public interprets references to the underclass – those who are poor, unwilling to work and looking for a handout – as referring particularly to Black women and their children. Further, the widely circulated image of a welfare queen perverted the public view of the average woman on welfare. She is almost universally imagined to be Black, poor, undeserving and in an intergenerational cycle of poverty that reflects her poor choices. As discussed in chapter 2, racial frames vilify Black women for being in poverty but obfuscate the cause. Rarely, if ever, in the public domain, do we join the history of unequal opportunity with persistent poverty. Instead, we draw on centuries-old racial stereotypes of worthiness and stigma that masks the truth – the majority of welfare recipients are White. White reliance on state support to navigate economic instability is framed sympathetically; recipients are hardworking, victims of economic exploitation and governmental negligence. Blacks, however, are portrayed simplistically and negatively as inherently lazy, and the programs that help them as "waste, fraud, and abuse" (Unnever, Cullen and Jones 2008; Nielsen, Bonn and Wilson 2010).

These competing frames and the misguided view that Blacks were disproportionately benefiting from and abusing welfare eroded the societal will to support the poor. The 1990s marked an end to federal interest in the War on Poverty, which began in the 1960s. An underlying assumption that provided the motivation for the Personal Responsibility and Work Opportunity Reconciliation Act of 1996 was that the nation's poor were universally underclass, unemployed individuals willing to live off of the nation's dole indefinitely, unless their behavior was regulated. Hence, the title of the bill pays homage to the notion of the need for increased personal responsibility as a means of reforming welfare. The characterization of all poor people as underclass and in need of increased personal responsibility is false, but was driven by racially familiar undertones. The same stereotypes that excluded Black women from labor market opportunity shredded the social safety net that could stabilize them economically.

These contemporary trends of Black exclusion have deep historical roots. Recall, from chapter 2, that racial frames attempt to normalize racial oppression (e.g. slavery) by making it seem "cultural" or natural to assign blame. Frames "hold individuals responsible for certain issues, or episodes that occur in society," but frames are not universally applied (Eargle, Esmail and Sullivan 2008). Power, in particular the ability of a group or individual actor to transmit their ideas to or through a population, determines whether and how broadly a frame is adopted, and whether and to what degree it is challenged. Let's take, for example, the evolution in public support for welfare. Judging through a contemporary lens, it is conceivable to think that welfare is at odds with American beliefs about hard work, but that is false.

The Origins of Welfare and Black Women's Exclusion

The original federal welfare policy of the early twentieth century (then called "widows' pensions") reflected White Victorian mores of gender relations and the household division of labor – an ideal of womanhood defined by domesticity and nurturing offspring. The "cult of domesticity" crystallized gender roles and idealized the notion that a woman's role was limited to the home – the private sphere (Reskin and Padavic 1994). Labor occurred in the public sphere and was the domain of men. Middle-class, mostly urban, women were encouraged to attain this ideal, although many working-class women attempted to follow suit, often to their detriment (Landry 2000). Aid programs were predicated on notions of "deserving poor" women who were poor "through no fault of their own," and public benefits were intended to spare "good mothers" from having to enter the labor force – at the expense of childrearing – following the loss of a spouse (Hancock 2004). These patriarchal policies, in essence replacing male breadwinners with the state, were lauded for their support of the traditional family.

However, lawmakers in the South insisted upon provisions preventing Black women from receiving benefits, in part in an attempt to ensure that Black women's labor remained available and cheap, and probably also to maintain – through policy – the distinction between Black women and *womanhood* (Landry 2000). Black women were vilified when choosing to stay at home since they were excluded from the ideals of White womanhood and full-time domesticity, and not regarded as "true" women (Branch 2011). Further, Black men did not earn a breadwinner's wage that would have enabled them to support their families in the absence of their wife's earnings. Restrictive provisions in the federal bill included the disqualification of domestic or agricultural workers (the occupational mainstays of Black women), and less-than-subtle local amendments included the suspension of Black women's benefits during cotton harvesting season (Kohler-Hausmann 2007; Cammett 2014). The interweaving of chivalry and the prohibition of Black women from receiving benefits made these programs as popular in the South as they were across the country.

Welfare did not become controversial, and trigger the sustained, racialized backlash that surrounds it today, until the 1960s, when the systematic exclusion of Black mothers ceased under President Johnson. Following these reforms, conservative candidates and lawmakers concertedly portrayed welfare, food stamps and Black Americans as near-synonymous, centering the discussion on personal responsibility, self-sufficiency and, most of all, deservedness (Cammett 2014; Pied 2018). The provision of benefits to qualifying Black mothers quickly shifted public perception against recipients and the program itself, despite the predominance of White recipients (Hancock 2004; Foster 2008; Cammett 2014). The program that was once valorized for paying mothers to stay home with their children was now castigated for enabling "lazy" and "exploitative" "welfare queens," and the acceptance of Black mothers onto the rolls more or less coincided with the program being decried as wasteful, and its recipients fraudulent (Hancock 2004; Cammett 2014).

The shift in political sentiment against welfare was near-contemporaneous with Senator Daniel Patrick Moynihan's 1965 report *The Negro Family: The Case for National Action*. While ostensibly sympathetic to Black Americans on the economic margins, Moynihan helped to provide what has proven to be an enduring post-Civil Rights framework for intertwining race and poverty, by describing Black poverty as a "tangle of pathology" resulting from a combination of Black mothers' supposed deviant sexual behavior, low marriage rates and employment patterns (Gustafson 2009; Carpenter 2012). While he blamed centuries of slavery for the destruction of Black family norms, his framing made Blacks' deviance a defining trait of their "culture," with implications for every aspect of their lives and for the policies that could ameliorate their negative outcomes (Carpenter 2012).

Others, far less sympathetic than Moynihan, eagerly adapted this line of thinking, apparently choosing the middle ground in the classic "nature vs. nurture" debate by downplaying slavery and the effects of structural inequality, and adding intent to the "tangle of pathology." Politicians and commentators suggested that poverty is a choice, a conscious rejection of commonly accepted means of self-determination (Derkas 2012). Political scientist Lawrence Mead (1986) went as far as to argue that Blacks prefer public assistance to the low-paying jobs that immigrants use to move out of poverty.

Contemporary Welfare and the Undeserving Black Woman

The media – often subtly and at times explicitly – framed Blacks negatively or unsympathetically (Lubin 2015), and stereotypes of Blacks as "lazy, poor, violent, unintelligent, and welfare dependent" can and did turn public opinion against otherwise fairly popular social policy once Blacks were imagined as the primary beneficiaries (Eargle et al. 2008). During the 1976 presidential primaries, candidate Ronald Reagan began recounting reports of "welfare queen" Linda Taylor, a Chicago resident who had been charged with defrauding the assistance program. He regaled crowds with tales of her collection of benefits under dozens of names, addresses and social security numbers, ultimately amassing over $150,000 (Kohler-Hausmann 2007). Reagan would continue to adapt his version of her story throughout his campaign until it reached folk status, scaling up the amount of money she had bilked, the number of children, husbands and paramours she had left in her wake, as well as the number of Cadillacs and other expensive signifiers of wealth she had amassed (Cammett 2014).

These tales were especially resonant with White working and

middle-class audiences, people whose own hard work often did not yield the rewards that an alleged "welfare queen" might reap (Foster 2008). While Taylor herself was racially ambiguous, Reagan didn't have to know or describe her race in his framing, as he had already painted – and his audiences imagined – a picture of an inner city-dwelling, criminally manipulative woman who could *only* be Black. His descriptions of her behavior drew upon existing stereotypes of Black matriarchs, with elements of "mammy," "Jezebel" and "Sapphire" (Carpenter 2012; Cammett 2014). The welfare queen's implicit partner in crime (if only in absentia) was the Black "deadbeat dad," the non-resident and non-involved father who had no place in the home, and their children were supported by taxpaying responsible citizens (Kohler-Hausmann 2007).

While the growing stereotype of the dishonest welfare queen probably represented a small fraction of actual recipients, the stereotype shaped local and national reforms nonetheless. Changes led to more punitive, fraud-focused policies that presumed criminality on the part of recipients (Kohler-Hausmann 2007; Gustafson 2009) and, accordingly, are oriented toward uniquely gendered behavioral control (Schram, Soss, Fording and Houser 2009; Derkas 2012). States' reforms often outwardly overlapped with the criminal justice system: New York jurisdictions in the 1960s forced recipients to pick up their monthly checks in police precincts, and, in the late 1990s, forced recipients to collect trash on the highways – while clad in orange prison jumpsuits – in exchange for their cash grants (Kohler-Hausmann 2007).

Politicians were often fond of scrutinizing Black culture and the personal lives and sexual behavior of recipients, and the execution of social aid programs often reflected this: whether through official policy or personal bias, case workers routinely engage recipients about their sexual behavior in ways middle-class women would not tolerate from the state (Masters, Lindhorst and Myers 2014), and marriage incentives, which are based now on a century-old assumption of male breadwinning and out-of-wedlock births as the *cause* of poverty, not an effect of it (Edin and Reed 2005), are often presented as the obvious alternatives to cash benefits. The roots of the contemporary focus on Black welfare recipients' sexual behavior and reproductive decisions (Masters et al. 2014) can be traced to the twentieth-century eugenics movement, which also "combined biology and behavior," and used science to rationalize inequality (McDaniel 1996).

In that period, eugenicists' focus on racial differentials in fertility (which occurs in contexts where race is already salient), coupled with pseudo-scientific definitions of racial superiority and inferiority, led to proposals for policies to decrease the birthrate among the "unfit," a group which included the poor, criminals, unmarried mothers but, more often, Blacks (McDaniel 1996). A century later, welfare reform proposals and actual policies continue to include provision for controlling the fertility of the poor, through economic penalties for additional births or compulsory birth control or sterilization, programs that in practice have far more to do with shaping behavior and signaling morals than actually addressing the causes of poverty (Thomas 1998).

While the outright elimination of public assistance for Black women is no longer possible, jurisdictions often have latitude regarding which recipients to sanction and how, with allegedly colorblind applications of sanctions nonetheless following patterns of race (Schuman et al. 2008; Masters et al. 2014). Studies have found that having limited education and being Black are the best predictors of sanctions when controlling for other factors, and increases in sanctions occurred in areas with the largest Black populations (Gustafson 2009), and, in the case of Florida, in more conservative regions, with chances of sanction there increasing with the duration of individuals' claims for assistance (Schram et al. 2008). The risk increases for Black mothers whose lifestyles comport with elements of the "welfare queen" stereotype, such as being unmarried and/or unemployed (Monnat 2010). Black recipients have also been found more likely than their White counterparts to have their cases closed – as opposed to their benefits reduced – and are more likely to be sanctioned for "unidentified" reasons, which often include behavioral requirements set by caseworkers (Monnat 2010).

As one might expect, having prior sanctions on one's record increases the risk of future sanctioning, which also disproportionately disadvantages Black recipients. In areas with stringent work requirements, Black women have experienced less support in getting off of welfare, and, while they are sometimes more likely than their White counterparts to get job interviews, they are also more likely to have to take pre-employment tests, and be tested for drug and alcohol use (Bonds 2006). Those who do get off generally land in low-wage work and must supplement their incomes with the Earned Income Tax Credit (EITC) or the Supplemental Nutrition Assistance Program (SNAP) (Wilson 2017). Leaving public assistance did not make them self-sufficient, as politicians contended; only securing a job with a living wage can do that.

Conclusion: Race and Class, Exploring the Prism of Difference

There is a widening gulf among Black Americans that has resulted from the class differentiation that increasing occupational opportunity has enabled since 1970. A well-educated and increasingly prosperous Black elite has become increasingly distinct – in interests and experiences – from an increasingly isolated and poor Black community (Ford 2009; Shelton and Wilson 2009). Some prominent Black conservatives, for example, have echoed politicians presenting the "culture of poverty" as the divide that separates the Black middle class from the Black poor. Entertainer Bill Cosby has argued that, since the Civil Rights era, personal responsibility (or the lack thereof) is far more relevant to Black success than transcending or ameliorating racism (Nunnally and Carter 2012).

Yet the reality remains that Blacks were bought and brought to the United States to serve as an exploitable and distinctive class of laborers – slaves – and there was no plan for their eventual societal integration as equals. This social fact has consequences. Historian Manning Marable, in his book *How Capitalism Underdeveloped Black America: Problems in Race, Political Economy, and Society*, argues: "Once 'freed,' Black Americans were not compensated for their 246 years of free labor . . . The only means of survival and economic development they possessed was their ability to work, their labor power, which they sold" (2000:7). Yet Blacks were never compensated equitably for their labor – even when performing identical jobs to Whites, they were not paid "White wages." Although slavery ended, the ideological underpinning that sustained slavery was never challenged. Racism helped manage the dissonance between American ideals of equality and Black exclusion, ideologically justifying the differential treatment of Blacks as free laborers. While Black slavery was wrong, Black labor equality with Whites was heresy. So the existence of rampant racial discrimination in the labor market is not at all a surprise. Yet consider the economic implications as posed by Marable: "Throughout the totality of economic relations, Black workers were exploited – in land tenure, in ownership of factories, shops and other enterprises, in the means of transportation, in energy, and so forth. *The constant expropriation of surplus value created by Black labor is the heart and soul of underdevelopment*" (2000:7, emphasis in original). The devastating consequences of underdevelopment are evident in the formation and persistence of the ghetto, which concentrates Black poverty.

Yet, more than ensuring equality, meritocracy points to America as the "land of opportunity." It is on this score that the divisions between the rising Black elite and the Black poor are most salient. They were evident throughout the twentieth century in various Black rights movements, with camps that favored integration arguing that all Blacks needed was a chance, the opportunity to compete, to demonstrate that they were equal. These views were juxtaposed against those advocating for the Black poor, recognizing they had no realistic prospects of being accepted into the White mainstream. These divisions and fundamental differences in real and perceived societal opportunity resulted in a differentiation in the types of racism Blacks experienced in the post-Civil Rights era. The racism suffered by middle-class Blacks (rising Black elite) – subtle bias, decreased access to networking opportunities and mentoring, and cool reception into largely White neighborhoods – became increasingly divorced from that faced by their poorer counterparts, who faced unemployment, violent crime, failing schools and increased health disparities (Ford 2009; Shelton and Wilson 2009).

While occupational opportunity was systematically denied to Black Americans – free Blacks before emancipation and all Blacks thereafter – the socioeconomic differentiation of the Black community has meant that, while middle-class Blacks still face racism and it does impact their occupational opportunities, they have access that is fundamentally denied to their marginalized counterparts (Feagin and Sikes 1995; Young 2004). Special judgment and cultural malignment are reserved for the Black poor. They are the group for whom the promise of America as the land of opportunity is most cruel and the present minimization of the role of racial discrimination in shaping the context for Black labor is most meaningful. Consider this, sociologist Devah Pager conducted an *audit study*, sending out paired participants with identical details with the exception of race to formally test whether a criminal record affects subsequent employment opportunities and how it may affect Whites and Blacks differently. Racism was alive and well, actively shaping the experiences of Black and White job-seekers. She found White job applicants with a criminal record were treated *more* favorably than Black applicants without a criminal record (Pager 2003). Although punditry often focuses on laziness and unwillingness of the Black poor to work, historically – and at present – Blacks have faced decades of blocked opportunity, the consequences of which define life for the Black poor today.

We have demonstrated how race fundamentally structures work in America, limiting Black occupational mobility; in the next chapter, we will similarly examine how race fundamentally structures engagement with the criminal justice system. Racial frames, which depict criminality as inherent to Blackness, have criminalized the Black body from the post-emancipation period to the contemporary schoolyard.

Critical Reflection Questions

1 Explain why race is fundamental to American conceptions of labor and how it manifested differently in the North and South.
2 Describe the causes and consequences of Blacks' overrepresentation in the public sector.
3 When and why did welfare become controversial?

6

Is Justice Blind?
Race and the Rise of Mass
Incarceration

with Lucius Couloute

Race, as a concept, has long been understood to be a product of soci-ohistoric processes involving power relations between social groups. From colonization, to chattel slavery, to the Jim Crow South, systems of racial classification have historically demarcated those in power from the powerless. Even today, as formal systems of racial control have gone by the wayside in the United States, power differentials in the form of income, employment and wealth inequality map easily onto the contours of race – pointing to its continued significance. Fundamentally, sociologist Howard Winant argues, **race** "signifies and symbolizes sociopolitical conflicts and interests in reference to different types of human bodies" (Winant 2000b:172). Like other categories, the concept of race does boundary work (Tilly 1998). It helps to group certain bodies together based on socially relevant criteria, while simultaneously differentiating them from other kinds of bodies. That is, race and other categories function relationally, gaining and giving meaning based on that which they exclude (Glenn 2002). To the extent that Blackness is associated with criminality, Whiteness represents the opposite – righteousness, law abidance and morality.

As such, it is impossible to understand the Black experience in the United States without interrogating the criminalization of Black bodies. Black feminist Angela Davis reminds us that "because of the persistent power of racism, 'criminals' and 'evildoers' are, in the collective imagination, fantasized as people of color" (Davis 2003:16). This has been true since emancipation and continues today, shaping many of the topics explored in this volume, including access to neighborhoods, schools, jobs and healthcare. The result is that millions of Black people in America find themselves wrapped in webs of criminal justice system control, locked out of social resources, and blocked from economic mobility structures not because they have not bought into the American Dream, but because systems of Black marginalization and White privilege require "problem people." In the United States, the millions of Black people under some form of criminal justice system control represent that problem.[1] Indeed, the Black body has been pathologized: the perpetual wrongdoer, the criminal element, the super-predator. Rarely, if ever, do Black bodies escape some form of criminalization, even amid increasing numbers of Black people in the middle class. Evidence for this claim lies in the extraordinary numbers of incarcerated Blacks relative to their overall representation in the American population. Let's take a closer look at mass incarceration and its outsized impact on the Black community.

Policing the Black Body: Race, Surveillance and Mass Criminalization

The use of prisons in the United States has grown precipitously in the last five decades. Today, around 1.5 million people are incarcerated in prisons across the country, up from about 100,000 in the 1970s.[2] Unfortunately, our carceral system doesn't end there. Over 600,000 people are incarcerated in local jails, and in most cases for low-level offenses or lack of funds to post bail. More times than not, they are awaiting a plea deal. Because of the transient nature of jails, which operate as a first stop for those who have been accused of crime, many more people *experience* jail than reside in them at any given time. In fact, over 10 million people go to jail each year. Additionally, another 4.5 million people in the United States are under some form of state surveillance, either probation or parole, where they are allowed to live somewhere in the community, but under rigid rules with limited rights.

The American criminal justice system is also racially disproportionate. Although Black people make up 13 percent of the United States population, they make up one-third of the prison population.[3] Of those on probation, 28 percent, and of those on parole, almost 40 percent, are also Black.[4] Alternatively, if we look at the entire United States population, we find that Whites have an incarceration rate of about 380 per 100,000 whereas the incarceration rate for Blacks is about six times higher at 2,207 per 100,000.[5] With such disproportionate statistics, many have argued that the American criminal justice system has a racism problem (Davis 2003; Brewer and Heitzeg 2008).

Maybe, though, the justice system's racial disproportionality and the exponential increase in incarceration rates are the product of increasingly criminal people. If we truly are in a period of mass incarceration, the logic goes, are we also maybe in a period of heightened crime? The answer, however, is simple: no. Overall, crime rates have been in decline since the 1990s, including violent crime which remains at near-historic lows.[6] Furthermore, the argument that Blackness (and any assumed criminal proclivities related to Blackness) is the cause of crime has long been debunked.

Take sociologists Lauren J. Krivo and Ruth D. Peterson's classic 1996 study of differences in crime rates among Black and White neighborhoods. They found that when Black and White neighborhoods "looked" similar (e.g. same levels of poverty and joblessness, same number of professionals and managers, etc.), crime rates were statistically indistinguishable. The results of Krivo and Peterson's study, and many others examining crime at the neighborhood level (Sampson and Groves 1989), are quite clear: Blackness does not produce crime, it is caused by the underlying structural disadvantages. But if crime rates are at an all-time low, and Black people are not committing crime simply because they are Black, what would account for such high incarceration rates, particularly within the Black community? The simple explanation is that concerted policy and practice changes led to the rise and maintenance of mass incarceration.

Beginning in the 1970s and early 1980s, we see a shift toward more punitive determinate sentencing, harsher federal sentencing guidelines, increasing correctional and police budgets, changes in prosecutorial behavior and more extensive use of pre-trial detention (Mauer 2001; Pfaff 2017). These policy changes disproportionately affected structurally disadvantaged communities, and thus those with relatively higher levels of crime. Nationally, criminal justice quickly became a game of punitivity, despite local variation in the way criminal justice systems operated. However, it is important to understand that these policies did not simply happen. Dominant cultural ideas surrounding crime and Blackness laid the ideological foundation from which many carceral policies sprouted. Despite colorblind laws and policies, the "looming criminal threat" has always been associated with Blackness in America.

Connecting the Past and Present: The Sociohistoric Roots of the "Black Crime Problem"

Although most accounts of mass incarceration begin in the 1980s, the full story requires an expanded look into what punishment scholar Ashley T. Rubin calls **prehistory**: "the ideational period in which an idea is created at the margins of criminal justice before manifesting on a wider scale" (2017:195) The criminalization of Black people in the United States goes at least as far back as emancipation, a period when the legal freeing of enslaved people was supposed to have created equality between Blacks and Whites. What occurred, however, was the implementation of newer oppressive institutions – such as lynching, sharecropping and convict leasing – that would reformulate inequality, not eliminate it, and provide the ideological space to link Blackness with criminality. These newer economic and social arrangements preserved a racial hierarchy in which Blacks remained anchored to the bottom and Whites at the top; absent Black enslavement, racism continued.

The passage of the 13th Amendment in 1865 catalyzed these shifts, ensuring that "neither slavery nor involuntary servitude, except as a punishment for crime whereof the party shall have been duly convicted, shall exist within the United States, or any place subject to their jurisdiction" (13th Amendment, US Constitution). Black people were no longer bound to slavery as a legitimate institution, but with a caveat – except for as a punishment of crime. When the crippling effects of the Union victory and 13th Amendment manifested themselves, the South found itself in the midst of an exploitable labor crisis (Hallet 2004). No longer could wealthy White landowners rely upon Black bodies to provide free work, yet there were now many thousands of slaves who were left landless and without employment.

As historian Douglas Blackmon (2008) explains, the limbo of a transforming social order threatened the economic wellbeing of Whites in the South. Enslaved Black people provided both the free physical labor and the expertise driving large-scale agricultural production there. Emancipation created massive uncertainty, on the farm and in the racial hierarchy; a new economic and judicial system was required to preserve White dominance. As W. E. B. Du Bois (1903) described in his seminal work, *The Souls of Black Folk*, "Almost every law and method ingenuity could devise was employed by the legislatures to reduce the Negroes to serfdom, – to make them the slaves of the State, if not of individual owners" (Du Bois 1903:20).

Without many options, free Blacks in the south were coerced, with the complicity of the newly formed Freedman's Bureau, into labor contracts with White plantation owners, stipulating slave-like rules with the promise of pay at the end of the harvest season (Blackmon 2008). "The Negro is not free," remarked Du Bois, "he may not leave the plantation of his birth; in well-nigh the whole rural South the Black farmers are peons, bound by law and custom to an economic slavery, from which the only escape is death or the penitentiary" (Du Bois 1903:23). Black sharecroppers would often find themselves in debt to White landowners after being charged exploitive fees for housing, farm tools and supplies, and losses. They were forced to work off their "debts" until they were paid, under threat of incarceration.

Additionally, a new legal apparatus was created, echoing old slave codes, designed to regulate the lives of post-emancipation Blacks. These newer Black Codes and vagrancy laws criminalized poverty and idleness so that anyone perceived to be without a job, or in violation of a labor contract, could then face penal servitude. As more and more of these codes came into being, Southern penitentiaries became increasingly Black. Black bodies were funneled into prisons for "crimes" that Whites were rarely convicted of and, once incarcerated, Blacks were often sent to the very plantations they had been freed from after the Civil War.

> Once imprisoned for petty crimes, former slaves, now inmates, were leased in large numbers to private vendors as a source of forced labor, to become the foundation of lucrative, profit-driven, White owned businesses. After imposing a service fee to the state for "lease" of the convicts, private vendors housed and fed laborers in their charge, with little or no wage costs and no practical state oversight. The first private for-profit imprisonment system in the US had emerged. (Hallet 2004:51)

With a constant supply of criminalized free Black labor, and without personal investment in any one convicted laborer, White landowners and other business operators had little interest in the wellbeing of their new unpaid "workers," but much to gain from this new system of Black criminalization.

As historian David Oshinsky (1997) documents in his book, *Worse than Slavery: Parchman Farm and the Ordeal of Jim Crow Justice*, systems of convict leasing – rampant with death and oppressive labor conditions – would have often felt worse than slavery. In some ways, the "slaveowner" was not eliminated, he simply had a new uniform, for "the men who now controlled squads of Black laborers available to the highest bidder were sheriffs" (Blackmon 2008:64). Southern criminal justice, operating "largely as a means of controlling Black labor," provided a solution to the economic and social uncertainty catalyzed by the freeing of enslaved people (Davis 2003:31). It delivered a reformulated racial stratification by providing the material from which flawed social statistics – used to criminalize *all* Black people – were constructed.

In *Thicker Than Blood: How Racial Statistics Lie*, sociologist Tufuku Zuberi (2001) argues that, following emancipation, "racially stratified societies had but one argument against yielding to the demand of humanity: they insisted on the importance of the racial difference and on its essential role in producing inequality between non-European-origin persons and the European-origin persons in Europe and in the areas of the European diaspora, especially in the Americas" (Zuberi 2001:3). The newly developing Southern carceral system fed fuel to this essentializing fire.

As Black people were funneled into prisons in order to fulfill the labor needs of the South, social scientists used racially disproportionate arrest and incarceration rates to provide evidence of what anecdote and Darwinist pseudo-science had long maintained: that Black people were inherently inferior. So-called statistical experts in the late nineteenth century, such as Frederick Hoffman, argued that census data and prison statistics "show without exception that the criminality of the negro exceeds that of any other race of any numerical importance in this country" (Muhammad 2010:51).

Historian Khalil Gibran Muhammad (2010) argues that it was not just the use and analysis of prison statistics by social scientists that gave rise to dominant connections between race and crime, but the framing of those statistics along moralistic, White-supremacist terms. The logic was that Black people were not simply incarcerated more often, they were incarcerated more often because they were inferior. By criminalizing vagrancy and incarcerating in a disproportionately racialized manner, the state legitimated a racial ideology purporting Black inferiority. Yet, as Black feminist historian Sarah Haley (2016) illustrates, Southern post-emancipatory carceral regimes not only legitimated a racial order, they maintained a mutually constitutive "racial–gender order" as well. Unequal constructions of Black women as aggressive, of low character, imbecilic and unfit mothers in newspapers, court rooms, clemency hearings and in popular discourse normalized their presence in penitentiaries and in chain gangs. This preserved the power of White men and the assumption of purity surrounding White womanhood (Gross 2015; Haley 2016). To put it frankly, the proof was in the pathologization.

These perceptions of criminality followed the movement of Blacks northward throughout the early twentieth century. In places where White immigrants, benefiting from the wages of Whiteness, achieved economic mobility, Black migrants were largely excluded from social welfare provisions on the basis of stereotypes related to a lack of initiative and criminal propensity (Fox 2012).

Racial terror was also used as a method to delineate the appropriate bounds of Black behavior, especially in the South where, between 1865 and 1965, an estimated 4,000–5,000 lynchings occurred (Brundage 2006). Underpinning this institution was the idea that America was suffering from the "Negro problem," yet in many cases the purported reasons for lynching Black bodies, such as rape, had no relationship to what actually occurred (Payne 2007). In 1945, sociologist Oliver C. Cox argued that what catalyzed the lynching of Blacks had more to do with Whites' anxieties about their economic wellbeing in relation to Blacks than the supposed crimes Blacks had committed. He writes that the lynching cycle begins with "A growing belief among Whites in the community that Negroes are getting out of hand – in wealth, in racial independence, in attitudes of self-assertion especially as workers; or in reliance upon the law. An economic depression causing some Whites to retrograde faster than some Negroes may seem a relative advancement of Negroes in some of the latter respects" (Cox 1945:577).

Sociologists E. M. (Elwood Meredith) Beck and Stewart E. Tolnay (1990) substantiate this claim, finding a relationship between the price of cotton and the prevalence of lynchings before the year 1900. Due to their racial and class position, Black laborers became the object of White scorn and terrorism. The intentional depiction of Blacks as criminals lent legitimacy to this racial terror and solidified the growing idea that there was a racialized crime epidemic. Yet, as historian W. Fitzhugh Brundage argues: "The myth of Black criminality, like many myths, was (and indeed remains) resistant to revision. Even while the practice of lynching changed significantly, Whites clung to the notion that it was the predictable, even justifiable, consequence of Black crime, and particularly sexual assaults" (Brundage 2006:30).

With more prosperous economic periods and the Civil Rights Movement activism of the 1950s and 1960s, lynching eventually lost its prevalence as a widespread method for social control (Brundage 2006; Payne 2007). But even during this era, Black organizing for a more equal society was framed by conservative commentators largely as lawless activity. As Michelle Alexander (2010) explains, Southern politicians and law enforcement officials branded direct-action tactics as a breakdown of law and order, in need of a tough-on-crime response. Although politicians were less likely to use explicitly racist terms, the "colorblind" law-and-order response to the Civil Rights Movement used coded language to reify the link between Blackness and crime. The White conservative backlash to the Civil Rights Movement aimed to preserve the existing social hierarchy as if privilege was understood as a zero-sum game.

Black Criminality and Racial Threat

Danger and violence have long been elements of the framing of Blacks in America, particularly Black men. With physicality – through labor – as their most marketable (and socially constructed) trait for most of the country's history, common ascriptions of Black deviance often center on the danger this physicality poses to Whites. Blacks are more likely to be portrayed as suspects on local TV, and attentiveness to crime news is associated both with concern about crime and with perceptions of Black suspects, which prime racial cues in White viewers (Goidel, Parent and Mann, 2011). The perceptions of the prevalence of crime are also skewed by local demographics, with Whites "systematically overestimating crime rates on the basis of the presence of Black and Latino residents" (Doering 2017:277).

This cycle of marginalization, crime, harsh policing, and protest, along with sensationalist media coverage of urban crime, serves to legitimate conservatives' veiled assertions that Black populations are dangerous, and perhaps even *more* dangerous due to civil rights reforms. Many of the proposed policing measures, while ostensibly geared toward lowering crime rates, in practice had far more to do with the continued social control of a people who had so loudly rejected the unfairness of that control (Williams 2007). Blacks are more likely than Whites to be arrested, charged, prosecuted and given long sentences for the same crimes. Yet, even when charges are unlikely, arrests alone are often employed as highly visible engagement by law enforcement in the Black community.

Los Angeles' 1988 "Operation Hammer," for example, was an arrest sweep that covered 10 square miles of South Central, netting over 1,000 arrests, mostly for minor offenses; but 90 percent of arrestees were released without charges, and of the hundreds of Black

youth logged into gang databases, most were found not to have affiliations (ibid.). Far from being a fruitless endeavor, however, a show
of force of this sort signals to voters outside of those communities
the need, willingness and ability to control Black populations. The
outcome of this overpolicing is racialized mass incarceration, which
serves a new kind of caste system that is more resistant to reform on
civil rights grounds because it is not explicitly based on race, and
willingness to recognize structural racism has shifted (Pickett and
Ryon 2017).

While most violent crime is not inter-racial, the notion of the inherent criminality of Blacks is accompanied by the mistaken presumption that their typical victim is White (Jacobs and Tope 2007, 2008).
Gender is often central to this framing, and the supposed inherent
danger posed to White women (themselves framed as fragile) by
Black men has traditionally been the pretext for violence against, and
prosecution of, Black men (McMahon and Kahn 2018), as demonstrated in the thousands of Black men killed by White mobs during
the post-Civil War Reconstruction period, the murder of Emmett Till
in the 1950s, and the swift arrest, prosecution and sentencing of the
so-called Central Park Five, who were later exonerated. The young
mass murderer who opened fire in a predominantly Black church in
South Carolina in 2015 highlighted this supposed threat – among
others – as one of his motivations (McMahon and Kahn 2018).

The cultural relevance – and believability – of this "Black
Boogeyman" who preys on White women has long been a popular
and often successful alibi for White criminals, as seen in the cases of
Charles Stuart of Boston in 1989, and Susan Smith of South Carolina
in 1994. Before Stuart's brother came forward to the authorities to
report that the former had shot his own wife, staged a robbery by
then shooting himself, and fabricated the mysterious "Black gunman
with a raspy voice," Boston police had already swept through predominantly Black neighborhoods and arrested or detained at least
two possible suspects fitting the description offered by Stuart. As the
police conducted their sweep, some Massachusetts lawmakers played
their part by calling for the return of the death penalty (Scalese
2014).[7]

Police showed greater restraint in the case of Smith, and did *not*
immediately seek Black men to arrest after she claimed that a Black
man had carjacked her and driven off with her two young sons. The
media and some officials were less skeptical of her story, reacting to
the danger her account elicited – at least until the boys and the car
were found submerged in a local lake, and Smith herself was arrested.

Given the power of prevailing racial narratives, that Stuart and Smith crafted the stories they did, with as little effort as they did, speaks to an at least partially correct presumption that their accounts would be accepted at face value.

"Tough on Crime"

The widespread belief in Black criminality and the immediacy of the Black threat set the stage for politicians to marshal racial fears for political gain. Though President Nixon opened the door to the "tough-on-crime" political framework through the mobilization of law enforcement militarization funding, under the veiled conflation of civil disobedience and street crime, it was really the Reagan-era Congress and administration that took aim at "Black Boogeyman" through the use of what sociologists call *moral panic*. Leading up to the 1986 Anti-Drug Abuse Act, which created mandatory minimum sentences for possessing about a sugar-packet's worth of crack-cocaine, members of Congress used media reports of Black drug dealers to construct a racialized threat to the wellbeing of American communities (Provine 2011).

Reagan himself relied upon racialized appeals to White America (and racialized fear of Black America) to garner support for both his election and policy restructuring. An emphasis on drug dealers and gangbangers provided a racially coded subtext from which a crime hysteria arose. Without saying so explicitly, the Reagan administration argued that the criminal (Black) element was ruining American communities. And, by 1989, 64 percent of America believed that drugs were the most significant issue facing the United States (Alexander 2010; Provine 2011). The federal government, with the help of other institutions such as the media, organized the drug problem along racialized lines and, thus, effectively re-articulated and reconstructed the "Black crime problem." A newer, punitive policy framework was needed.

Under Reagan, the federal government took a greater role in determining the character of local-level criminal justice, including funneling billions of dollars to the militarization of local police departments. Additionally, the Federal Crime Bill of 1984 created asset forfeiture laws allowing police departments to seize almost all of the property they could associate with people selling drugs (Parenti 2001). The aforementioned Anti-Drug Abuse Act of 1986 placed added emphasis on drug users, mandating that even the smallest amounts of crack would garner higher penalties than large amounts of cocaine. The most well-known sentencing mandate, the "100 to 1 rule," applied to possessing an ounce of crack the same penalty as for 100 ounces of powder cocaine. Considering that powder cocaine is the primary ingredient of crack, and has a far higher street value than crack, the apparent backward nature of this rule is paradoxical, unless creating a racially imbalanced outcome was the intent since crack proliferated in Black communities and cocaine in White ones.

Two years after the Anti-Drug Abuse Act, Congress created additional civil penalties for drug offenders, including the potential eviction of drug users from public housing and the exclusion of people with drug convictions from federal student aid and other social benefits (Alexander 2010). The carceral apparatus in America was changing, now with a greater emphasis on controlling a population that was all but named poor and Black. In 1990, young Black men had a 10 percent chance of going to prison – a number almost 2.5 times higher than similarly situated Black men just 20 years earlier (Pettit & Western 2004). To be the problem (poor and Black) meant experiencing the ravages of mass incarceration on a scale never before seen. To be middle-class and White meant relative insulation from the United States carceral system – regardless of personal behavior.

Even under the Clinton administration, frequently regarded as the polar opposite of the Nixon and Reagan administrations, mass incarceration grew to unprecedented heights. Under Clinton, over $30 billion in federal cash was given to law enforcement agencies across the nation (Parenti 2001). Additionally, undocumented immigrants were stripped of their rights to due process, the use of the death penalty expanded across the United States, lawyers lost their ability to receive legal fees in civil rights suits, and a host of other measures were employed to "take out what little remained for prisoners in the Bill of Rights" (Parenti 2001). From 1990 to 2000, the number of people incarcerated in state or federal prisons grew by over 600,000. As Michelle Alexander explains, "Clinton escalated the drug war beyond what conservatives had imagined possible a decade earlier" (Alexander 2010:55). (Un)remarkably, the connection between crime and color endured. Clinton's liberal administration, supported by First Lady Hillary Clinton's now infamous repudiation of "superpredators," continued a longstanding trend of coded language connecting inner-city Black people to epidemic levels of violent behavior.

Today, Black people are convicted more often than, and experience sentences that are substantially longer than the sentences experienced by, Whites who commit similar crimes; make up 82 percent of those convicted for crack offenses, despite being only 25 percent of users (Provine 2011); and are more likely to be stopped by the police, detained pretrial and charged with serious crimes (Hinton, Henderson and Reed 2018). Racial inequality structures the American carceral system – it isn't simply an outgrowth of it.

This uniquely American system of mass incarceration and criminalization has grown into something no one could have envisioned just 50 years ago, despite beginning over a century ago. But how do we make sense of the criminal justice system today? What role does the widespread criminalization, particularly of Black bodies, play in shaping life chances, social hierarchies and broader inequalities? Put plainly, how do we make sense of mass criminalization and the role it plays in structuring racial inequality in the United States?

Problem Produced: Caste, Citizenship and other Carceral Creations

In her groundbreaking book *The New Jim Crow: Mass Incarceration in the Age of Colorblindness*, Michelle Alexander argues that the contemporary carceral apparatus is not unlike an older system of social control – Jim Crow – that regulated the lives of Black people in maintenance of a racialized hierarchy. Indeed, Alexander (2010) contends that the criminal justice system is less about preventing crime and more about structuring society:

> The current system of control permanently locks a huge percentage of the African American community out of the mainstream society and economy. The system operates throughout criminal justice institutions, but it functions more like a caste system than a system of crime control ... Like Jim Crow (and slavery), mass incarceration operates as a tightly networked system of laws, policies, customs, and institutions that operate collectively to ensure the subordinate status of a group defined largely by race. (Alexander 2010:13)

Despite the fact that Black people make up only about 13 percent of the United States population, over 33 percent of the 20 million US citizens with felony records are Black. Of the over 5 million who have been to prison, nearly 40 percent are Black (Shannon et al. 2017). Imprisonment has become a life-course event for young Black men, who must face the reality that about one in three will at some point serve time (Bonczar 2003; Pettit and Western 2004). But if, indeed, Alexander's argument is valid, we must interrogate the extent to which the lives of criminalized and racialized people truly operate in a manner consistent with the subordination produced by a caste system.

Having been formally criminalized, people with felonies are forced to navigate a world with added barriers bestowed upon no other social group. For example, formally criminalized people are subject to a myriad of rules and regulations restricting their access to fundamental resources necessary for simple survival. Laws restrict their ability to attain occupational licenses and secure federal financial aid, such as Pell grants, that would otherwise fund a college education for those from lower socioeconomic backgrounds. Public housing authorities and landlords can legally deny housing based on prior convictions, and many are excluded from social welfare benefits. Most states go on to restrict the ability of incarcerated, formerly incarcerated or otherwise criminalized people from participating in the democratic process through voting. Many ex-offenders are also mandated by parole stipulations to attain employment, pay rent as mandated by transitory housing services, and relinquish substantial portions of their wages to various entities along the criminal justice pipeline (Caputo 2004; Harris, Evans and Beckett 2010). If they are unable to do so, additional fines and penalties may be imposed. To be criminalized is to experience the world under a unique set of conditions, legally subject to a restrictive set of rules that govern where former convicts can work and live, with whom they can associate, and which social supports they can access.

Individuals under criminal justice supervision – for example, on parole or probation – can be subject to curfews and electronic ankle monitoring, prevented from consuming otherwise legal substances, and are frequently restricted from associating with other people who have felony records. For those leaving prison, almost all are released under parole supervision which typically involves further subjugation, and rarely facilitates reintegration. Based on her experience as a mentor to formerly incarcerated African American men and women, Marie Pryor (2010) attests to the ways in which parole stipulations conflict with one's ability to maintain employment, activate network resources and manage the logistical concerns of daily life. Rather than providing the flexibility necessary for ex-offenders to exercise some semblance of economic, social and political agency familiar to full citizens, the re-entry apparatus' focus is instead upon the "therapeutic management and control" of individuals (Nixon et al. 2008:30). Upon release, former offenders become subjects of the state, forced to abide by a set of constraints unknown to free citizens.

Spotlight on Resistance

Case Study 6 Black Men Making Good: Re-entry in the Fillmore Neighborhood

Black San Franciscans migrated into the city as wartime workers, and when they remained after the war, they were seen as a social and civic problem. Attempts were made to contain the Black problem through employment exclusion and constraining them to public housing in the hope that they would not threaten the city. Urban renewal, redevelopment and law enforcement possessed a firm grip on Black neighborhoods like the Fillmore and Bayview – Hunters Point, labeling them as *bad places* marked by crime and violence. In ethnographer and sociologist Nikki Jones' most recent book, *The Chosen Ones: Black Men and the Politics of Redemption*, she describes how Black men in the Fillmore neighborhood who have served time re-enter, desiring to "make good" in the midst of a newly introduced gang injunction and continuing renewal projects which cause them to feel like "targets for removal by incarceration, eviction or both" (Jones 2018:24).

Brothers Changing the Hood (BCH) is a small community-based organization, created by a local resident named Eric, that aids Black men with records who desire to change their lives. BCH helps them to navigate court cases and targeted police initiatives, as well as to heal and deepen their interpersonal networks in their families and communities. BCH enables men to redefine their place in the neighborhood as buffers from institutional control (law enforcement, redevelopment efforts) as well as contribute to the social life and health of their spaces (Jones 2018).

Post-incarceration life is more akin to a routine of circulation whereby individuals are subject to a nearly unbreakable extension of "punitive containment" (Wacquant 2010). Indeed, a maze of collateral consequences and barriers await those who have been officially designated by the state as "criminal," disrupting their "socioeconomic rights," or an individual's "ability to support [themselves] and/ or to utilize the social safety net" (Archer and Williams 2006:528).

Once marked, criminalized people experience a very punitive form of paternalism. That is, the state's criminal justice arm endeavors to dominate and control all aspects of the criminalized body necessary to ensure the protection of the status quo. Through surveillance and the threat of punishment, the criminal justice system seeks to manage those officially deemed threatening. But, as recent analyses from the Prison Policy Initiative suggest, the contemporary criminal justice apparatus does little to improve the lives of criminalized people. Compared to the general public, formerly incarcerated people are eight times less likely to have a college degree and ten times more likely to be homeless (Couloute 2018a, 2018b). Ex-prisoners are also five times more likely to be unemployed than the general public. The results are worse for Black ex-prisoners. Formerly incarcerated Black women, for example, face the highest unemployment penalties of any racial group (Couloute and Kopf 2018).

Numerous constraints pose challenges to gaining employment. Hourly wages, employment hours, annual earnings and earnings growth decrease substantially for those who have experienced incarceration (Western 2006). Part of the problem is that all states have policies restricting the kinds of occupational licenses or forms of employment people with criminal records may attain (Petersilia 2003; Pager 2006; Alexander 2010). The ability of employers who might otherwise hire an ex-offender is further limited by employer liability policies whereby employers can be penalized for failing to check criminal backgrounds and exposing the public to potentially dangerous environments (Solomon et al. 2004; Weiman 2007).

Being criminalized is a permanent, dehumanizing condition. Criminologists Daniel S. Murphy, Brian Fuleihan, Stephen C. Richards and Richard S. Jones refer to this system, aided by technological advancements, as the "electronic scarlet letter," "[conferring] a stigmatized identity upon the bearer and [rendering] him or her forever suspect by others" (Murphy et al. 2011:104). Inmate numbers, labels such as "criminal" or "felon," and the difficulty in attaining even a minimally stable economic footing contribute to what sociologist Joshua Price calls "spirit murder"; the "psychosocial, material, and legal complex of paternalism, disregard, resentment, and pitiless derision" defining the lives of criminalized people (2015:127).

The work of sociologist Reuben Miller and colleagues on re-entry and criminalization (Miller 2014; Miller and Alexander 2016; Miller and Stuart 2017) further emphasizes how the American carceral state has created new forms of living and being altogether. They argue that the range of collateral consequences facing ex-prisoners, in addition to the expectations attached to those marked as criminal, have created not a second-class citizenry, but an entirely new form of attachment to the American polity: carceral citizenship. Racialized and formally criminalized people must not only negotiate separate and unequal social barriers, such as criminal records, but also the informal requirements demanded of them. Under the presumption of poor moral character, those marked as criminal are expected to repay a symbolic debt to account for their civil sins, which might include fines and fees, self-help programs and other forms of civic engagement to prove a newfound trustworthiness. These informal expectations placed upon carceral citizens informally delineate the trusted "us" from the untrusted "them," rearticulating relationships with not only the state, but the organizations, families and individuals around them.

Criminalized people exist as an altogether separate class (or caste) of individuals, excluded from the social and economic resources of full citizens, and subject to an alternate range of social expectations (Alexander 2010; Miller and Stuart 2017). But we would argue that this isn't simply about creating a "new" group of disadvantaged people (although the rise and continuance of mass criminalization is historically unprecedented and unique). The systemic funneling of Black bodies into the criminal justice system, and then out into the world where they experience continued oppression, contributes to a larger system of race-making, of socially (mis)constructing Blackness.

Historically, mechanisms of social control, such as convict leasing, have operated as projects contributing to American racial formation, or, as Omi and Winant define them: "the sociohistorical process by which racial categories are created, inhabited, transformed, and destroyed" (1994:55). The association of Blackness with criminality hardened as more Black people were trapped in racist post-emancipatory systems of criminal justice to fulfill burgeoning labor needs, and as social scientists used disproportionate prison statistics to prove their own biases. Similarly, contemporary criminal justice practices, policies and outcomes function collectively as a racial project.

Normalizing Surveillance: Racial Formation and the Forces Driving Mass Incarceration

Mass incarceration has had a direct impact on the production of racial inequality, or process of racial formation, in America. Whether or not communities exhibit high levels of crime, as the number of Black men in any one community increases, perceptions of rising crime tend to follow (Quillian and Pager 2001). Indeed, studies show that, in general, Whites tend to overestimate crime rates among Black people by upward of 20 percent (Ghandnoosh 2014). The **broken**

windows theory of policing holds that visible signs of crime, anti-social behavior, and civil disorder create an urban environment that encourages further crime and disorder. As a result, urban hubs such as Oakland, Chicago and New York have historically subjected people of color to over-policing under the assumption that it prevents larger, more serious crimes. In practice, strategies like stop-and-frisk disproportionately subject poor Blacks to invasive policing tactics and perpetuate the idea that Black communities require punitive social control. In some communities, despite the fact that crime has been declining for decades, over 1 million dollars per year goes into policing and incarcerating people of color.[8]

The assumption of Black criminality endures even in the absence of criminal behavior. Researchers have also found ample evidence that non-Blacks connect Blacks to guns and violence more often than they do Whites (Payne 2001). One study even found that, after being incarcerated, ex-prisoners are more likely to identify and be seen as Black, and less likely to identify and be seen as White (Saperstein and Penner 2010). Being Black puts you at risk of formal criminalization, through arrest, incarceration or supervision, *and* guarantees that, even if you have never come into contact with the criminal justice system – you're assumed to be dangerous.

The linkages between Blackness and other tenets of constructed inferiority – such as laziness – also find reinforcement in the ongoing criminalization of Black bodies. Western and Pettit (2005), for example, estimate that 7-20 percent of the Black–White wage gap from 1980 to 1999 was due to joblessness arising from mass incarceration. Furthermore, among those who have experienced incarceration, 35 percent and 40 percent of Black men and women respectively are unemployed (Couloute and Kopf 2018).[9] Despite the fact that jobless formerly incarcerated people are more likely to be looking for employment than the jobless general public, mass incarceration has produced mass unemployment among criminalized Black people who largely face individualistic decrees to lift themselves up by their bootstraps and become more productive workers (see Thompson and Bobo 2011).

The structural conditions awaiting poor Black ex-prisoners, who largely return to the impoverished areas from which they came, tend to create a perfect storm of disadvantage and recidivism (Kubrin, Squires and Stewart 2007; Hipp, Jannetta, Shah and Turner 2011; Mears, Wang and Bales 2014). Yet high rates of prison returns, particularly among Black ex-prisoners, are frequently explained away by using the language of choice and responsibility, positioning those who cycle in and out of prison as lazy or bad people (boogeymen), reinforcing the need for a punitive paternalist state. Faced with immense social barriers to economic stability, the linkages between joblessness, laziness and Blackness harden in the context of mass criminalization.

Historian W. Fitzhugh Brundage argues (2006) that, mindful of prisons crowded with Blacks in the post-emancipation period, Whites concluded that a new class of criminal Blacks was responsible for the epidemic of crime which threatened to overwhelm the region. Similarly, the massive increase in the number of Black bodies wrapped into the criminal justice system since the 1980s has served to harden the perception that criminalized Black bodies are inappropriate in the labor market (Acker 2006; Wooten and Branch 2012).

Take Devah Pager's (2003) pathbreaking study, "The Mark of a Criminal Record," for example. Pager found that job applicants with criminal records were 50 percent less likely to receive callbacks from employers than those without records. Critical to understanding the link between Blackness and criminality is the fact that, in Pager's sample, job applicants who were Black and *did not* have a criminal record were less likely to receive callbacks than Whites *with* criminal records. Employers use markers such as race to disaggregate between low-skilled applicants assumed to be involved in criminal activity and those marked "White," skilled and stable (Neckerman and Kirschenman 1991; Moss and Tilly 2001). Adding to this wealth of data, in research examining "Ban-the-Box" initiatives (Agan and Starr 2017; Doleac and Hansen 2017), researchers are finding that, in the absence of the ability to decipher which applicants have criminal records, employers engage in increased statistical discrimination against Blacks – using race as a proxy for criminality.

It is in this context that we must situate Black life in America. With millions of people under its control, all assumed to straddle the socially ambiguous line between criminality and Blackness, the criminal justice system also exists as a race-making institution. That is, the American criminal justice system produces race just as much as it relies upon it to deal out American justice. Absent proof, historical connections between race and criminality – reinforced in the current context by decontextualized discussions of so-called "Black-on-Black" crime and media constructions of dangerous Black communities – reinforce systems of discrimination based in the kind of pseudo-evidence used to oppress Black bodies since the post-emancipation era. From periods of explicit racial subjugation to what many have called the era of colorblind racism, being Black in America continues to mean being dangerous.

Conclusion: Becoming Criminal, the Role of the School-to-Prison Pipeline

The suspicion of and danger attributed to the Black body is apparent even for Black children. In his book *Punished: Policing the Lives of Black and Latino Boys*, sociologist Victor Rios (2011) explores the lives of 40 young Black and Latino men in Oakland, California, and paints an illustrative picture of what he calls the "Youth Control Complex." Before the youth Rios studied ever formally came into contact with the criminal justice system, they had experienced informal criminalization at the hands of teachers, police officers and other adults who assumed the youths were indeed criminal. Over the course of his three-year study, aggressive policing which led to minor citations (e.g., for loitering or public drinking) funneled the young men deeper into the criminal justice system, perpetuating the narrative that they were, in fact, deviant.

Similarly, research on the experiences of Black girls increasingly suggests that punitive school disciplinary policies, heightened surveillance, and racialized and gendered expectations around femininity have also resulted in their disproportionate justice system contact (Morris 2012; Crenshaw 2015; Epstein, Blake and González 2017; Kajstura 2018). Black women represent 29 percent of women in prison or jail despite comprising less than 7 percent of the general US population. Importantly, about half of women who end up in state prisons report experiencing prior physical abuse and almost 40 percent report a history of sexual abuse, compared to 13 percent and 6 percent, respectively, among men (Harlow 1999). Recent cases involving Black women attempting to escape from abuse, such as Cyntoia Brown who killed her sex trafficker when she was 16, illustrate what African American studies scholar Kali Gross (2015) calls the "exclusionary politics of protection." Black girls rarely enjoy the protection of laws and organizational policies, but often feel the full weight of their punishments (Gross 2015: 25).

In total, over 50,000 youths are held in United States correctional or quasi-correctional facilities, and nearly 10 percent of them are held in adult facilities (Sawyer 2018). But, rather than a juvenile justice system that addresses only the most severe crimes, young Black youths often face criminal penalties for behaviors that wouldn't be crimes – such as running away or violating curfew – if they weren't already on probation, if they were just a few years older or if they were from a different neighborhood. This racially specific reality of normalized surveillance is highly consequential and shapes the early life experiences of Black Americans. Communities that could be targeted for social investment to improve schools and neighborhood conditions are instead overpoliced and further marginalized.

These outcomes are not the result of neutral actors; politicians, as we have shown, often led the way, framing the issue for the public and steering federal funds toward a particular end. Disproportionate investment in the carceral system was tightly bound up with political actors from both the Republican and Democratic parties. In the final chapter, we examine the role of racism in shaping politics and policy sustaining racial inequality.

Critical Reflection Questions

1 What are the origins of ideas about Black criminality?
2 How are the experiences of Black women and girls in the criminal justice system unique?
3 Describe how Presidents Nixon and Reagan used *moral panic* to justify criminalizing Black communities.

7

Reifying the Problem: Racism and the Persistence of the Color Line in American Politics

with Emmanuel Adero

Politics and policy play a key role in the persistence of racial inequality in the US. The framing of Blacks and the subsequent approaches to civil rights continue to shape the alignments of the Democratic and Republican parties, as well as the parameters through which Black candidates and politicians can operate. However, we have yet to see Black people and their issues fully and equally incorporated into the American political sphere. Both parties have perfected the art of the "dog-whistle" to energize their base. There is often recognition of and willingness to name Blacks as the problem, but unwillingness to acknowledge the structural underpinnings that contribute to the problem, or promote policy that will ameliorate it.

Race is commonly reduced, each election cycle, to an implicit – at best – wedge issue in policy proposals and campaigns, allowing the politics of race to persist in a colorblind society. Simply raising the specter of race and the supposed racial alignment of politicians (most often assumed by party affiliation) has proven more than sufficient in driving voter turnout, from national-level elections to small-town referendums. Attempts at social and legal race-conscious reforms have prompted swift backlash and are a recurring theme in American politics that serves as a yardstick of how far we've come and a mirror that demonstrates how far we still have to go.

To understand how racial avoidance as a means to pander to White voters began, we have to begin at the beginning and understand race – specifically, advocating for the equality of Blacks – as a historical dividing line that fundamentally shaped American politics. In the following section, we examine how the unrest leading up to and following the emancipation of Black slaves created a turbulent American political landscape shaped in large part on what to do about the Black problem: persist in subjugation or pursue equality? This irreconcilable tension defined our contemporary political parties and drove the racial realignments of the two major political parties.

The "Southern Strategy," the Grand Realignment and the Backlash Against Civil Rights

The ideological fissures of the late nineteenth century over **federalism** – the division of power between states and the federal government – and equal rights for Black Americans led to a formal split between Northern and Southern Democrats. By the latter third of the twentieth century, the outgrowth of the ideological split regarding the legal status and engagement of Blacks led to the two major parties as we know them today.

During the build-up to the Civil War, legislators and landowners in the South lamented what they saw as federal intrusion into regional social and economic relations. As otherwise colorblind Republicans are eager to point out during contemporary national campaigns, theirs was the party of Lincoln, the author of the Emancipation Proclamation. In contrast, Democrats in the South resisted post-war reforms. Isolated by Republicans' avowedly pro-Black policies, Southern Democrats continued to resist what they felt were violations of their states' rights (Herman and Peterson 2008), and pushed back on reforms through a combination of local policies and conventions and selective enforcement of federal policies. Despite elimination of equality from both parties' agenda by the 1876 election, Republican support from Blacks remained strong through the end of the nineteenth century (Hoffman 2015).

As the twentieth century dawned, the Democratic Party made some in-roads into the North, albeit with somewhat more egalitarian platform positions than their Southern colleagues. The New Deal policies proposed by Franklin Delano Roosevelt (a New York Democrat) in the 1930s did not always sit well with party lawmakers in the South, and in order to appease the latter, many key New Deal initiatives – including Social Security, the "widow's pension" that preceded Aid to Families with Dependent Children (AFDC), and urban renewal – were watered down so as not to benefit Blacks in the South. Nonetheless, throughout his terms, Roosevelt continued to pursue civil rights as a major Democratic position, further eroding his support among Southern Democrats (Hoffman 2015).

The party would split further under Roosevelt's successor, Harry

Truman, with Blacks influencing the latter's work to end discrimination, work that had begun with desegregating the armed forces during World War II with the establishment of Executive Order 8802, signed by Roosevelt. The Party's ultimate fracturing occurred in the 1960s under John F. Kennedy and was codified under Lyndon Johnson. The Civil Rights and Voting Rights Acts pushed by Kennedy and signed into law by Johnson, as well as the *Brown* decision and the ensuing desegregation of schools, eschewed the regional compromises of previous Democrat-led reforms, and instead openly affirmed the federal government's commitment to racial equality. Given the arguably disproportionate impact they would have on the South, Johnson correctly surmised that these reforms would cost the Democratic party the support of the South going forward (Hoffman 2015).

The extension of civil rights to Blacks was a crisis for White supremacy and spelled the end of state-sanctioned racial oppression, triggering counter-mobilization (Doane 2006). In the midst of what seemed to be a new order dawning in the 1960s South, a movement of racial resentment arose, a shift from traditional "old-fashioned racism, or Jim Crow racism," to an ethos hinging "on the perception of Blacks as 'violating cherished values'" (Sniderman, Piazza, Tetlock and Kendrick 1991), particularly "the kind of traditional American moral values embodied in the Protestant Ethic" (Kinder and Sears 1981). As this resentment frayed the long-tenuous bonds between Southern and Northern Democrats, Republican politicians seized on these fissures when and where they could.

Presidential candidate Richard Nixon and his team carried out the most direct and successful campaign to this end in 1968. Fully aware of the race-fueled disaffection of Southern Democrats, and their fear that theirs was now "the party of Blacks" in the South (Herman and Peterson 2008), Republican strategist Kevin Phillips introduced a plan to capitalize on this disaffection, literally appealing to racists by targeting anti-Black sentiments among Southern White voters (Jacobs and Tope 2008). The ensuing racialized discourse (including a renewed emphasis on crime) resonated with its target audience, and ultimately allowed Republicans to "peel large numbers of southern White voters away from the Democratic Party" (Drakulich and Crutchfield 2013:9). This migration continued from the 1970s through the end of the twentieth century, and culminated in a near-total racial split in the electorate (Hawley 2015). Despite – or, perhaps, due to – the popularity of colorblind politics, this realignment completely changed the role of race, both in policy *and* in the "rules of the game" of campaigning.

Following the success of the "Southern Strategy" and the resulting realignment, there have been persistent, well-organized ideological and legal campaigns to scale back the gains achieved by the Civil Rights Movement, with both the means *and* goals of diversity under assault (Cokorinos 2003). This anti-civil rights agenda operates on the principle that the government should have little or no role in ensuring racial equity. The 1970s saw significant challenges to the policies of the 1960s, including the *Bakke* decision, which called into question the fairness of race as a determining factor in admissions (with implications for hiring as well). Republican reframing of racism all but necessitated colorblind policies, which were presented through a corruption of classic civil rights discourse, but the accompanying proposals for reform protected the structures that the 1960s policies were intended to ameliorate.

The legal assault on affirmative action is illustrative of the organized push-back on the progressive policies of the 1960s. Crafted at the direction of – and federally implemented by – President Nixon in 1969, the program established timelines for employers to achieve "proportionate representation" in their labor forces (Kotlowski 1998), and to cease rejecting qualified candidates merely on the basis of race. During and after the long implementation period, opponents decried the program as nothing more than a system of racial quotas, despite Nixon's insistence that quotas were not the intent. Less than a decade after the program's implementation, the plaintiff in *Bakke* v. *Regents of the University of California* alleged that racial quotas designed to help non-White applicants were the basis of his rejection from the university.

Numerous similar cases have since followed – most recently *Fisher* v. *University of Texas* – each challenging the use of race in admissions by invoking and inverting the meaning of civil rights, with appeals to an "even playing field" where White identity is treated "no different from any other racial group identity" (Berrey 2015). These appeals necessarily ignore the far longer history of policies designed to disadvantage Blacks, de jure and de facto policies whose historical effects largely persist. Still, in this discourse, race-conscious policies are now "a perversion of civil rights" that enforces if not *mandates* "reverse discrimination" (Berrey 2015). This framing presents progress as zero-sum, where any group's opportunity must automatically mean disadvantage for another. While this particular framing necessarily deemphasizes the role of racism, similar framings – those of the increasingly visible extremist and supremacist groups – do not, while otherwise still adopting zero-sum discourse.

Despite the propensity of some to complain of reverse-discrimination (Mayrl and Saperstein 2013),[1] colorblindness is the preferred ethos, politically. Racial equity is generally supported by White Americans as long as the pursuit of equity in policy doesn't threaten advantages traditionally enjoyed by them. Race-neutrality in policy is understood as the stated intent *and* public perception: welfare is arguably more race-neutral in practice than affirmative action, but both are widely viewed as "unfair" and "Black-oriented" (Unnever et al. 2008). Policies that appear to benefit non-Whites the most are less likely to receive support by White voters, and those with racial prejudice are particularly unlikely to support explicitly race-targeted programs (including busing and the aforementioned affirmative action) but are more likely to support harsher criminal justice outcomes (Jacobs and Tope 2007; Unnever et al. 2008). They are also more likely, especially when living in areas with large Black populations, to support conservative candidates, especially those who appear hostile to non-Whites (Jacobs and Tope 2007). A dedication to colorblind policies and apparently racially neutral language (code words notwithstanding) typified much of Republican discourse at the turn of the twenty-first century.

Challenges to the political pursuit of racial equality extended beyond politicians' mindfulness of the sensibilities of White voters to the outright repression of the Black vote. With Blacks almost exclusively supporting Democrats since the 1960s (McFayden 2013), arch-conservatives – with 2050's census projections on their minds – see the composition of the electorate as a "last stand" for ensuring their material and racial advantage in the decades to come (King and Smith 2016). While free and fair elections are in the best interests of American democracy, and the right to vote has always been central to American principles of liberty, freedom and self-expression, purposeful exclusion of the Black vote is a key part of America's history and present (Ochs 2006). The Voting Rights Act of 1965 guaranteed the right of Blacks to vote, yet it did not withstand legal challenge. The Supreme Court's 2013 decision in *Shelby County* v. *Holder*, which upheld a challenge to the Voting Rights Act and scaled back its impact, has only reinforced Republican efforts to make voting more difficult, and may clear the way for similar initiatives already in the pipeline (King and Smith 2016).

Republicans generally assume they will not have the support of Black voters (Prisock 2015), and instead put their political and legal energy into keeping them from voting at all (Burmila 2017). The measures of the past that impeded one Black voter at a time have given way to measures that categorically affect large numbers of

Black citizens before they ever arrive at polling precincts. These include the proposed ceasing of automatic registration when obtaining drivers' licenses, legal assaults on organizations dedicated to voter registration in underrepresented populations, the implementation of new voter ID requirements close to the date of elections, and the disenfranchisement of felons.

While surmountable, given sufficient time and resources, the voter ID and registration measures force prospective voters – including those who were already registered – to contend with an already-clogged bureaucracy, one that Black citizens often feel is (re)oriented to prevent them from registering in time. These measures ostensibly exist to prevent election fraud – voting by those who are not legally eligible to do so. Fears of fraud by Republicans tend to follow elections where Democrats were victorious and/or where Blacks voted in higher than average numbers, or, in the case of Trump's victory in 2016, when candidates had openly campaigned on the threat presented by non-Whites. While fraud is presented as a racially neutral threat, voters have long been primed to "see" or "hear" race when discussing it. Surveys of White poll workers indicated greater support for ID laws when they are shown images of Black voters than when shown White voters or no image at all (Wilson, Brewer and Rosenbluth 2014).

The criminal justice system has been instrumental in maintaining Whites' advantage in the political sphere, in part through the criminalization of protest, and voter registration, voter intimidation and the revocation of felon voting rights (Miller 2015). While these policies outwardly operate in a race-neutral fashion (Burmila 2017), Black citizens are disproportionately more likely to face arrest and imprisonment, and thus disproportionately affected by felon disenfranchisement (Ochs 2006). Court challenges were often rebuffed for their failure to link disproportionate effect to racist intent: while the Supreme Court ruled in favor of a plaintiff challenging the constitutionality of felon disenfranchisement in *Hunter* v. *Underwood* in 1985, these policies, with their carefully crafted language and disproportionate effects, persist (Burmila 2017).

While patently unconstitutional in spirit, felon disenfranchisement has proven a valuable strategy for Republicans. Black votes that were *not* cast in Florida in 2010 and 2014 essentially elected and re-elected Governor Rick Scott, and allowed for a Republican Party agenda that, among other things, helped implement or scale back policies in ways that disadvantaged Blacks, including restrictions on welfare and access to education (Philips and Deckard 2016). The use of disenfranchisement policies has become increasingly partisan:

pre-2000, there was less of a difference in rates between Democratic- and Republican-controlled states, and post-2000, disenfranchisement rates no longer correlate with local or state-level crime rates. Similarly, Southern states, which are generally more conservative *and* have significant Black populations, place more restrictions on felon voting rights, during and after incarceration (Burmila 2017).

Through the horrors of slavery, crime victimization, fatal encounters with law enforcement and the penal system, and numerous acute and long-term health disparities, Black Americans have long experienced shorter life expectancy, and this too has a powerful effect on the composition of the electorate. Those who die before reaching the age of 18 – which Black youth are disproportionately likely to do – will never get to vote, and those dying after 18 but before the typical life expectancy have a shorter "electoral life," creating a cumulative dilution of Blacks' electoral voice (Rodriguez et al. 2015). The effect of this disparity is powerful: for example, the participation of voting-aged Blacks who died prematurely might have sustained Democratic control of the Senate from 1986 to 2012 (ibid.).

In addition to these measures and trends, **gerrymandering** – manipulating the boundaries of an electoral constituency to favor one party – has become increasingly partisan. At the time of writing, numerous states' practices of racial and political redistricting – drawing electoral district boundaries – were either under review, headed to the Supreme Court, or already found to be unconstitutional. In an era of changing demographics, redistricting, like disenfranchisement, is one of the final options for Republicans to maintain electoral advantages in jurisdictions where they are numerically the minority. The current administration's flat-funding of the Census Bureau – when increased funds are crucial – will only impede officials' ability to make better-informed redistricting decisions. Despite these many factors, Black electoral participation has only increased through the decades, as has the number of Black elected officials at the sub-national level – particularly in the regions traditionally most hostile to Black empowerment (Lewis 2008). Nonetheless, for some time to come, it appears that much of Black political engagement will be through fighting to engage at all.

Racial Appeals and Presidential Politics

Race for both political parties presents a conundrum managed best by avoidance. Yet presidential campaigns are characterized by racial appeals – often poignant moments that illuminate an underlying racial frame. Hence, examining racial appeals across presidential campaigns provides a unique opening to examine how political parties understand and are willing to use race and racism to target White voters, shaping presidential politics and policies. A particularly poignant and decidedly effective racial appeal was used against Democratic presidential candidate, Michael Dukakis.

Late in the 1988 presidential race between Vice President George H. W. Bush and Massachusetts Governor and Democratic challenger Michael Dukakis, the National Security Political Action Committee (NSPAC), a conservative PAC, began running ads linking Dukakis to Willie Horton, a convicted killer who, while on furlough from prison, traveled to Maryland and brutally assaulted a young couple, repeatedly raping the female victim after stabbing her fiancé. Since this furlough program was part of Massachusetts prison policy, NSPAC was able to present this incident as the result of the "soft-on-crime" policies one might expect from the Democratic Governor who oversaw the program.

While never explicitly mentioning race, the ad campaign and the incident itself were saturated with racial meaning: Horton's victims were White, whereas Horton, as the menacing mugshot that punctuated the commercials made clear, was Black. Dukakis campaign manager Susan Estrich would later write, "There is no stronger metaphor for racial hatred in our country than the Black man raping the White woman. If you were going to run a campaign of fear and smear and appeal to racial hatred you could not have picked a better case to use than this one."[2] Almost overnight, Horton transcended from inmate to *symbol*, with Bush and his surrogates making the most of these allusions in their subsequent campaigning, and with Bush campaign manager Lee Atwater gleefully declaring, "By the time we're finished, they're going to wonder whether Willie Horton is Dukakis' running mate" (ibid.). This approach resonated with voters: by fall, the 17-point lead Dukakis had built in the polls during the summer disappeared, and Bush went on to win the election by 8 points.

The coupling of overt discussions of crime and more covert allusions to race were not a new tactic for Republicans in 1988. Against the backdrop of political protests that in part drove the then-ongoing Civil Rights Movement, the 1964 presidential election was the moment where "tough-on-crime" rhetoric entered Republicans' toolkit, with Black criminality linked to the frequent political protests taking place in the streets. This appeal played upon the resentments that many harbored toward the apparent beneficiaries of the contemporary civil rights legislation (Jacobs and Tope 2007). The "descendants" of this rhetoric, the "War on Crime" of the 1980s and the "War on Drugs" of the 1990s, relied on similar undertones, often accompanied by imagery of Black criminals – and allusions to real or imagined White victims – painting a particularly vivid and continuous image of America's true enemy in these "wars."

Key to this framing is the *implicitness*: as Republican strategists like Atwater recognized, 1950s-style overt racial appeals would backfire by the end of the twentieth century (Jacobs and Tope 2007). Political scientists Jon Hurwitz and Mark Peffley argue that "White Americans, despite their resentment toward Blacks, are committed to a 'norm of equality,' which causes them to reject blatantly racial appeals, but not those that are implicit – that is, those not recognized as racial" (Hurwitz and Peffley 2005:100). Crime is among the most direct race-based topics that conservatives can raise without naming Blacks – and given this historical association, they do not have to (Jacobs and Tope 2007). Juxtaposing Black killers and White victims elicits support from the racially resentful without appearing racist (Unnever et al. 2008). While the Horton ad would probably not be considered implicit by today's standards, more subtle approaches can and do strongly influence positions on policy and candidate preferences (Hurwitz and Peffley 2005); after all, the influence of individuals' racial resentment on their support for national policies increased with their exposure to the Horton ads (Unnever et al. 2008).

Barack Obama's 2009 presidency brought far more overt racial discourse – and the tolerance of such discourse – to the surface (McCamey and Murty 2013). Much of the Tea Party's resistance to Obama's real or imagined policies focused on his "un-Americanism," which could be defined in part through a combination of his perceived race, presumed religion, African heritage, and multicultural and international upbringing (Leone and Presaghi 2018). The influence of the Tea Party pulled the Republican Party further from its roots in fiscal and social conservatism toward policies that were thinly veiled appeals to a traditional American racial order. That veil became significantly less thin by the 2016 election, when candidate Donald Trump distinguished himself from the rest of the large Republican field with openly racist appeals to voters (Bobo 2017; Swain 2018). In the run-up to the election, the media and the candidates were actively re-imagining the "White working class" as a rhetorical device and as a theoretical voter base with particular sets of economic concerns, with much made of the bloc's "economic anxiety." Still, in case there was any question of what segments of the base the Trump campaign had sought to mobilize, the first year of his term saw the return – to the public and the headlines – of unabashedly White-supremacist organizing and dialogue, to which Trump made clear he was at least sympathetic.

While the emergence of these groups was not solely a feature of that year or decade, it came amid a similarly prominent national discourse over the importance of and/or need for Confederate monuments in public spaces. While many Republicans at the national level (such as Representatives Paul Ryan and Tom Rooney) correctly identified the deep racialized meanings of the monuments and called for their removal, Trump and others downplayed or ignored the racial implications and painted them as important parts of American history. This is an idealized American history and a display of privilege that is racially and culturally specific – while defending the historical importance of Confederate monuments, Trump scaled back Native American monuments and decried the (Obama-era) policies that created them as governmental overreach (Bobo 2017).[3] This ideology "lies beyond the realm of traditional conservatism, despite claiming that mantle" (Cokorinos 2003:3), even as it comports with the most extreme elements of the Republican Party at the time of this writing.

It is no accident that post-Civil War, Confederate monuments and symbolism most often appear during moments of racial conflict or Black civil rights progress (Strother, Piston and Ogorzalek 2017), and appeals to their historical significance are often inversely proportional to knowledge of history (ibid.). In this way, we can see both the increased (albeit 100 years late) support of the Confederacy, and the renewed rise of hate groups, as a continued manifestation of civil rights backlash, and as reaction to the racial progress that Obama's presidency supposedly signaled (ibid.).

Obama and the Mirage of Post-racial Politics

Despite the lack of prominent Black politicians at the national level, the rise and success of Barack Obama tells us a great deal about the role, utility and limits of racial and post-racial politics in 21st-century America. The trends in the framing of race, along with social and legal race-conscious reforms – and the swift backlash to those reforms – all set the stage for what has been a unique moment in American politics. The Civil Rights Movement succeeded in decreasing the acceptability of blatant displays of racism (Doane 2006), and the individual successes of Black figures in high office allow many to herald the decline of racism (Bonilla-Silva and Ray 2009). While President George W. Bush's domestic and foreign policies were hardly among the most progressive, his cabinet was the most diverse in history. In the context of his policies, this diversity to some critics was little more than "White supremacy in Blackface" (ibid.). One can also see this demonstrated in George H. W. Bush's nomination of conservative Clarence Thomas to fill the Supreme Court seat vacated by the retiring Thurgood Marshall, a former civil rights pioneer.

Before discussing more directly how Obama ascended to the White House in 2009, we should establish the political, social and economic climate in which he did so. Simply put, his victory required "a perfect storm" (Pettigrew 2009): the state of the economy under Bush inspired a backlash against his Republican Party (Taylor 2011) and hurt nominee John McCain, and two unpopular wars showed no signs of ceasing, all while a younger and more progressive segment of the electorate was increasingly amenable to mobilization (ibid.). Obama's race was hardly ignored by the electorate: while he received significant support from White voters in 2008 (including from those whose racial views were anything but progressive), his share was lower than the 2000 and 2004 party totals (ibid.), and he failed to win the majority of White voters' support in either of his victories (Baodong 2014). He particularly struggled in the South, where the racial context was far more traditional than nationally, and even as he carried the states of Nebraska, Michigan and Washington, concurrent referendums in those states banned or limited race-based affirmative action (Pettigrew 2009). The significance of geography to party alignment in the South, which emerged with the Southern strategy, has yet to fully decline.

Those with bigoted views who did vote for Obama largely did so because economic concerns, in that moment, outweighed their racial concerns, and we have heard much about their resentment and "economic anxiety" since (Pettigrew 2009). Media attention to Obama's background during his campaigns differed from that paid to his opponents; neither Mitt Romney's Mormonism in 2012, nor the regressive doctrine of the leading evangelical figures supporting McCain in 2008, received the same attention that Jeremiah Wright or supposed Islamic beliefs did for Obama (Herman and Peterson 2008). This is the context through which we will explore Obama's success and impact: one in which the form, but not the substance, of race matters shifted (Bonilla-Silva and Ray 2009), and in which a "modern alliance on racial issues, and *not* a lack of racial concerns," moved race to the margins during his first election (Smith and King 2009:25).

Obama was the first President of known African descent in the Americas, the Global West or Asia, and it is impossible to ignore the significance of race in his moment (Smith and King 2009). Despite this, he ran a decidedly race-neutral campaign, informed by a "practical idealism" (Winant 2009) that highlighted shared values and underscored the importance of the American Dream. His race-neutral strategy, while consciously inclusive of all Americans, masked the issues facing the Black communities who hoped he would embody the progress they had sought for so long. His emphasis on the economic concerns of middle-class workers resonated with the electorate as the country looked to climb out of the Great Recession, but, in doing this, he equated those concerns with the economic marginalization that Blacks had disproportionately faced prior to the recession (Johnson, Dowe, and Fauntroy 2011).

Spotlight on Resistance

Case Study 7 Mobilizing and Forcing Justice: Political Accountability in San Francisco

In San Francisco, sociologist Christina Jackson conducted an ethnography from 2008 to 2010 in Black neighborhoods – in particular, Bayview – Hunters Point. She joined a diverse community group called Stop Redevelopment Corporations Now (SRCN) that organizes against the de-population of Black San Francisco and other low-income groups of color in the Bay area by putting pressure on politicians to address the injustice toward their communities, among other organizing efforts. Jackson participated in a meeting that specifically addressed organizing around the killing of Oscar Grant, a 22-year-old Black man who was shot by Bay Area Rapid Transit (BART) officer Johannes Mehserle in Oakland, California, in 2009. One movement tactic was to put pressure on Black and Brown politicians who did not serve the interests of the community, forcing them to speak up for justice for Oscar Grant. Jackson comments in her field notes:

[One resident] talked about how they forced politicians to speak on it, and take a stand. "We were tricked into believing politics would solve our problems!" This group had to take this killing into their own hands because the "politics" of it would not do Grant justice

... They discussed how leaders that you think would stand up for justice don't because of their financial connections to the city. They went on to say "bums like Black, Latino, and progressive caucuses don't act in your interest when it goes against big business! ... You can't rely on those who you put in office to defend your interests and protect you." They quoted Frederick Douglass saying, "Power concedes nothing without a demand ... we got to put together an agenda to organize and mobilize to put presence on our legislators starting with the ones who look like us. They need to choose!"

How local Black residents *do politics* is largely dependent on their class status and whether they perceive themselves as absent or ignored at the decision-making table. In an earlier project, Jackson explored the city-initiated African American Out Migration task force in which the most politically connected Blacks were asked to contribute their solutions. Members of SRCN were not asked to participate, but they organized locally on their own to demand justice from Black and Brown politicians with more social capital in the city's government. These organizers point out how financial opportunities and connections interfere with obtaining justice for low-income Black residents in the city.

It is, of course, not necessary that a Black candidate make their Blackness central to their campaigning or policy, as Obama demonstrated as he captured 90 percent of the Black vote while downplaying race. If nothing else, he handily proved the utility of deracialized campaigns by candidates of color (Belkhir 2011). Obama was viewed as a kind of "savior" among many Black Americans, despite his race-neutral campaign. Yet, as post-racial as his victory was, it remained an improbable racial moment. While middle-class Whites embraced the historic significance of his candidacy, working-class Whites remained reluctant to support him for the same reason (Parker, Sawyer and Towler 2009).

Despite his colorblind strategy, race thoroughly saturated Obama's campaign, which seemed consciously poised to "identify with the Black community but not be defined by it" (Walters 2007:26). His initial reception included questions as to whether he was Black at all, in part due to a combination of Blacks' unfamiliarity with him (Walters 2007), his mixed-race ancestry, international upbringing and social class. Even before Black voters came to see Obama as one of their own (Carter and Dowe 2015), his Blackness was far *less* ambiguous to critics and outsiders. Whereas McCain in 2008 stoked

enthusiasm among supporters with his "maverick" persona while
Obama sought to placate critics and be as non-controversial as possible, the combination of the latter's race, background, progressive
leanings and less predictable constituency bestowed upon him an
outsider status that made him a far more polarizing figure (Herman
and Peterson 2008).

While McCain promised to disrupt the Washington status quo, his
more mainstream associations with lobbyists and the military were
far more familiar than what Obama represented. The focus on the
critiques of the American social system in Jeremiah Wright's sermons,
coupled with Obama's connection to radicals in the 1970s, and time
spent in Indonesia as a child, in part allowed critics to brand him as
an un-American "Other," be it Socialist, Muslim or radical (Herman
and Peterson 2008; Parker et al. 2009). Even Hillary Clinton, his
2008 Democratic challenger, alluded to patriotism and her distinctly
middle-class American upbringing and values in the primaries to
draw a distinction between her background and Obama's (Parker et
al. 2009; Lowndes 2013). Ultimately, the "Obama effect" may have
harmed Democrats in the South (Taylor 2011).

American Presidents' "presentations of self" have at once directly
represented the government and metaphorically represented the
people of the nation (Lowndes 2013). A particular configuration
of race, sexuality, masculinity and vulnerability has traditionally connected the presidency to the American political culture.
Contemporary Republican imagery, for example, wraps patriotism in
a cloak of hypermasculinity, informing foreign and domestic policy
(Winter 2010; Lowndes 2013). Obama, in his unique form of masculinity that was not (stereo)typically Black, presented a bridge between
Republican hypermasculinity and the less-than-masculine liberalism
often ascribed to Democrats: his was a "moral and controlled manli-
ness" (Winter 2010:610–11).

In his appeals to shared American values, especially the importance
of strong families in-and-of-themselves and to their wider communities, and the need for an economic system that rewards hard work
and provides security to households, Obama clearly sought to both
represent and usher in a more unified America. His family narratives
– from the aspirational platitudes to his castigations of non-resident
Black fathers – served two purposes. First, they spoke to the goal
of cross-racial political unity (Collins 2012). That his family's race
differed from that of any previous First Family would never be lost
on observers and detractors, but a distinctly conservative appeal that
linked family to traditional marriage and economic security created

a race-mute bridge between himself and any who would otherwise see him as "Other." This was an appeal to *inclusivity* in a culture that had, to that point, not gone further than *diversity* (Collins 2012).

Second, and similarly, the Black family had long been presented as a key example of Black deviancy, and as a leading cause of poverty, as discussed in chapter 2. Obama's presentation of his highly traditional and highly successful Black family simultaneously offered rebuttals to conservative critics who pathologized Black families as dysfunctional, *and* to Black Americans who contended that structural obstacles still precluded Black success. Here was a family that in all ways (besides race) was indistinguishable from the theoretical depiction of a good American family. Black Americans need only "be like Barack" to "find wealth, fame, and fortune" (ibid.), and now had "no more excuses" because White racism was now apparently no longer a meaningful barrier to Black success (Reed and Louis 2009). Obama, in short, tried to interweave traditionalism with diversity and inclusion into a living example of what the American Dream *could* look like for a Black family.

With this particular framing of himself against the traditional meaning of the presidency, Obama represented to his critics the most profound fissuring of his "presentation of self" as President representing the government and metaphorically representing the people of the nation (Lowndes 2013). The numerous ways in which he differed from the traditionally *idealized* American – either actual (race) or assumed (Socialist, Muslim) – could not be obscured by his aspirational models. A great many voters (41 percent of Republicans in 2010) believed that he either "probably or definitely wasn't born in the US," and this belief of his un-American, perennial outsider status disqualified him from policymaking in their eyes (Maxwell and Shields 2014:293). During the 2008 presidential primaries, Hillary Clinton's aide Mark Penn dismissed the notion of Obama's campaign with "save it for 2050," referring to the census projections of a more racially and ethnically diverse population by then (Lowndes 2013).

Personifying metaphorically the people of the nation, Obama could have made the case that he *embodied* American racial unity by highlighting his mixed-race heritage, as he was singularly Black and Not Black (Ford 2009). Instead, he was branded as the cause of racial divisions since his election, symbolically for his race, but more particularly – and, largely, rhetorically – for the relatively rare moments when he directly *referred to* his race, as he did after Trayvon Martin's murder (ibid.). Because of his post-racial framing, critical audiences expected *complete* colorblindness from him. But, despite his post-racial framing, the economic and material realities for most Black families did not improve simply because Obama was successful (Ford 2009; Carter and Dowe 2015). Indeed, measures that offered support to the poorest Americans "were designed to help his primary constituency – the middle class" (Johnson et al. 2011:146).

Obama's presidency began during a surge of hyper-partisanship, and while many of the attacks on his policies were political in nature, he was subject to an unprecedented wave of "overwhelming rhetoric, overt opposition of political ideology, racial overtones, lack of bipartisanship, and disrespect for the Oval Office" (McCamey and Murty 2013:80). Continuous focus on his birth name and requests for his birth certificate, on his failure to wear a lapel flag pin (Fishman 2013) and even his audacity in wearing a tan suit, made clear his critics' belief that no one like him belonged – either as President or in their idealized America. Republicans' malleable and evolving critiques gradually bore no resemblance to the principles of fiscal and social conservatism that they claimed to stand upon (McCamey and Murty 2013), harkening instead to the racialized politics of retrenchment that characterized the post-Civil War and civil rights eras (Fishman 2013).

Obama's signature act, the Affordable Care Act (ACA), offered opponents the opportunity to mount a racialized resistance wrapped in colorblind politics and supposed fiscal responsibility. Despite the fact that the reforms were presented by the administration as race-neutral, and – like Clinton's attempt in 1993 – were shaped largely in part by conservative policy proposals in order to garner bipartisan support, the ACA, pejoratively referred to as Obamacare, was framed at times as socialism, or "Big Government." It was also framed as reparations, a demand rhetorically ascribed to militant Blacks who are supposedly unwilling to work for economic equality (Lubin 2015).

Ethnocentrists who saw Obama as the "Other" viewed his policies through that same lens, and alleged that they were crafted out of concern for non-Whites in particular, potentially leading to outcomes that would hurt Whites by default (Maxwell and Shields 2014). Conservative opponents made reference to the fact that Americans would be "forced" under the ACA to subsidize the care of citizens on welfare, with HIV and with drug addictions, and immigrants, groups with strong racial – and in the case of the former three, Black – connotations (ibid.; Lubin 2015). This echoes much of the prevailing opposition to welfare. Critics, of course, were not entirely consistent in their opposition: many Tea Party members who opposed the ACA as welfare supported Medicare (Lubin 2015), and many who were polled were less favorable to Obama's plan for universal coverage than they were to Bill Clinton's similar plan (Maxwell and Shields 2014). Racially resentful Whites were especially likely to oppose Obamacare (ibid.), further indicating that race drove sentiments as powerfully as, if not more powerfully than, knowledge of the elements of the policy itself. Indeed, surveys suggested that a third of Republicans were unaware that Obamacare and the ACA were the same policy.[4]

Healthcare was but one example of a reform that was highly controversial – and around which the debate became deeply racialized – simply because Obama wanted it; racial resentment negatively correlated with White support for the reform, controlling for a host of alternative explanations (Maxwell and Shields 2014). Barack Obama's avenue of ascent was the culmination of a colorblind and presumably post-Southern strategy – but in an anti-civil rights American political landscape (Edge 2010). But, as was soon made painfully apparent, the election of the first Black President did not free the nation of current or future racism, and instead stirred up the most reactionary elements among conservatives (ibid.). The dual beasts of racial resentment and retrenchment, and hyper-partisanship, have made the political color line as indelible as it has ever been.

Racial Politics and Race(d) Policy

As was evident in the case of the Affordable Care Act (ACA), perceptions of policy and its racial targets can lead to resistance regardless of its actual aims. These perceptions are actively shaped by media frames that appeal to either **egalitarianism** (namely, equal opportunity to individual prosperity) or **individualism** (and the importance of one's work ethic), which can signal to a consumer whom a proposed policy may benefit most greatly, and whether the latter "deserves" such assistance (Eargle et al. 2008). Race-conscious policies are generally most popular when presented through an egalitarian frame, while an individualistic frame tends to garner support for conservative, colorblind policies (Kellstedt 2000). Politicians have long been adept in their use of coded language "to prime voters for biases, not toward policy itself" (Lubin 2015).

Numerous studies indicate that assumptions of whom a policy serves or applies to greatly influence public support, even when *only* code is used to refer to race (Hurwitz and Peffley 2005; Eargle, et al. 2008). Newt Gingrich, for example, kicked off his 2012 presidential campaign before a cheering Georgia crowd by describing then-President Barack Obama as "the most successful food stamps president in American history."[5] No further context or discussion of US social policy was necessary for Gingrich's crowd to understand the connection he was making between US poverty, the public benefits "hand-outs" unpopular among conservatives, and Obama's Black heritage (Cammett 2014). The art of the dog-whistle has long been perfected by conservative opponents to anti-poverty policies and civil rights, and, as Gingrich demonstrated, not even a sitting Black President was off-limits. Such imagery is not evoked just for the sake of provocation; this language can and absolutely does shape social, economic and criminal justice policy, often with results that are as regressive and disproportionate as proponents intended. And, as we will see, this use of racial sentiments to move policy is exclusive to no single party.

To illustrate, let's begin with the Black "crime" problem and the racial politics of drug policy. References to "crime" or "inner city" have long been treated as synonymous with "Black," and associations of this language with proposed policies will link one's preferences for this policy to one's feelings toward Black Americans (Hurwitz and Peffley 2005). The "tough on crime" political rhetoric that emerged in the 1950s and 1960s gave politicians a way to discuss race relations without making race explicit. Crime is a popular tool of racial politics for its ability to "mobilize resentment and fears among White voters," without the direct appeals to racial superiority that might have typified pre-Civil Rights Movement discourse (Doering 2017:280).

Against a backdrop of increased urban deindustrialization and deeper economic marginalization among Black families, America in the 1970s shifted from a "War on Poverty" to what was essentially a war on the poor, fought through political rhetoric that framed the Black poor as dangerous, and led to increased imprisonment, the curtailing of social and political rights *post*-incarceration, the rolling back of the safety net and deepening social and economic disparities (Miller 2015; De Giorgi 2017). The next domestic wars that were declared – on crime in the 1980s, and on drugs in the 1990s – were typified by conservative support for, and actual campaigns of, aggressive policing tactics that focused on Black urban communities in particular (Drakulich and Crutchfield 2013).

Drug policy in the US is traditionally **Janus-faced**, having two sharply contrasting characteristics, with race influencing how politicians frame and regulate drug use. Generally, drug addiction has been treated as a disease, with treatment preferred as the ideal mitigation. But drugs – dealing, use and possession – have traditionally been conflated with crime, as markers of deviance said to be inherent to Blacks. For over a generation, addiction to drugs like heroin has been described as a feature of inner-city life and a pathology of Blacks in particular, and drugs share much of the blame for the crime said to await White and non-poor visitors to the inner city.

Conversely, recent increases in the rates – and especially the visibility – of addiction to heroin among White and middle-class Americans has been met largely with sympathy, with their addiction presented not as a problem to be solved through the arrests of users, but rather as an epidemic to be rallied against through investment in treatment and the arrests of drug dealers. When drug policies are punitive, the results are more generally felt most severely along racial lines. The same is generally true of public support for drug policies, which politicians can and do influence: views toward Blacks and Latinos correlate with attitudes for spending on rehabilitation, and Whites who blame structure – and not individual behavior – are likely to believe that more must be spent (Nielsen, Bonn and Wilson 2010).

The response by Reagan, national and local lawmakers, and law enforcement, to the crack epidemic of the 1980s, was swift and punitive, with public-service announcements playing up the addictiveness and risk of overdose as acute dangers even for those just experimenting. Mandatory minimum sentences for possession were established for crack, leading to long sentences for those caught with quantities – for personal use *or* distribution – on their person. White support for more punitive sentencing, furlough, and rehabilitation policies, are tied to global stereotypes about Blacks (Eargle et al. 2008). This is equally true for lawmakers, including former US Senator and Vice President Joe Biden who admitted that, in the midst of the War on Drugs, media reports influenced lawmakers' support for mandatory minimum sentences for crack-related offenses, a policy that, given the relative differences in price and accessibility for crack and powder cocaine, all but targeted Black defendants.

The intense criminalization of crack – and comparative neglect of powder cocaine – accompanied special focus on the behavior of Black mothers. In the mid 1980s, the "Crack mother" emerged as a pejorative with similar racial and gendered coding to the "Welfare Queen," and soon led to politicians' support for and implementation of various procedures to police the bodies of pregnant Black mothers on the margins (Derkas 2012). Prosecutors called for the death penalty for drug users whose babies were stillborn, and jurisdictions enforced mandatory reporting of mothers in hospitals who tested positive for drugs – testing that, while theoretically applicable to *any* pregnant mother, was in practice used most often for women of color (Carpenter 2012). Similarly, despite the demonstrated severe harm of tobacco and alcohol (which White pregnant mothers use more frequently than crack) on the developing fetus, there was generally no mandate to report women who used those substances (ibid.).

As we saw in the racial politics of drug policy, the race of the target of enforcement framed the response of the state as either punitive when they were Black or benevolent/sympathetic when White. This trend toward disparate treatment is also evident in government crisis support, an instance of stereotypes informing policy provisions producing unnatural disasters from natural devastation. The current governmental – especially conservative and Republican – commitment to colorblindness requires race-neutral responses to crises. Because the US was founded on egalitarian principles – notwithstanding slavery, and Blacks' or women's lesser legal and political rights pre-1960s – conservatives now argue that policies are best carried out neutrally (Lieberman 2006). Of course, when the *effect* of a crisis disproportionally affects those of a particular racial or ethnic group, a colorblind response – that is, a response that is not scaled to the magnitude of the effect on that group – will probably be ineffective and demonstrably discriminatory (ibid.). Our most recent example of such a response is the Trump administration's managing of Hurricane Maria, where the insufficient and sloppy administering of resources was rivaled only by the President's constant blaming of the affected population for the scope of their suffering; as his behavior suggests, previous antipathy toward a group can make one resistant to beneficial policies that seemingly target that group. While Trump's response to Maria seemed racialized in its intent, the Bush administration's response to Hurricane Katrina in 2005 brings into sharp relief the impotence of colorblindness in the face of a crisis, laying bare the impact of historical discrimination and neglect.

While Katrina cut a swath across Florida and other Gulf states, the prospect of a New Orleans landfall was especially troubling to officials in the region. Unlike national distributions of wealth and poverty, where only 10 percent of the poor – and 19 percent of Blacks – are concentrated in urban cores, the distribution of poverty in New Orleans was far starker, with residents of the 9th Ward by and large the poorest of the poor (Danziger and Danziger 2006). Even without a hurricane, extreme residential segregation, racially discriminatory social policy, the disengagement of the federal government and uneven local political policy and urban development (Lieberman 2006) had created a chronic state of crisis for poor Black residents of New Orleans. Regardless of any warnings by officials to evacuate, these residents would be least likely to do so. Similarly, due to New Orleans' geological placement (below sea level), and the conditions of its levees and infrastructure, forecasts suggested that it was all but a given that even a low-category hurricane would be catastrophic. (Katrina was a category 3; devastating damage was fairly certain.)

Nonetheless, the administration gave no special attention to the Gulf as the storm approached, arguably – proportionally – less than it had to the parts of Florida that were hit by, but spared from the worst of, the storm. By the time Bush finally toured the devastation, national media had already spent days covering the unfolding humanitarian crisis, albeit in what should now be familiar racialized fashion: Black survivors retrieving food and supplies from destroyed markets were described as "looters," while White survivors doing the same were described as "finding" food and supplies (Belkhir and Charlemaine 2007; Jackson 2008). Still, commentators and media figures immediately highlighted the possible connections between the disproportionate effect the storm had on Black Gulf residents and the administration's slow and insufficient response, and in his address the night he arrived in the city, even Bush spoke to the role that generations of racial segregation and neglect played in the disproportionate suffering. National political attention soon turned from the region, however, and by some accounts communities – both people and structure – have yet to fully recover. Katrina remains a metaphor for the tension between colorblind and race-conscious politics and policies (Lieberman 2006). While a phenomenon as vast and aimless as a hurricane cannot possibly be racist, and policymakers are unlikely to intend for Blacks to be in the path of such a storm, the collision of race, class and politics made for a situation that was in every way about race.

Colorblind policy can and does reproduce racial inequality. We have examined several race-neutral policies that were race-conscious in their impact, either directly or indirectly disadvantaging Black Americans and other groups of color. Colorblind policies alone are insufficient to reduce the material disadvantage faced by Blacks, produced by political malignment since emancipation. Yet this view is contested: the amelioration of inequity is commonly said to be unnecessary given the assertion that racism was "solved" in the 1960s. As decades of colorblind policy have made painfully clear, economic growth alone is not sufficient in addressing racially disproportionate poverty while economic and educational barriers and disparities remain (Danziger and Danziger 2006). To this end, public policy must be expanded beyond legislation and regulation, to include leadership, community engagement, activism and organizational endeavors, a reorientation that also necessitates a rejection of the interests that led to and maintain the present – and, evidently, deepening – alignments of our current political parties (Lewis and Embrick 2016).

Conclusion: Black Protest, the Politics of Representation, and Resistance

With voting rights and political access historically curtailed, Black engagement with the political system has often been from the outside, through grassroots organizing and protest (Jackson 2018). There is a history of mistrust in the political system among Black Americans that lends itself to participation in protests, a fairly "high-initiative" form of political engagement (Avery 2006; Jackson 2018). Protests demonstrate people's sense that the government has failed to address the problems afflicting their communities, or to enforce the system that is supposed to make the traditional channels of engagement viable (ibid.). Because Black protest includes demands for equality, which in a colorblind frame has already been achieved, it has not always found sympathy among White audiences or even middle-class Black audiences (ibid.).

For example, during the final year of his tenure as President, and amid a seemingly endless number of unarmed Black citizens experiencing fatal encounters with police, Barack Obama admonished Black Lives Matter protesters to "stop yelling" and push for change through official channels (Jones 2016). While this admonishment was consistent with his clear dedication to colorblind politics, it reflected his lack of understanding of how official channels had contributed to the events preceding those protests (ibid.). Black protest demonstrates a displeasure with the current political system (Avery 2006), a system that the nation's first Black President came to symbolize more than transcend or disrupt.

Black political candidates provide a unique lens through which to view the politics of representation and examine the impacts of the divergent Black experience, in terms of how candidates frame themselves and appeal to the Black community. Black political candidates compete for office in a historical context of racism that has defined them as other-than-American, and, politically, as problems to contain or solve. This context influences how Black candidates run, and their approaches to policy. While Black candidates who came out of the 1960s Civil Rights Movement may have consciously played up their experiences as Black Americans, contemporary Black candidates with White opponents often deracialize themselves and their campaigns, and are more willing to invoke their race against other Black candidates (Eargle et al. 2008).

In *From #BlackLivesMatter to Black Liberation*, Keeanga-Yamahtta Taylor writes: "Black elected officials obscure their actions under a cloak of imagined racial solidarity, while ignoring their role as arbiters of political power who willingly operate in a political terrain designed to exploit and oppress Black and other working-class people" (2016:79). According to Taylor, Blacks in high and powerful positions serve the role of arbiters, or, as lower-class community residents might say, puppets of White political power (Taylor 2016). This places Blacks, themselves, in the position of doing the dirty work of oppressing other racial minorities for their own personal benefit and capitalist accumulation (Taylor 2016).

Whether they invoke their own race or not, Black conservative politicians downplay the persistence and significance of racism, carefully constructing "an idealized society that obfuscates White Conservatives' historic role in making America's exceptionalism work in theory but not in practice for Blacks" (Prisock 2015). Candidates such as Herman Cain, who unsuccessfully ran for the Republican presidential nomination in 2012, represent their success in business as the fruit of a Horatio Alger-esque ethos, suggesting that hard work trumps commonly discussed structural barriers – and, at times, outright discrimination – that have long been linked to economic disparities (ibid.).

Thus, the increased representation of Blacks in more powerful positions can at times obfuscate and perpetuate severe and entrenched racial inequality. Implicit in the choices and actions of Black political candidates is an awareness of the racial frame and the denigration of Blackness in the American imaginary. By distancing themselves from Blackness distinctly, they position themselves as American and not "Other," leaving the denigrating frame intact. By pointing to themselves as "self-made," and appealing to the American ideal of pulling themselves up by their "bootstraps," they indirectly place blame on those who fail to do the same. These tendencies extend beyond Black politicians to some successful Black Americans. Fundamentally different life experiences can and have influenced policy support. For example, Black Americans with advanced degrees are less likely than similarly situated Whites to favor social policy aimed at helping

Blacks in particular, but high-income and well-educated Blacks are more favorable than Whites to policies helping the poor in general (Shelton and Wilson 2009).

Racial frames do the essential maintenance work of collectively reinforcing ideology, naturalizing inequality by shaping how we comprehend the inequality we see, what we attribute it to, and, most importantly, whether we believe anyone is at fault. Black resistance, in all of its forms, does the essential work of making the color line and the framing around it visible. It calls attention to the holes in a meritocratic frame and the paradox that exists within the Black community, resulting at times in an uncomfortable tension between the Black poor and the Black elite. The result is that we are reminded that the fight for Black equality must be nuanced, intersectional, continuously expanded and transnational to encompass the entangled relationship between racism, capitalism and oppression. Amid centuries of structural violence and racism, Black American persistence *is* resistance in and of itself.

Critical Reflection Questions

1 How have the affirmative action cases *Bakke* v. *Regents of the University of California* and *Fisher* v. *University of Texas* impacted the public's understanding of reverse discrimination?
2 Why was the Southern strategy a form of racial retrenchment?
3 What was the relationship between race-neutral and post-racial narratives in Barack Obama's presidential campaign?
4 How did the War on Poverty become a War on the Poor, especially on poor Black Americans?

Epilogue

While Blacks in America are no longer legally inhibited from full citizenship, the movement from slavery to freedom was never carried through to full equality. W. E. B. Du Bois described the color line – the legal separation and segregation of Blacks and Whites that defined American life – in 1903 as the problem of the twentieth century. Though separate but equal may no longer be the law of the land in the twenty-first century, separate and unequal we remain. Therein lies the paradox, and the question of who is to blame?

While the color line has been imbued with significance since Blacks set foot on the Southern shore, marking those bodies that were fit to be enslaved, it was the threat of freedom and the fight against abolition that produced the paradox. There was no place for the formerly enslaved to coexist as equals within American society. Emancipation did not change the fact that anti-Blackness was foundational to the forming of America and remains entrenched in its institutions today, producing disproportionately marginalizing effects on Black communities and other poor communities of color.

Anti-blackness manifests in a myriad of ways, as we have outlined in each chapter, but most importantly by framing Black people as *the* problem. The color line still persists, but what it delineates has been reconfigured as society has changed. Racial integration has meant that Blacks can be found in almost all industries, even if in small numbers, and there has been undeniable growth in the number of middle- and upper-class Blacks. Yet these measures of racial progress still reflect the existence of a racial hierarchy, in which mostly White and/or fair-skinned people fare better than Black and/or dark-skinned people in America and across the globe (Glenn 2009). Racism, colorism and classism largely dictate one's access to resources and quality of life.

We often measure Black progress based on the relatively small, yet increasing, number of Black millionaires and other positive indicators that orient our view toward those at the top. Yet this obscures the reality and permanence of the Blacks who are anchoring the bottom. Black Americans are still *disproportionately* one of the most isolated and segregated groups in America, experiencing extraordinary rates of concentrated poverty (Quillian 2012). These dual realities of growing wealth and persistent poverty coexist.

Focusing on the presence of Blacks in the entertainment industry (i.e. Oprah) or elected positions (i.e. President Obama) as a measure of racial progress is too narrow a lens for understanding racial inequality. Now, 153 years after the abolishment of slavery, and 54 years after the passage of the Civil Rights Act, the permanence of White wealth and continuing discrimination reverses gains Blacks have made through personal achievement, working hard and fighting for fuller inclusion in the American system (Shapiro 2004). In other words, due to increasing inequality, it is impossible for Black people and other groups of color to gain equal wealth to White families through high salaries and advanced degrees because of the geography of accumulated advantages and disadvantages in our society (Feagin 2000; Shapiro 2004; Conley 2009). Systematic structural racism and discrimination as perpetuated through the educational system, racial residential and occupational segregation, and inheritances have prevented full inclusion and equal access to a better life.

Du Bois' proclamation that "the problem of the twentieth century is the problem of the color line" remains true in the twenty-first century, but precipitated and maintained by other means (1903:7). Today, we must understand how class *and* race are used to continue to exploit and oppress the vulnerable, despite a societal belief in equality. Conservative shifts among Black Americans since 1980 have led to a convergence with Whites in person-centered (human capital, motivation) as opposed to structuralist (discrimination) explanations for income inequality (Hunt 2007). The American Dream espouses an ahistorical and post-racial ideal that hard work and effort are all that is required for success, where meritocracy wins out in the end and cumulative advantages and disadvantages are not relevant. Alas, America's racial reality complicates this dream. Our racial legacy has left footprints on our present that reinforce the centrality of race and racism, necessitating resistance in post-civil rights America, in order to achieve Martin Luther King's dream.

Glossary

Black Codes Laws enacted to specify the rights of former slaves that were often framed with the express goal of attempting to stabilize and control Black labor.

Black placemaking Sites of resistance in urban Black neighborhoods by residents who use joy and culture to reframe what their spaces mean to them.

broken windows theory of policing The theory that visible signs of crime, anti-social behavior and civil disorder create an urban environment that encourages further crime and disorder.

colorblindness The racial ideology that suggests the best way to end discrimination is by treating individuals as equally as possible (without regard to race).

controlling images Stereotypes that are both pervasive and persistent, and that serve to justify and naturalize inequality.

convict leasing Forcing prisoners to perform uncompensated labor.

cultural racism A view in which subordinated minorities are judged to be culturally deficient, and this cultural deficiency/inferiority is the basis of their demeaned social position, not racism or discrimination.

de facto segregation Segregation that is not enforced by the government but is socially upheld through private practices in everyday life.

de jure segregation Intentional and government-sanctioned segregation.

discourse An attempt to influence both the rules of the game and others' perceptions of social reality.

discursive redlining Ways of expressing racial attitudes with language that might be sanitized and subtle but still affects how we think about the redevelopment and gentrification of Black neighborhoods.

egalitarianism Media frame emphasizing equal opportunity to individual prosperity.

eminent domain A legal practice used by the government to obtain private land for public use.

federalism The division of power between states and the federal government.

frames Crucial shorthand for making sense of and navigating the great complexities in our lived realities and interactions.

gentrification A process in which urban neighborhoods inhabited by the poor and/or people of color are replaced by wealthier and/or White people, changing the culture of the neighborhood.

gerrymandering Manipulating the boundaries of an electoral constituency to favor one party.

ghetto A subsection of a larger urban metropolitan area that is cumulatively racially and economically disadvantaged.

ghettoization The othering process of a space becoming a ghetto, or becoming disinvested in due to racial and classed attitudes, coupled with the withdrawal of jobs, industries, public offices and other forms of investment, creating more isolation.

individualism Media frame emphasizing the importance of one's work ethic.

intersectionality Interdependent systems of advantage and disadvantage that further marginalize some Blacks while privileging others.

Janus-faced Description of drug policy as having two sharply contrasting characteristics, with race influencing how politicians frame and regulate drug use.

occupational achievement The occupation and compensation an individual attains.

population and structural change thesis A theory that posits that changes in the relative sizes of the minority and majority populations interact with changes in the social structure to exacerbate racial and ethnic inequality.

power Within a racialized social system, this is a racial group's capacity to push for its racial interest in relation to other races.

prehistory The ideational period in which an idea is created at the margins of criminal justice before manifesting on a wider scale.

race A concept that signifies and symbolizes sociopolitical conflicts and interests in reference to different types of human bodies. Race can also be defined as an *ideological construct*, a shared societal understanding of racial ideologies that manifest materially and socially within society, resulting in differential power along racial lines; a *sociohistorical construct*, developed over hundreds of years, producing a shared global understanding and reinforcement of relationships of domination and subordination along racial lines (Winant 2000a); an *ideology*, a manner of thinking, a system of complex ideas about power that justifies who should have it along racial lines; or an *objective fact*, one is simply one's race.

racetalk Racially coded words.

racial formation The sociohistorical process by which racial categories are created, inhabited, transformed and destroyed.

racial frames Overarching common-sense beliefs that consist of racial stereotypes, ideas, narratives and actions.

racial groups A subcategory of racialized minorities for whom the race dimension is the salient marker.

racial retrenchment The process by which racial progress obtained through policy gains is challenged or undermined by individual and collective actions.

racialization A process during which physical characteristics are imbued with racial significance.

racialized ethnic groups A subcategory of racialized minorities for whom ethnicity can also be a prominent feature of their identity, alongside race.

racialized minorities Minority groups who are defined by and infused with racial meaning.

racialized social system A social system in which economic, political, social and ideological levels are partially structured along racial lines, where races are socially constructed and typically determined by phenotypic characteristics.

redevelopment The rehabilitation or building of new physical structures in a place.

redlining A process that associated Black people, Blackness and other communities of color with being a financial risk and encouraged *disinvestment* in those areas by evaluating them as declining and hazardous.

restrictive (racial) covenants Agreements among property owners that stated they would not permit Blacks to own, occupy or lease their property for a period of time.

shade discrimination Preference for people who are light-skinned.

symbolic ethnicity This form of ethnicity is voluntary and peripheral in the lives of White ethnics, primarily because they express their identity in ways that do not conflict with other facets of their lives.

Notes

Introduction: Are We "Post-racial" Yet?

1 www.merriam-webster.com/dictionary/post-racial.
2 www.archives.gov/files/press/exhibits/dream-speech.pdf.
3 context.newamerica.org/there-is-the-south-then-there-is-mississippi-6cb154ee3843.

1 How Blacks Became the Problem: American Racism and the Fight for Equality

1 Franklin and Brooks Higginbotham (2011:100).
2 Sociologist Eduardo Bonilla-Silva (1996) introduced the concept of a racialized system to provide a theoretical framework through which racism could be viewed as having a *structural interpretation*. He asserts that, in a racialized social system, "economic, political, social, and ideological levels are partially structured" along racial lines, where races are socially constructed and typically determined by phenotypic characteristics (Bonilla-Silva 1996:469). The ultimate purpose of this categorization is to provide a basis for the formation of a social hierarchy along racial lines that justifies the unequal distribution of social goods (economic and political) amongst races by reference to their place in the hierarchical structure. The end result of this is that the life chances of racial groups are dissimilar, and the degree of racialization of a social system is indicated by this dissimilarity in life chances (Bonilla-Silva 1996:470).
3 https://medium.com/@matthewjohn_36675/White-supremacy-and-capitalism-the-two-headed-dragon-that-must-be-slain-dc55fc5e8ccf.
4 https://socialistworker.org/2011/01/04/race-class-and-marxism.
5 An example can be drawn by examining the role of the state: Oliver and Shapiro (1995) in their examination of the racialization of state policy demonstrate how state policy has simultaneously impaired the ability

of Black Americans to accumulate wealth, while promoting the accumulation of wealth amongst White Americans. Thus, members of the dominant group can profess a belief in racial equality and still reap the material benefits of their dominant position (Bonilla-Silva 1996; Blauner 2001).

6 Lieberson (1980:137) states: "Georgia passed laws in 1770, 1829, and 1853 that prohibited their education; Virginia in 1849; and South Carolina in 1740, 1800, and 1834. The latter prohibitions also applied to free Blacks."

2 Crafting the Racial Frame: Blackness and the Myth of the Monolith

1 https://billmoyers.com/content/the-vanishing-family-crisis-in-Black-am erica.
2 www.nytimes.com/1986/01/25/arts/tv-cbs-reports-examines-Black-fami lies.html.
3 www.pewresearch.org/fact-tank/2018/01/24/key-facts-about-Black-im migrants-in-the-u-s.
4 www.essence.com/news/politics/trump-travel-ban-Black-muslims.
5 www.politico.com/story/2016/05/obamas-howard-commencement-trans cript-222931.
6 www.census.gov/quickfacts/fact/note/US/RHI425217.
7 www.pewresearch.org/fact-tank/2017/11/01/how-wealth-inequality-has-changed-in-the-u-s-since-the-great-recession-by-race-ethnicity-and-inc ome.
8 https://ips-dc.org/report-ever-growing-gap.
9 www.esquire.com/news-politics/a6857/rod-blagojevich-interview-0210.
10 www.pewresearch.org/fact-tank/2014/12/12/racial-wealth-gaps-great-rec ession.
11 https://hbr.org/2015/02/how-americas-wealthiest-Black-families-invest-money.
12 https://money.cnn.com/2016/10/14/news/economy/Black-1-unstereotyp ed/index.html.
13 www.fastcompany.com/40513613/why-these-three-southern-cities-at tract-the-most-Black-entrepreneurs.
14 www.georgiaencyclopedia.org/articles/counties-cities-neighborhoods/au burn-avenue-sweet-auburn.
15 www.pewresearch.org/fact-tank/2017/06/13/5-key-findings-about-lgbt-american.
16 www.glaad.org/publications/whereweareontv11/characters.
17 www.thedailybeast.com/why-Black-ish-has-a-gay-problem.
18 www.thetaskforce.org/new-analysis-shows-startling-levels-of-discrimina tion-against-Black-transgender-people.
19 https://daily.jstor.org/chimamanda-ngozi-adichie-i-became-Black-in-am erica.

20 www.cnn.com/2018/01/11/politics/immigrants-shithole-countries-trum p/index.html.
21 www.pewresearch.org/fact-tank/2016/03/01/afro-latino-a-deeply-rooted -identity-among-u-s-hispanics.
22 www.npr.org/templates/transcript/transcript.php?storyId=597455444.
23 www.instagram.com/p/9L4DzMGwak/?taken-by=blaxicansofla.
24 www.nhs.uk/conditions/selective-mutism.
25 https://advopps.org/Black-history-month-prominent-african-americans-disabilities.
26 www.cdc.gov/ncbddd/disabilityandhealth/disability.html.
27 www.cdc.gov/ncbddd/disabilityandhealth/materials/infographic-disabili ties-ethnicity-race.html.

3 Whose Life Matters? Value and Disdain in American Society

1 The "crime" committed by *Buck* v. *Bell* plaintiff Carrie Buck that resulted in her sterilization was giving birth to a child out of wedlock while a ward of the state.
2 www.pbs.org/independentlens/blog/unwanted-sterilization-and-eugen ics-programs-in-the-united-states.
3 http://articles.chicagotribune.com/2014-05-13/health/ct-met-sterilizat ion-denied-20140513_1_tubal-ligation-sterilization-young-women/2. Doctors followed a rubric known as the "rule of 120," in which the product of a mother's age and number of births had to equal or exceed 120 before they could be considered for sterilization.
4 www.theatlantic.com/politics/archive/2018/01/when-the-south-was-the-most-progressive-region-in-america/550442.
5 www.slate.com/blogs/the_vault/2013/06/28/voting_rights_and_the_supr eme_court_the_impossible_literacy_test_louisiana.html.
6 www.history.com/news/free-school-breakfast-Black-panther-party.
7 http://explorepahistory.com/displayimage.php?imgId=1-2-1710.
8 www.history.com/this-day-in-history/riot-at-attica-prison.
9 www.phillytrib.com/news/after-years-move-still-in-prison/article_71ce2 3ad-892a-55e6-8bcb-eee06b643432.html.
10 www.phillytrib.com/news/after-years-move-still-in-prison/article_71ce2 3ad-892a-55e6-8bcb-eee06b643432.html.
11 www.theguardian.com/us-news/2015/may/13/osage-avenue-bombing-philadelphia-30-years.
12 www.cnn.com/2016/12/20/health/black-men-killed-by-police/index. html.
13 www.pewinternet.org/2016/08/15/the-hashtag-Blacklivesmatter-emerg es-social-activism-on-twitter/; www.pewinternet.org/2018/07/11/an-anal ysis-of-Blacklivesmatter-and-other-twitter-hashtags-related-to-political-or -social-issues.
14 http://wapo.st/KzQ7Fo?tid=ss_tw&utm_term=.e2da6b07cb9f.

5 Who Gets to Work? Understanding the Black Labor Market Experience

1 The exclusion of Black men persisted until the industrial movement in the 1930s, spearheaded by the Congress of Industrial Organizations (CIO) (Lieberson 1980:339).

6 Is Justice Blind? Race and the Rise of Mass Incarceration

1 www.naacp.org/criminal-justice-fact-sheet.
2 https://sentencingproject.org/wp-content/uploads/2016/01/Trends-in-US-Corrections.pdf.
3 www.bjs.gov/content/pub/pdf/p16.pdf.
4 www.bjs.gov/content/pub/pdf/ppus16.pdf.
5 www.prisonpolicy.org/graphs/raceinc.html.
6 See www.brennancenter.org/sites/default/files/publications/Crime%20 Trends%201990-2016.pdf, and www.pewresearch.org/fact-tank/2018/ 01/30/5-facts-about-crime-in-the-u-s.
7 Roberto Scalese, "The Charles Stuart Murders and the Racist Branding Boston Just Can't Seem to Shake," October 22, 2014, www.boston.com/ news/local-news/2014/10/22/the-charles-stuart-murders-and-the-racist-branding-boston-just-cant-seem-to-shake.
8 https://chicagosmilliondollarblocks.com.
9 Unemployment, in this case, refers to the rate of formerly incarcerated people who are jobless but are actively looking for jobs.

7 Reifying the Problem: Racism and the Persistence of the Color Line in American Politics

1 The authors note regional and cultural variations in likelihood: male, well-educated, in professional classes and religious outside the South, vs. economically marginalized and more emphasis on politics in the South; conservative and Republican in either case.
2 www.politico.com/story/2015/05/jeb-bush-willie-horton-118061 ("The GOP and Willie Horton: Together Again").
3 www.washingtonpost.com/news/the-fix/wp/2017/12/06/trump-argued-for-keeping-confederate-monuments-then-he-scaled-back-those-of-nati ve-americans/?utm_term=.2f89ed3fdfe.
4 www.nytimes.com/2017/02/07/upshot/one-third-dont-know-obamac are-and-affordable-care-act-are-the-same.html.
5 www.politifact.com/truth-o-meter/statements/2011/may/16/newt-gingri ch/newt-gingrich-defends-calling-barack-obama-food-st.

References

Acker, Joan. 2006. "Inequality Regimes: Gender, Class, and Race in Organizations." *Gender & Society* 20(4), 441–64.

Agan, Amanda, and Sonja Starr. 2017. "Ban the Box, Criminal Records, and Racial Discrimination: A Field Experiment." *The Quarterly Journal of Economics* 133(1), 191–235.

Alba, Richard. 1990. *Ethnic Identity: The Transformation of White America.* New Haven, CT: Yale University Press.

Alexander, Michelle. 2010. *The New Jim Crow: Mass Incarceration in the Age of Colorblindness.* New York: The New Press.

Anderson, Beverley. 1994. "Permissive Social and Educational Inequality 40 Years after Brown." *The Journal of Negro Education* 63(3), 443–50.

Anderson, Elijah. 2011. *The Cosmopolitan Canopy: Race and Civility in Everyday Life.* New York: Norton.
    2012. "The Iconic Ghetto." *The ANNALS of the American Academy of Political and Social Science* 642(8).

Anderson, Karen Tucker. 1982. "Last Hired, First Fired: Black Women Workers during World War II." *The Journal of American History* 69(1), 82–97.

Andrews, Kenneth. 2002. "Movement–Countermovement Dynamics and the Emergence of New Institutions: The Case of 'White Flight' Schools in Mississippi." *Social Forces* 80(3), 911–36.

Archer, Deborah N., and Kele S. Williams. 2006. "Making America 'The Land of Second Chances': Restoring Socioeconomic Rights for Ex-Offenders." *NYU Review of Law and Social Change* 30, 527–84.

Austin, Algernon. 2004. "Doing Race and Class." *Journal of African American Studies* 8(3), 52–61.

Avery, James. 2006. "The Sources and Consequences of Political Mistrust Among African Americans." *American Politics Research* 34(5), 653–82.

Banks, Ingrid, Gaye Johnson, George Lipsitz, Ula Taylor, Daniel Widener and Clyde Woods, eds. 2012. *Black California Dreamin': The Crises of California's African-American Communities.* University of California–Santa Barbara, Center for Black Studies Research.

Baodong, Liu. 2014. "Postracial Politics? Counterevidence from the Presidential Elections, 2004–2012." *DuBois Review* 11(2), 443–63.

Beck, E. M., and Stewart E. Tolnay. 1990. "The Killing Fields of the Deep South: The Market for Cotton and the Lynching of Blacks, 1882–1930." *American Sociological Review* 55(4), 526–39.

Bell, Derrick. 1992. *Faces at the Bottom of the Well: The Permanence of Racism.* New York: Basic Books.

Bell, Jeannine. 2017. "Hate Thy Neighbor: Lessons for Neighborhood Integration for the Post-Obama Era and Beyond." *Law & Social Inquiry* 42(2), 577–81.

Belkhir, Jean Ait, and Christiane Charlemaine. 2007. "Race, Gender, and Class Lessons from Hurricane Katrina." *Race, Gender & Class* 14(½), 120–52.

Bennett, Larry. 2018. "Ghettoization." *Encyclopedia of Chicago.* www.encyclopedia.chicagohistory.org/pages/514.html.

Bennett, Pamela, and Amy Lutz. 2009. "How African American is the Net Black Advantage? Differences in College Attendance among Immigrant Blacks, Native Blacks, and Whites." *Sociology of Education* 82, 70–100.

Berrey, Ellen. 2015. "Making a Civil Rights Claim for Affirmative Action: Bamn's Legal Mobilization and the Legacy of Race-Conscious Policies." *Du Bois Review* 12(2), 375–405.

Blackmon, Douglass. 2008. *Slavery by Another Name: The Re-Enslavement of Black Americans from the Civil War to World War 2.* New York: Anchor Books.

Blackwell, James E. 1975. *The Black Community: Diversity and Unity.* New York: Dodd, Mead and Company.

Blau, Peter M., and Otis D. Duncan. 1967. *The American Occupational Structure.* New Jersey: John Wiley & Sons, Inc.

Blauner, Robert. 2001. *Still the Big News: Racial Oppression in America.* Philadelphia: Temple University Press.

Blum, Edward J. 2011. "'Look, Baby, We Got Jesus on Our Flag': Robust Democracy and Religious Debate from the Era of Slavery to the Age of Obama." *The ANNALS of the American Academy of Political and Social Science* 637(1), 17–37.

Bobo, Lawrence D. 2017. "The Empire Strikes Back: Fall of the Postracial Myth and Stirrings of Renewed White Supremacy." *Du Bois Review* 14(1), 1–5.

Bogle, Donald. 2001. *Toms, Coons, Mulattoes, Mammies, and Bucks: An Interpretive History of Blacks in American Films.* London: Bloomsbury Publishing.

Bonczar, Thomas P. 2003. "Bureau of Justice Statistics (BJS)." *Bureau of Justice Statistics (BJS).* N.p. Aug., 2003.

Bond, Horace Mann. 1934. *The Education of the Negro in the American Social Order*. New York: Prentice-Hall.

Bonds, Michael. 2006. "The Continuing Significance of Race: A Case Study of the Impact of Welfare Reform." *Journal of African American Studies* 9(4), 18–31.

Bonilla-Silva, Eduardo. 1996. "Rethinking Racism: Toward a Structural Interpretation." *American Sociological Review* 62(3), 465–80.

2001. *White Supremacy and Racism in the Post-Civil Rights Era*. London: Lynne Rienner Publishers.

2003a. *Racism without Racists: Color-blind Racism and the Persistence of Racial Inequality in the United States*. Lanham, MD: Rowman & Littlefield.

2003b. "'New Racism,' Color-Blind Racism, and the Future of Whiteness in America." In *White Out: The Continuing Significance of Racism*, ed. Ashley W. Doane and Eduardo Bonilla-Silva.

2015. "The Structure of Racism in Color-Blind, 'Post-Racial' America." *American Behavioral Scientist* 59(11): 1358–76.

Bonilla-Silva, Eduardo, and Tyrone A. Forman. 2000. "'I Am Not a Racist But . . .': Mapping White College Students' Racial Ideology in the USA." *Discourse & Society* 11(1), 50–85.

Bonilla-Silva, Eduardo, and Victor Ray. 2009. "When Whites Love a Black Leader: Race Matters in Obamerica." *Journal of African American Studies* 13(2), 176–83.

Boutwell, L. 2015. "'I Don't Want to Claim America': African Refugee Girls and Discourses of Othering." *Girlhood Studies* 8(2), 103–18.

Branch, Enobong Hannah. 2007. "The Creation of Restricted Opportunity Due to the Intersection of Race & Sex: Black Women in the Bottom Class." *Race, Gender & Class* 14(3–4), 247–64.

2011. *Opportunity Denied: Limiting Black Women to Devalued Work*. New Brunswick, NJ: Rutgers University Press.

2018. "Racism, Sexism, and the Constraints on Black Women's Labor in 1920." *Research in the Sociology of Work* 32, 91–112.

Branch, Enobong Hannah, and Melissa Wooten. 2012. "Suited for Service: Racialized Rationalizations for the Ideal of the Domestic Servant from the Nineteenth Century to the Early Twentieth Century." *Social Science History* 36(2), 169–89.

Brandt, Allan M. 1978. "Racism and Research: The Case of the Tuskegee Syphilis Study." *The Hastings Center Report* 8(6), 21–9.

Brewer, Rose, and Nancy A. Heitzeg. 2008. "The Racialization of Crime and Punishment: Criminal Justice, Color-Blind Racism, and the Political Economy of the Prison Industrial Complex." *American Behavioral Scientist* 51(5), 625–44.

Broussard, Albert. 1993. *Black San Francisco: The Struggle for Racial Equality in the West, 1900–1954*. Lawrence: University of Kansas Press.

Brown, DeNeen. 2017. "You've Got Bad Blood: The Horror of the Tuskegee Syphilis Study." *Washington Post*. May 16, 2017. www.washingtonpost.

com/news/retropolis/wp/2017/05/16/youve-got-bad-blood-the-horror-of-the-tuskegee-syphilis-experiment/?utm_term=.2c6534c7f45e.

Browne, Irene Cynthia Hewitt, Leann Tigges and Gary Green. 2001. "Why Does Job Segregation Lead to Wage Inequality Among African Americans? Person, Place, Sector, or Skills," *Social Science Research* 30, 473–95.

Brundage, W. Fitzhugh. 2006. "The Ultimate Shame: Lynch-law in Post-civil War American South." *Social Alternatives* 25(1), 28–32.

Buehler, James W. 2017. "Racial/Ethnic Disparities in the Use of Lethal Force by US Police, 2010–2014." *American Journal of Public Health* 107(2), 295–7.

Bullock, Henry Allen. 1967. *A History of Negro Education in the South.* Cambridge, MA: Harvard University Press.

Burbridge, Lynn C. 1994. "The Reliance of African-American Women on Government and Third Sector Employment." *The American Economic Review* 84(2), 103–7.

Burmila, Edward M. 2017. "Voter Turnout, Felon Disenfranchisement and Partisan Outcomes in Presidential Elections, 1988–2012." *Social Justice Research* 30(1), 72–88.

Cammett, Ann. 2014. "Deadbeat Dads & Welfare Queens: How Metaphor Shapes Poverty Law." *Boston College Journal of Law & Social Justice* 34, 233.

Camp, Stephanie H. 2004. *Closer to Freedom: Enslaved Women and Everyday Resistance in the Plantation South.* Chapel Hill: University of North Carolina Press.

Cancio, Silvia, David T. Evans and David Maume Jr. 1996. "Reconsidering the Declining Significance of Race: Racial Differences in Early Career Wages." *American Sociological Review* 61(4), 551.

Caputo, Gail A. 2004. *Intermediate Sanctions in Corrections.* Denton: University of North Texas Press.

Carney, Nikita. 2016. All Lives Matter, but So Does Race? Black Lives Matter and the Evolving Role of Social Media. *Humanity & Society* 40(2), 180–99.

Carpenter, Tracy R. 2012. "Construction of the Crack Mother Icon." *Western Journal of Black Studies* 36(4), 264–75.

Carter, Niambi M., and Pearl F. Dowe. 2015. "The Racial Exceptionalism of Barack Obama." *Journal of African American Studies* 19(2), 105–19.

Clark, Kenneth. 1965. *The Dark Ghetto: Dilemmas of Social Power.* Hanover, NH: Wesleyan University Press.

Coates, Ta-Nehisi. 2015. *Between the World and Me.* New York: Spiegel & Grau.

Cobb, Jelani. 2014. "Between the World and Ferguson." *The New Yorker.* August 26, 2014.

Cokorinos, L. 2003. *The Assault on Diversity: An Organized Challenge to Racial and Gender Justice.* Lanham, MD: Rowman & Littlefield.

Collins, Patricia Hill. 2000. *Black Feminist Thought: Knowledge, Consciousness, and the Politics of Empowerment*. 2nd edition. New York: Routledge.

2012. "Just Another American Story? The First Black First Family." *Qualitative Sociology* 35(2), 123–41.

Conley, Dalton. 2009. *Being Black, Living in the Red: Race, Wealth, and Social Policy in America*. Berkeley: University of California Press.

Couloute, Lucius. 2018a. *Nowhere to Go: Homelessness among Formerly Incarcerated People*. Northampton: Prison Policy Initiative.

2018b. *Getting Back on Course: Educational Exclusion and Attainment among Formerly Incarcerated People*. Northampton: Prison Policy Initiative.

Couloute, Lucius, and Dan Kopf. 2018. *Out of Prison & Out of Work: Unemployment among Formerly Incarcerated People*. Northampton: Prison Policy Initiative.

Cox, Jonathan M. 2017. "The Source of a Movement: Making the Case for Social Media as an Informational Source Using Black Lives Matter." *Ethnic and Racial Studies* 40(11), 1847–54.

Cox, Oliver C. 1945. "Lynching and the Status Quo." *The Journal of Negro Education* 14(4), 576–88.

Crenshaw, Kimberlé Williams. 2000. "Race, Reform and Retrenchment." In *Theories of Race and Racism*, ed. Les Back and John Solomos. New York: Routledge.

2015. *Black Girls Matter: Pushed Out, Overpoliced and Underprotected*. New York: African American Policy Forum.

Cruise, Harold. 1968. *Rebellion or Revolution*. Minneapolis: The University of Minnesota Press.

Daniels, Douglass Henry. 1980. *Pioneer Urbanites: A Social and Cultural History of Black San Francisco*. Philadelphia, PA: Temple University Press.

Danziger, Sheldon, and Sandra K. Danziger. 2006. "Poverty, Race, and Antipoverty Policy Before and After Hurricane Katrina." *Du Bois Review* 3(1), 23–6.

Davis, Adrienne. 2002. "'Don't Let Nobody Bother Yo' Principle': The Sexual Economy of Slavery." In *Sister Circle: Black Women and Work*, ed. Sharon Harley and the Black Women and Work Collectives. New Brunswick, NJ: Rutgers University Press.

Davis, Angela. 1981. *Women, Race and Class*. New York: Vintage Books.

2003. *Are Prisons Obsolete?* New York: Seven Stories Press.

2016. *Freedom is a Constant Struggle: Ferguson, Palestine and the Foundations of a Movement*. Chicago, IL: Haymarket Books.

De Giorgi, Alessandro. 2017. "Back to Nothing: Prisoner Reentry and Neoliberal Neglect." *Social Justice* 44(1): 83–120.

Dennis, Andrea. 2016. "Black Contemporary Social Movements, Resource Mobilization and Black Musical Activism." *Law and Contemporary Social Problems* 79(3), 29–51.

Derkas, Erika. 2012. "'Don't Let Your Pregnancy Get in the Way of Your

Drug Addiction': Crack and the Ideological Construction of Addicted Women." *Social Justice* 38(3), 125–44.

Doane, Ashley W. 2003. "Rethinking Whiteness Studies". In *White Out: The Continuing Significance of Racism*, ed. Ashley W. Doane and Eduardo Bonilla-Silva.

2006. "What is Racism? Racial Discourse and Racial Politics." *Critical Sociology* 32(2–3), 255–74.

Doane, Ashley W., and Eduardo Bonilla-Silva. 2003. *White Out: The Continuing Significance of Racism*. New York: Routledge.

Doering, Jan. 2017. "'Afraid of Walking Home From the "L"at Night?' The Politics of Crime and Race in Racially Integrated Neighborhoods." *Social Problems* 64(2), 277–97.

Doleac, Jennifer L., and Benjamin Hansen. 2017. "Moving to Job Opportunities? The Effect of 'Ban the Box' on the Composition of Cities." *American Economic Review* 107(5), 556–9.

Donato, Rubén, and Jarrod S. Hanson. 2012. "Legally White, Socially 'Mexican': The Politics of De Jure and De Facto School Segregation in the American Southwest." *Harvard Educational Review* 82(2), 202–25.

Dorr, Gregory. 2011. "Protection or Control? Women's Health, Sterilization Abuse, and *Relf* v. *Weinberger*." In *A Century of Eugenics in America: From the Indiana Experiment to the Human Genome Era*, ed. Paul A. Lombardo. Indiana University Press.

Douglass, Frederick. n.d. "Address to the People of the United States." Speech by Frederick Douglass, n. pag.

Drake, St. Clair, and Horace Cayton. 1945. *Black Metropolis: A Study of Negro Life in a Northern City*. The University of Chicago Press.

Drakulich, Kevin M., and Robert D. Crutchfield. 2013. "The Role of Perceptions of the Police in Informal Social Control: Implications for the Racial Stratification of Crime and Control." *Social Problems* 60(3), 383–407.

Du Bois, William Edward Burghardt. 1898. "The Study of Negro Problems." *The ANNALS of the American Academy of Political and Social Science* 11(1), 1–23.

1899. *The Philadelphia Negro: A Social Study*. Philadelphia: The University of Pennsylvania Press.

1901. *The Negro Common School*. Atlanta University Press.

1903. *The Souls of Black Folk*. Chicago, IL: A. C. McClurg & Co.

1935. *Black Reconstruction in America 1860–1880*. New York: The Free Press.

Du Bois, William Edward Burghardt, and Augustus Granville Dill, eds. 1911. *The Common School and the Negro American*. Atlanta University Press.

Duncan, Otis D. 1968. "Inheritance of Poverty or Inheritance of Race." In *On Understanding Poverty*, ed. Daniel P. Moynihan. New York: Basic Books.

Eargle, Lisa A., Ashraf M. Esmail and Jas M. Sullivan. 2008. "Voting the Issues or Voting the Demographics? The Media's Construction of Political Candidates' Credibility." *Race, Gender & Class* 15(¾), 8–31.

Edge, Thomas. 2010. "Southern Strategy 2.0: Conservatives, White Voters, and the Election of Barack Obama." *Journal of Black Studies* 40(3), 426–44.

Edin, Kathryn, and Joanna M. Reed. 2005. "Why Don't They Just Get Married? Barriers to Marriage among the Disadvantaged." *The Future of Children* 15(2), 117–37.

Epstein, Rebecca, Jamilia Blake and Thalia González. 2017. "Girlhood Interrupted: The Erasure of Black Girls' Childhood." *Center on Poverty and Inequality*, Georgetown Law.

Erevelles, Nirmala. 2011. "The 'Other' Side of the Dialectic: Toward a Materialist Ethic of Care." In *Disability and Difference in Global Contexts*, ed. Nirmala Erevelles. New York: Palgrave Macmillan.

Esposito, Luigi, and J. W. Murphy. 2010. "Post Civil Rights Racism and the Need to Challenge Racial/Ethnic Inequality beyond the Limits of Liberalism." *Theory in Action* 3(2), 38–63.

Fainstein, Norman, and Susan Fainstein. 1985. "Economic Restructuring and the Rise of Urban Social Movements." *Urban Affairs Quarterly* 21(2), 187–206.

Feagin, Joe. 2000. *Racist America: Roots, Current Realities, & Future Reparations*. New York: Routledge.

Feagin, Joe, and Melvin P. Sikes. 1995. *Living with Racism: The Black Middle-Class Experience*. New York: Beacon Press.

Fields, Barbara Jeanne. 1990. "Slavery, Race and Ideology in the United States of America." *New Left Review* 181, 95–118.

Fischer, Claude S., and Michael E. Hout. 2007. *Century of Difference: How America Changed in the Last One Hundred Years*. New York: Russell Sage Foundation.

Fishman, Darwin. 2013. "Racial Attacks on President Obama and the White Nationalist Legacy." *Western Journal of Black Studies* 37(4), 236–348.

Follins, Lourdes D., Ja'Nina J. Walker and Michele K. Lewis. 2014. "Resilience in Black Lesbian, Gay, Bisexual, and Transgender Individuals: A Critical Review of the Literature." *Journal of Gay & Lesbian Mental Health* 18(2), 190–212.

Foner, Eric. 1988. *Reconstruction: America's Unfinished Revolution 1863–1877*. New York: Harper Row.

Ford, Richard T. 2009. "Barack Is The New Black: Obama and the Promise/Threat of the Post-Civil Rights Era." *Du Bois Review* 6(1), 37–48.

Forman, Tyrone A., and Amanda E. Lewis. 2015. "Beyond Prejudice? Young Whites' Racial Attitudes in Post-Civil Rights America, 1976 to 2000." *American Behavioral Scientist* 59(11), 1394–1428.

Foster, Carly Hayden. 2008. "The Welfare Queen: Race, Gender, Class, and Public Opinion." *Race, Gender, & Class* 15(¾): 162–79.

Fox, Cybelle. 2012. *Three Worlds of Relief: Race, Immigration, and the American Welfare State from the Progressive Era to the New Deal.* Princeton University Press.

Franklin, John Hope. 1956. *From Slavery to Freedom.* New York: Alfred A. Knopf.

Franklin, John Hope, and Evelyn Brooks Higginbotham. 2011. *From Slavery to Freedom: A History of African Americans.* New York: McGraw-Hill.

Fredrickson, George M. 2002. *Racism: A Short History.* Princeton University Press.

Freeman, Lance. 2006. *There Goes the Hood: Views of Gentrification from the Ground Up.* Philadelphia, PA: Temple University Press.

Fullilove, Mindy. 2005. *Root Shock: How Tearing Up City Neighborhoods Hurts America, and What We Can Do About It.* New York: Ballantine Books.

Gans, Herbert. 1979. "Symbolic Ethnicity: The Future of Ethnic Groups and Cultures in America." *Ethnic and Racial Studies* 2, 1–20.

2008. "Involuntary Segregation and the Ghetto: Disconnecting Process and Place." Symposium on the Ghetto. *City and Community* 7(4), 353–7.

Gates Jr., Henry L. 2012. *Black Cool: One Thousand Streams of Blackness.* Soft Skull Press.

Ghandnoosh, Nazgol. 2014. *Race and Punishment: Racial Perceptions of Crime and Support for Punitive Policies.* Washington, DC: The Sentencing Project.

Glaser, Jack. 2015. *Suspect Race: Causes and Consequences of Racial Profiling.* New York: Oxford University Press.

Glazer, Nathan, and Daniel P. Moynihan. 1970. *Beyond the Melting Pot: The Negroes, Puerto Ricans, Jews, Italians, and Irish of New York City.* Cambridge, MA: MIT Press.

Glenn, Evelyn Nakano. 2002. *Unequal Freedom: How Race and Gender Shaped American Citizenship and Labor.* Cambridge, MA: Harvard University Press.

2009. *Shades of Difference: Why Skin Color Matters.* Stanford University Press.

Goffman, Erving. 1955. "On Face-Work: An Analysis of Ritual Elements in Social Interaction." *Psychiatry* 18(3), 213–31.

Goidel, Kirby, Wayne Parent and Bob Mann. 2011. "Race, Racial Resentment, Attentiveness to the News Media, and Public Opinion Toward the Jena Six." *Social Science Quarterly* 92(1), 20–34.

Goldberg, David Theo. 1998. "The New Segregation." *Race and Society* 1(1), 15–32.

Graham, Lawrence O. 2000. *Our Kind of People: Inside America's Black Upper Class.* New York: HarperCollins.

Graham, Louis F. 2014. "Navigating Community Institutions: Black Transgender Women's Experiences in Schools, the Criminal Justice System, and Churches." *Sexuality Research and Social Policy* 11(4), 274–87.

Grant, Nicholas. 2017. *Winning Our Freedoms Together: African Americans and Apartheid, 1945–1960.* Raleigh: The University of North Carolina Press.

Green, Laurie B. 2006. "'Where Would the Negro Women Apply for Work?': Gender, Race, and Labor in Wartime Memphis." *Labor: Studies in Working-Class History of the Americas* 3(3), 96.

Gross, Kali Nicole. 2015. "African American Women, Mass Incarceration, and the Politics of Protection." *Journal of American History* 102(1), 25–33.

Gustafson, K. 2009. "The Criminalization of Poverty." *The Journal of Criminal Law and Criminology*, 643–716.

Gutman, Herbert G. 1976. *Black Family in Slavery and Freedom, 1750–1925.* Pantheon Books.

Haberman, Margaret A. 2018. *White Kids: Growing Up with Privilege in a Racially Divided America.* New York University Press.

Hacker, Andrew. 1995. *Two Nations: Black and White, Separate, Hostile, and Unequal.* New York: Ballantine Press.

Hahn, Steven. 2003. *A Nation Under Our Feet: Black Political Struggles in the Rural South from Slavery to the Great Migration.* Cambridge, MA: Belknap Press.

Haley, Sarah. 2016. *No Mercy Here: Gender, Punishment, and the Making of Jim Crow Modernity.* Chapel Hill: University of North Carolina Press.

Hallett, Michael. 2004. "Commerce with Criminals: The New Colonialism in Criminal Justice." *Review of Policy Research* 21(1), 49–62.

2012. "Reentry to What? Theorizing Prisoner Reentry in the Jobless Future." *Critical Criminology* 20(3), 1–16.

Hallihan, Maureen T. 2001. "Sociological Perspectives on Black–White Inequalities in American Schooling." *Sociology of Education* 74, 50–70.

Hammond, James Henry. 1866. *Selections from the Letters and Speeches of the Hon. James H. Hammond of South Carolina.* New York: John F. Trow & Co.

Hancock, Ange-Marie. 2004. *The Politics of Disgust: The Public Identity of the Welfare Queen.* New York University Press.

Harlow, Caroline Wolf. 1999. "Prior Abuse Reported by Inmates and Probationers." *Bureau of Justice Statistics*.

Harris, Alexes, Heather Evans and Katherine Beckett. 2010. "Drawing Blood from Stones: Legal Debt and Social Inequality in the Contemporary United States." *American Journal of Sociology* 115(6), 1753–99.

Hartman, Chester. 2002. *City for Sale: The Transformation of San Francisco.* Los Angeles: University of California Press.

Hawley, George. 2015. *White Voters in 21st-Century America*. New York: Routledge.

Haynes, Bruce, and Ray Hutchinson, eds. 2011. *The Ghetto: Contemporary Global Issues and Controversies*. Boulder, CO: The Westview Press.

Herman, Edward S., and David Peterson. 2008. "Jeremiah Wright in the Propaganda System." *Monthly Review* 60(4), 1–21.

Hill, Jane H. 1998. "Language, Race and White Public Space." *American Anthropologist* 100(3), 680–9.

Hill II, Sean. 2017. "Precarity in the Era of #BlackLivesMatter." *Women's Studies Quarterly* 45(3), 94–109.

Hinton, Elizabeth, LeShae Henderson and Cindy Reed. 2018. *An Unjust Burden: The Disparate Treatment of Black Americans in the Criminal Justice System*. Vera Institute of Justice.

Hipp, John R., J. Jannetta, R. Shah and S. Turner. 2011. "Parolees' Physical Closeness to Social Services: A Study of California Parolees." *Crime & Delinquency* 57(1), 102–29.

Hippler, Arthur E. 1974. *Hunter's Point: A Black Ghetto*. New York: Basic Books Inc.

Hirsch, Arnold. 1983. *Making of the Second Ghetto: Race and Housing in Chicago, 1940–1960*. Cambridge University Press.

Hochshild, Jennifer. 1995. *Facing Up to the American Dream: Race, Class, and the Soul of the Nation*. Princeton University Press.

Hoffman, Timothy J. 2015. "The Civil Rights Realignment: How Race Dominates Presidential Elections." *Political Analysis* 17(1).

Honey, Michael Keith. 1999. *Black Workers Remember: An Oral History of Segregation, Unionism, and the Freedom Struggle*. Berkeley: University of California Press.

Horton, Hayward Derrick. 1998. "Toward a Critical Demography of Race and Ethnicity: Introduction of the 'R' Word." Earlier version of paper presented at the 1998 annual meeting of the American Sociological Association in San Francisco, California.

Horton, Hayward D., Beverlyn Lundy Allen, Cedric Herring and Melvin E. Thomas. 2000. "Lost in the Storm: The Sociology of the Black Working Class, 1850–1990." *American Sociological Review* 65(1), 128–37.

Hunt, Matthew O. 2007. "African American, Hispanic, and White Beliefs about Black/White Inequality, 1977–2004." *American Sociological Review* 72, 390–415.

Hunter, Daniel. 2015. *Building a Movement to End the New Jim Crow: An Organizing Guide*. The Veterans of Hope Project.

Hunter, Marcus Anthony. 2013. *Black Citymakers: How the Philadelphia Negro Changed Urban America*. New York: Oxford University Press.

Hunter, Marcus Anthony, Mary Pattillo, Zandria F. Robinson and Keeanga-Yamahtta Taylor. 2016. "Black Placemaking: Celebration, Play and Poetry." *Theory, Culture & Society* 33(7–8), 31–56.

Hunter, Marcus Anthony, and Zandria Robinson. 2016. "The

Sociology of Urban Black America." *Annual Review of Sociology* 42, 385–405.

Hunter, Tera W. 1995. "Domination and Resistance: The Politics of Wage Household Labor in New South Atlanta." In *"We Specialize in the Wholly Impossible": A Reader in Black Woman's History*, ed. Darlene Clark Hines. Brooklyn, NY: Carlson Publishing.

Hurwitz, Jon, and Mark Peffley. 2005. "Playing the Race Card in the Post-Willie Horton Era: The Impact of Racialized Code Words on Support for Punitive Crime Policy." *Public Opinion Quarterly* 69(1), 99–112.

Imoagene, Onoso. 2015. "Broken Bridges: An Exchange of Slurs Between African Americans and Second Generation Nigerians and the Impact on Identity Formation among the Second Generation." *Language Sciences* 52, 176–86.

Ioanide, Paula. 2015. *The Emotional Politics of Racism: How Feelings Trump Facts in an Era of Colorblindness*. Stanford University Press.

Jackson, Christina. 2010. "Black Flight from San Francisco: How Race, Community and Politics Shape Urban Policy." Master's thesis. University of California–Santa Barbara, Santa Barbara, CA.

2014. "Black San Francisco: The Politics of Race and Space in the City." Doctoral dissertation. University of California–Santa Barbara, Santa Barbara, CA.

2018. "The Effect of Urban Renewal on Fragmented Social and Political Engagement in Urban Environments." *Journal of Urban Affairs*. https://doi.org/10.1080/07352166.2018.1478225.

Jackson, Christina, and Nikki Jones. 2012. "Remember the Fillmore: The Lingering History of Urban Renewal in Black San Francisco." In *Black California Dreamin': The Crises of California's African-American Communities*, ed. Ingrid Banks, Gaye Johnson, George Lipsitz, Ula Taylor, Daniel Widener and Clyde Woods.

Jackson, John. 2008. *Racial Paranoia: The Unintended Consequences of Political Correctness*. New York: Basic Civitas Books.

Jacobs, David, and Daniel Tope. 2007. "The Politics of Resentment in the Post-Civil Rights Era: Minority Threat, Homicide, and Ideological Voting in Congress." *American Journal of Sociology* 112(5), 1458–94.

2008. "Race, Crime, and Republican Strength: Minority Politics in the Post-Civil Rights Era." *Social Science Research* 37(4), 1116.

Johnson, Allan G. 2005. *Privilege, Power, and Difference*. New York: McGraw-Hill.

Johnson, Tekla Ali, Pearl K. Ford Dowe and Michael K. Fauntroy. 2011. "One America? President Obama's Non-Racial State." *Race, Gender & Class* 18(¾): 135–49.

Jones, Brian P. 2016. "Black Lives Matter and the Struggle for Freedom." *Monthly Review* 68(4), 1.

Jones, Chenelle A., and Renita L. Seabrook. 2017. "The New Jane Crow: Mass Incarceration and the Denied Maternity of Black Women."

In *Race, Ethnicity and Law*, ed. Matieu Deflem. Bingley: Emerald Publishing Limited.

Jones, Jacqueline. 1986. *Labor of Love, Labor of Sorrow: Black Women, Work, and the Family, from Slavery to the Present*. New York: Vintage Books.

Jones, Nikki. 2008. "Working 'the Code': On Girls, Gender, and Inner City Violence." *Australian and New Zealand Journal of Criminology* 41(1), 63–83.

2018. *The Chosen Ones: Black Men and the Politics of Redemption*. Oakland: The University of California Press.

Jones, Nikki, and Christina Jackson. 2011. "'You Just Don't Go Down There': Learning to Avoid the Ghetto in San Francisco." In *The Ghetto: Contemporary Global Issues and Controversies*, ed. Ray Hutchinson and Bruce Haynes. Boulder, CO: The Westview Press.

Judd, Dennis R., and Todd Swanstrom. 1998. *City Politics: Private Power and Public Policy*. Longman Publishers.

Kalleberg, Arne L. 2011. *Good Jobs, Bad Jobs: The Rise of Polarized and Precarious Employment Systems in the United States, 1970s to 2000s*. New York: Russell Sage Foundation.

Kajstura, Aleks. 2018. "Women's Mass Incarceration: The Whole Pie 2018." Northampton: Prison Policy Initiative.

Katzman, David M. 1978. *Seven Days a Week: Women and Domestic Service in Industrializing America*. New York: Oxford University Press.

Kaufman, Robert L. 1986 "The Impact of Industrial and Occupational Structure of Black–White Employment Allocation". *American Sociological Review* 51(3), 310–23.

2002. "Assessing Alternative Perspectives on Race and Sex Employment Segregation." *American Sociological Review* 67(4), 547–72.

Keith, Verna, and Cedric Herring. 1991. "Skin Tone and Stratification in the Black Community." *American Journal of Sociology* 47, 518–32.

Kellstedt, P. M. 2000. "Media Framing and the Dynamics of Racial Policy Preferences." *American Journal of Political Science* 44(2), 245–60.

Kinder, D. R., and D. O. Sears. 1981. "Prejudice and Politics: Symbolic Racism Versus Racial Threats to the Good Life." *Journal of Personality and Social Psychology* 40(3), 414–31.

King, Desmond S., and Rogers M. Smith. 2016. "The Last Stand? *Shelby County* v. *Holder*, White Political Power, and America's Racial Policy Alliances." *Du Bois Review* 13(1), 25–44.

King, Ryan S., and Marc Mauer. 2007. *Uneven Justice: State Rates of Incarceration by Race and Ethnicity*. Washington, DC: The Sentencing Project.

Kletzer, Lori G. 1991. "Job Displacement, 1979–86: How Blacks Fared Relative to Whites." *Monthly Labor Review* 114(7), 17–25.

Kohler-Hausmann, Julilly. 2007. "'The Crime of Survival': Fraud Prosecutions, Community Surveillance, and the Original 'Welfare Queen.'" *Journal of Social History* 41(2), 329–54.

Kotlowski, D. 1998. "Richard Nixon and the Origins of Affirmative Action." *The Historian* 60(3), 523–41.

Kozol, Jonathan. 2012. *Savage Inequalities: Children in America's Schools.* New York: Broadway Books.

Krivo, Lauren J., and Ruth D. Peterson. 1996. "Extremely Disadvantaged Neighborhoods and Urban Crime." *Social Forces* 2(1), 619–48.

Kubrin, C., G. Squires and E. Stewart. 2007. "Neighborhoods, Race, and Recidivism: The Community Reoffending Nexus and its Implications for African Americans." *Sage Race Relations Abstracts* 32(2), 7–37.

Landry, Bart. 2000. *Black Working Wives: Pioneers of the American Family Revolution.* Berkeley: University of California Press.

Leonard, Jonathan S. 1990. "The Impact of Affirmative Action Regulation and Equal Employment Law on Black Employment." *Journal of Economic Perspectives* 4(4), 47–63.

Leone, Luigi, and Fabio Presaghi. 2018. "Tea Party Support, Racial Resentment, and Evaluations of Obama: A Moderation Analysis." *Race and Social Problems* 10(2), 91–100.

Lewis, Amanda E., and David G. Embrick. 2016. "Working at the Intersection of Race and Public Policy: The Promise (and Perils) of Putting Research to Work for Societal Transformation." *Sociology of Race and Ethnicity* 2(3), 253–62.

Lewis, Arnold. 2008. "Has the Revolution Been Specified? A Critical Assessment of the Status of Research on the Voting Rights Act and Black Politics." *Western Journal of Black Studies* 32(1), 53–61.

Lieberman, Robert C. 2006. "'The Storm Didn't Discriminate': Katrina and the Politics of Color Blindness." *Du Bois Review* 3(1), 7–22.

Lieberson, Stanley. 1980. *A Piece of Pie.* Berkeley: University of California Press.

Liebow, Elliot. 2003. *Tally's Corner: A Study of Negro Streetcorner Men.* New York: Rowman and Littlefield.

Lincoln, Abraham, and Stephen Arnold Douglas. 1894. *Political Debates between Abraham Lincoln and Stephen A. Douglas in the Celebrated Campaign of 1858 in Illinois: Including the Preceding Speeches of Each at Chicago, Springfield, Etc., Also the Two Great Speeches of Abraham Lincoln in Ohio in 1859.* Cleveland, OH: Burrows Bros. Co.

Lipsitz, George. 2011. *How Racism Takes Place.* Philadelphia: Temple University Press.

2015. "From Plessy to Ferguson." *Cultural Critique* 90 (Spring).

Logan, John, and Harvey Molotch. 1987. *Urban Fortunes: The Political Economy of Place.* Berkeley: University of California Press.

Lord, Brielle, and Christina Jackson. 2017. "Black Lives Matter AC on Affirming Black LGBTQ Lives." Media Mobilizing Project's NJ Platform Blog. http://njplatform.org/black-lives-matter-ac-affirming-black-lgbtq-lives.

Lorde, Audre. 1983. "There Is No Hierarchy of Oppressions." *Bulletin: Homophobia and Education*, 14(3/4), 9.

Loughran, Kevin. 2015. "The Philadelphia Negro and the Canon of Classical Urban Theory." *DuBois Review* 12(2), 249–67.

Lowndes, J. 2013. "Barack Obama's Body: The Presidency, the Body Politic, and the Contest over American National Identity." *Polity* 45(4), 469–98.

Lubin, Judy M. 2015. "Race and the Politics of Health Reform: Antigovernment Opposition to National Health Insurance from the New Deal to the Affordable Care Act." Dissertation. Proquest, Ann Arbor, MI.

Mah, Theresa. 1999. "Buying into the Middle Class: Residential Segregation and Racial Formation in the United States, 1920–1964." Doctoral dissertation. Department of History, University of Chicago, Chicago, IL.

Marable, M. 1999. *How Capitalism Underdeveloped Black America: Problems in Race, Political Economy, and Society*. Boston, MA: South End Press.

Massey, Douglass, and Nancy Denton. 1993. *American Apartheid: Segregation and the Making of the Underclass*. Cambridge, MA: Harvard University Press.

Masters, N. Tatiana, Taryn P. Lindhorst and Marcia K. Meyers. 2014. "Jezebel at the Welfare Office: How Racialized Stereotypes of Poor Women's Reproductive Decisions and Relationships Shape Policy Implementation." *Journal of Poverty* 18(2), 109–29.

Mauer, Marc. 2001. "The Causes and Consequences of Prison Growth in the United States." *Punishment & Society* 3(1), 9–20.

Maxwell, Angie, and Todd Shields. 2014. "The Fate of Obamacare: Racial Resentment, Ethnocentrism and Attitudes about Healthcare Reform." *Race and Social Problems* 6(4), 29–304.

Mayer, Kenneth R. 2002. *With the Stroke of a Pen: Executive Orders and Presidential Power*. Princeton University Press.

Mayrl, Damon, and Aliya Saperstein. 2013. "When White People Report Racial Discrimination: The Role of Region, Religion, and Politics." *Social Science Research* 42(3), 742–54.

McAdam, Doug. 1982. *Political Process and the Development of Black Insurgency*. University of Chicago Press.

McCamey, Jimmy D., and Komanduri S. Murty. 2013. "A Paradigm Shift in Political Tolerance Since President Obama Was Elected." *Race, Gender & Class* 20(¾), 80–97.

McCune, Jeffrey. 2014. *Sexual Discretion: Black Masculinity and the Politics of Passing*. University of Chicago Press.

McDaniel, Antonio. 1996. "Fertility and Racial Stratification." *Population and Development Review* 22, 134–50.

McFayden, Elgie C. 2013. "The Politics of Race During the Obama Era." *Race, Gender, & Class* 20(¾), 7–17.

McGovern, Stephen. 1998. *The Politics of Downtown Development: Dynamic Political Culture in San Francisco and Washington D.C.* The University of Kentucky Press.

McMahon, Jean M., and Kimberly B. Kahn. 2018. "When Sexism Leads to Racism: Threat, Protecting Women, and Racial Bias." *Sex Roles* 78(9–10), 591–605.

Mead, Lawrence M. 1986. *Beyond Entitlement: The Social Obligations of Citizenship.* New York: Free Press.

Mears, Daniel P., Xia Wang and William D. Bales. 2014. "Does a Rising Tide Lift All Boats? Labor Market Changes and Their Effects on the Recidivism of Released Prisoners." *Justice Quarterly* 31(5), 822–51.

Mickelson, Roslyn A. 1990. "The Attitude–Achievement Paradox among Black Adolescents." *Sociology of Education* 63(1), 44–61.

Milkman, Ruth. 1987. *Gender at Work: The Dynamics of Job Segregation During World War II.* Champaign: University of Illinois Press.

Miller, Lisa L. 2015. "What's Violence Got to Do with It? Inequality, Punishment, and State Failure in US Politics." *Punishment & Society* 17(2), 184–210.

Miller, Reuben J. 2014. "Devolving the Carceral State: Race, Prisoner Reentry, and the Micro-Politics of Urban Poverty Management." *Punishment & Society* 16(3), 305–35.

Miller, Reuben J., and Amanda Alexander. 2016. "The Price of Carceral Citizenship: Punishment, Surveillance, and Social Welfare Policy in an Age of Carceral Expansion." *Michigan Journal of Race & Law* 21, 291.

Miller, Reuben J., and Forrest Stuart. 2017. "Carceral Citizenship: Race, Rights and Responsibility in the Age of Mass Supervision." *Theoretical Criminology* 21(4), 532–48.

Mollenkopf, John H. 1983. *The Contested City.* Princeton University Press.

Monnat, Shannon M. 2010. "The Color of Welfare Sanctioning: Exploring the Individual and Contextual Roles of Race on TANF Case Closures and Benefit Reductions." *The Sociological Quarterly* 51(4), 678–707.

Moore, Mignon. 2011. *Invisible Families: Gay Identities, Relationships, and Motherhood among Black Women.* University of California Press.

Morgan, Jennifer L. 2011. *Laboring Women: Reproduction and Gender in New World Slavery.* Philadelphia: University of Pennsylvania Press.

Morris, Aldon. 2017. "W. E. B. DuBois at the Center: From Science, Civil Rights Movement to Black Lives Matter." *The British Journal of Sociology* 68(1), 3–16.

Morris, M. 2012. *Race, Gender and the School-To-Prison Pipeline: Expanding Our Discussion to Include Black Girls.* African American Policy Forum.

Morris, M., and Bruce Western. 1999. "Inequality in Earnings at the Close of the Twentieth Century." *Annual Review of Sociology* 25, 623–57.

Moss, Philip, and Chris Tilly. 2001. *Stories Employers Tell: Race, Skill, and Hiring in America.* New York: Russell Sage.

Muhammad, Khalil G. 2010. *The Condemnation of Blackness: Race, Crime, and the Making of Modern Urban America*. Cambridge, MA: Harvard University Press.

Mullings, Leith. 2005. "Interrogating Racism: Toward an Antiracist Anthropology." *Annual Review of Anthropology* 34, 667–93.

Murphy, Daniel S., Brian Fuleihan, Stephen C. Richards, and Richard S. Jones. 2011. "The Electronic 'Scarlet Letter': Criminal Backgrounding and a Perpetual Spoiled Identity." *Journal of Offender Rehabilitation* 50(3), 101–18.

Neckerman, Kathryn M., and Joleen Kirschenman. 1991. "Hiring Strategies, Racial Bias, and Inner-City Workers." *Social Problems* 38(4), 433–47.

Newbold, Nathan C. 1928. "Common Schools for Negroes in the South." *Annals of the American Academy of Political and Social Science* 140, 209–23.

Newsome, Yvonne D., and F. Nii-Amoo Dodoo. 2002. "Reversal of Fortune: Explaining the Decline in Black Women's Earnings." *Gender and Society* 16(4), 442–64.

Nielsen, Amie L., Scott Bonn and George Wilson. 2010. "Racial Prejudice and Spending on Drug Rehabilitation: The Role of Attitudes Toward Blacks and Latinos." *Race and Social Problems* 2(3–4), 149–63.

Nixon, Vivian, Patricia T. Clough, David Staples et al. 2008. "Life Capacity Beyond Reentry: A Critical Examination of Racism and Prisoner Reentry Reform in the US." *Race/Ethnicity: Multidisciplinary Global Contexts* 21–43.

Noland, Edward William, and Edward Wight Bakke. 1977. *Workers Wanted: A Study of Employers' Hiring Policies, Preferences and Practices in New Haven and Charlotte*. New York: Harper & Brothers.

Nunnally, Shayla C., and Niambi M. Carter. 2012. "Moving from Victims to Victors: African American Attitudes on the 'Culture of Poverty' and Black Blame." *Journal of African American Studies* 16(3), 423–55.

Ochs, Holona Leanne. 2006. "'Colorblind' Policy in Black and White: Racial Consequences of Disenfranchisement Policy." *Policy Studies Journal* 34(1), 81–93.

Ogbu, John U. 2004. "Collective Identity and the Burden of 'Acting White' in Black History, Community, and Education." *The Urban Review* 36(1), 1–35.

Oliver, Melvin L., and Thomas M. Shapiro. 1995. *Black Wealth / White Wealth: A New Perspective on Racial Inequality*. New York: Routledge.

Omi, Michael, and Howard Winant. 1994. *Racial Formation in the United States: From the 1960s to the 1980s*. New York: Routledge.

Oshinsky, D. 1997. *Worse than Slavery: Parchman Farm and the Ordeal of Jim Crow Justice*. New York: Free Press.

Pager, Devah. 2006. "Evidence-based Policy for Successful Prisoner Reentry." *Criminology & Public Policy* 5(3), 505–14.

2003. "The Mark of a Criminal Record." *American Journal of Sociology* 108(5), 937–75.

Parenti, Christian. 2001. "The 'New' Criminal Justice System: 1968 to 2001." *Monthly Review*, 19–28.

Parker, Christopher S., Mark Q. Sawyer and Christopher Towler. 2009. "A Black Man in the White House? The Role of Racism and Patriotism in the 2008 Presidential Election." *Du Bois Review* 6(1), 193–217.

Pascoe, Peggy. 1996. "Miscegenation Law, Court Cases, and Ideologies of 'Race' in Twentieth-Century America." *The Journal of American History* 83(1), 44–69.

Patillo-McCoy, Mary. 2000. *Black Picket Fences: Privilege and Peril among the Black Middle Class*. University of Chicago Press.

Paul-Emile, Kimani. 2018. "Blackness as Disability?" *Georgetown Law Journal* 106, 293.

Payne, B. Keith. 2001. "Prejudice and Perception: The Role of Automatic and Controlled Processes in Misperceiving a Weapon." *Journal of Personality and Social Psychology* 81(2).

Payne, Charles M. 2007. *I've Got the Light of Freedom: The Organizing Tradition and the Mississippi Freedom Struggle*. Berkeley: University of California Press.

Perry, Andre, Jonathan Rothwell and David Harshbarger. 2018. "The Devaluation of Assets in Black Neighborhoods: The Case of Residential Property." Washington, DC: Brookings Institute, Metropolitan Policy Program.

Petersen, Amy J. 2009. "'Ain't Nobody Gonna Get Me Down': An Examination of the Educational Experiences of Four African American Women Labeled with Disabilities." *Equity & Excellence in Education* 42(4), 428–42.

Petersilia, J. 2003. *When Prisoners Come Home: Parole and Prisoner Reentry*. Oxford University Press.

Pettigrew, Thomas F. 2009. "Post Racism? Putting President Obama's Victory in Perspective." *Du Bois Review* 6(2), 279–92.

Pettit, Becky, and Stephanie Ewert. 2009. "Employment Gains and Wage Declines: The Erosion of Black Women's Relative Wages Since 1980." *Demography* 46(3), 469–92.

Pettit, Becky, and Bruce Western. 2004. "Mass Imprisonment and the Life Course: Race and Class Inequality in U.S. Incarceration." *American Sociological Review* 69(2), 151–69.

Pfaff, J. 2017. *Locked In: The True Causes of Mass Incarceration – and How to Achieve Real Reform*. New York: Basic Books.

Philips, Anthony Jamal, and Natalie Deckard. 2016. "Felon Disenfranchisement Laws and the Feedback Loop of Political Exclusion: The Case of Florida." *Journal of African American Studies* 20(1), 1–18.

Pickett, Justin T., and Stephanie B. Ryon. 2017. "Race, Criminal Injustice

Frames, and the Legitimation of Carceral Inequality as a Social Problem." *Du Bois Review*, 14(2), 577–602.

Pied, Claudine M. 2018. "Conservative Populist Politics and the Remaking of the 'White Working Class' in the USA." *Dialectical Anthropology* 42(2), 193–206.

Pierre, Jemima. 2004. "Black Immigrants in the United States and the 'Cultural Narratives' of ethnicity." *Identities: Global Studies in Culture and Power* 11(2), 141–70.

Portes, Alejandro, and Min Zhou. 1993. "The New Second Generation: Segmented Assimilation and its Variants." *The ANNALS of the American Academy of Political and Social Science* 530, 74–96.

Price, Joshua. 2015. *Prison and Social Death*. New Brunswick, NJ: Rutgers University Press.

Prince, Sabiyha. 2014. *African Americans and Gentrification in Washington D.C: Race, Class and Social Justice in the Nation's Capital*. Burlington, VT: Ashgate Publishing Company.

Prisock, Louis. 2015. "The CEO of Self: Herman Cain, Black Conservatism and the Achievement Ideology." *Journal of African American Studies* 19(2), 178–91.

Provine, Doris Marie. 2011. "Race and Inequality in the War on Drugs." *Annual Review of Law and Social Science* 7(1), 41–60.

Pryor, Marie 2010. "The Unintended Effects of Prisoner Reentry Policy and the Marginalization of Urban Communities." *Dialectical Anthropology* 34(4), 513–17.

Pulido, Laura. 2006. *Black, Brown, Yellow and Left: Radical Activism in Los Angeles*. Berkeley: University of California Press.

Quillian, Lincoln. 2012. "Segregation and Poverty Concentration: The Role of Three Segregations." *American Sociological Review* 77(3), 354–79.

Quillian, Lincoln, and Devah Pager. 2001. "Black Neighbors, Higher Crime? The Role of Racial Stereotypes in Evaluations of Neighborhood Crime." *American Journal of Sociology* 107(3), 717–67.

Ransby, Barbara. 2003. *Ella Baker and the Black Freedom Movement: A Radical Democratic Vision*. Chapel Hill: University of North Carolina Press.

Reskin, Barbara F., and Irene Padavic. 1994. *Women and Men at Work*. Thousand Oaks: Pine Forge Press.

Rios, Victor. 2011. *Punished: Policing the Lives of Black and Latino Boys*. New York University Press.

Roberts, Dorothy. 1997. *Killing the Black Body: Race, Representation and the Meaning of Liberty*. New York: Vintage Books.

Robinson, Cedric. 1983. *Black Marxism: The Making of the Black Radical Tradition*. Chapel Hill: University of North Carolina Press.

Robinson, Eugene. 2010. *Disintegration: The Splintering of Black America*. New York: Anchor Books.

Rockquemore, Kerry Ann. 2002. "Negotiating the Color Line: The

Gendered Process of Racial Identity Construction among Black/White Biracial Women." *Gender & Society* 16(4), 485–503.

Rodriguez, Javier M., Arline T. Geronimus, John Bound and Danny Dorling. 2015. "Black Lives Matter: Differential Mortality and the Racial Composition of the U.S. Electorate, 1970–2004." *Social Science & Medicine* 136–7, 193.

Roedinger, David. 2007. *The Wages of Whiteness: Race and the Making of the American Working Class*. New York: Verso Books.

Rose, T. 2004. *Longing to Tell: Black women Talk about Sexuality and Intimacy*. New York: Farrar, Straus and Giroux.

Rothstein, Richard. 2017. *The Color of Law: A Forgotten History of How Our Government Segregated America*. New York: W. W. Norton and Company.

Rubin, Ashley, and Michelle S. Phelps. 2017. "Fracturing the Penal State: State Actors and the Role of Conflict in Penal Change." *Theoretical Criminology* 21(4), 422–40.

Rugh, Jacob S., Len Albright and Douglas S. Massey. 2015. "Race, Space, and Cumulative Disadvantage: A Case Study of the Subprime Lending Collapse." *Social Problems* 62(2), 186–218.

Rumbaut, Ruben G., and Alejandro Portes, eds. 2001. *Ethnicities: Children of Immigrants in America*. Berkeley: University of California Press.

Sampson, Robert J., and W. Bryon Groves, 1989. "Community Structure and Crime: Testing Social-Disorganization Theory." *American Journal of Sociology* 94(4), 774–802.

Saperstein, Aliyah, and Andrew M. Penner. 2010. "The Race of a Criminal Record: How Incarceration Colors Racial Perceptions." *Social Problems* 57(1), 92–113.

Sawyer, Wendy. 2018. "Youth Confinement: The Whole Pie." Northampton: Prison Policy Initiative. www.prisonpolicy.org/reports/youth2018.html.

Schram, Sanford F., Joe Soss, Richard C. Fording and Linda Houser. 2009. "Deciding to Discipline: Race, Choice, and Punishment at the Frontlines of Welfare Reform." *American Sociological Review* 74(3), 398–422.

Schuman, Howard, Charlotte Steeh, Lawrence Bobo and Maria Krysan. 1998. *Racial Attitudes in America: Trends and Interpretations*. Cambridge, MA: Harvard University Press.

Schwartz, M. J. 2006. *Birthing a Slave: Motherhood and Medicine in the Antebellum South*. Cambridge, MA: Harvard University Press.

Scott, Emily. 2017. "Mark Lamont Hill Speaks in Student Center about Palestine." *The Temple News*. October 7. https://temple-news.com/marc-lamont-hill-speaks-student-center-palestine.

Scott, James. 1990. *Domination and the Art of Resistance: Hidden Transcripts*. New Haven, CT: Yale University Press.

Scott, Lottie. 2018. *Deep South, Deep North: A Family's Journey*. Pittsburgh, PA: Dorrance Publishing Co.

Sernett, Milton C. 1997. *Bound for the Promised Land: African American Religion and the Great Migration.* Durham, NC: Duke University Press.

Sewell, William H. 1971. "Inequality of Opportunity for Higher Education." *American Sociological Review* 36(5), 793–809.

Shannon, Sarah K., Christopher Uggen, Jason Schnittker, Melissa Thompson, Sara Wakefield and Michael Massoglia. 2017. "The Growth, Scope, and Spatial Distribution of People with Felony Records in the United States, 1948–2010." *Demography* 54(5), 1795–1818.

Shapiro, Thomas. 2004. *The Hidden Cost of Being African American: How Wealth Perpetuates Inequality.* New York: Oxford University Press.

Sharp, Gregory, and Matthew Hall. 2014. "Emerging Forms of Racial Inequality in Homeownership Exit, 1968–2009." *Social Problems* 61(3), 427–47.

Sharkey, Patrick. 2013. *Stuck in Place: Urban Neighborhoods and the End of Progress Toward Racial Equality.* University of Chicago Press.

Shelton, Jason E., and George Wilson. 2009. "Race, Class, and the Basis of Group Alignment: An Analysis of Support for Redistributive Policy among Privileged Blacks." *Sociological Perspectives* 52(3), 385–408.

Shibutani, Tamotsu, and Kian M. Kwan. 1965. *Ethnic Stratification.* New York: Macmillan Press.

Skloot, Rebecca. 2011. *The Immortal Life of Henrietta Lacks.* New York: Broadway Books.

Sniderman, Paul M., Thomas Piazza, Philip E. Tetlock and Ann Kendrick. 1991. "The New Racism." *American Journal of Political Science* 35(2), 423–447.

Smith, Rogers M., and Desmond S. King. 2009. "Barack Obama and the Future of American Racial Politics." *Du Bois Review* 6(1) (Spring), 25–35.

Solomon, Amy L., Kelly D. Johnson, Jeremy Travis and Elizabeth McBride. 2004. "From Prison to Work: The Employment Dimensions of Prisoner Reentry." Washington, DC: Urban Institute, Justice Policy Center.

Stainback, Kevin, Corre L. Robinson and Donald Tomaskovic-Devey. 2005. "Race and Workplace Integration: A Politically Mediated Process?" *American Behavioral Scientist* 48(9), 1200.

Standley, Fred, and Louis H. Pratt, eds. 1989. *Conversations with James Baldwin.* Jackson: The University of Mississippi Press.

Steinberg, Stephen. 1998. "The Role of Social Science in the Legitimization of Racial Hierarchy." *Race and Society* 1, 5–14.

Strother, Logan, Spencer Piston and Thomas Ogorzalek. 2017. "Pride or Prejudice? Racial Prejudice, Southern Heritage, and White Support for the Confederate Battle Flag." *Du Bois Review*, 14(1), 295–323.

Swain, R. D. 2018. "Negative Black Stereotypes, Support for Excessive Use of Force by Police, and Voter Preference for Donald Trump During the 2016 Presidential Primary Election Cycle." *Journal of African American Studies* 22(1), 109–24.

Taylor, Keeanga-Yamahtta. 2016. *From #Blacklivesmatter to Black Liberation.* Chicago, IL: Haymarket Books.

2017. *How We Get Free: Black Feminism and the Combahee River Collective.* Chicago, IL: Haymarket Books.

Taylor, Steven. 2011. "Racial Polarization in the 2008 U.S. Presidential Election." *Western Journal of Black Studies* 35(2), 118–27.

Thomas, Jamie, and Christina Jackson, eds. 2019. *Embodied Difference: Divergent Bodies in Public Discourse.* Lanham, MD: Lexington Books.

Thomas, Susan L. 1998. "Race Gender, and Welfare Reform: The Antinatalist Response." *Journal of Black Studies* 28(4), 419–46.

Thompson, Victor R., and Lawrence D. Bobo. 2011. "Thinking about Crime: Race and Lay Accounts of Lawbreaking Behavior." *The ANNALS of the American Academy of Political and Social Science* 634(1), 16–38.

Tilly, Charles. 1978. *From Mobilization to Revolution.* Prentice-Hall.

1998. *Durable Inequality.* Berkeley: University of California Press.

Timberlake, Jeffrey M. 2000. "Still life in black and white: Effects of racial and class attitudes on prospects for residential integration in Atlanta." *Sociological Inquiry* 70(4), 420–5.

Tomaskovic-Devey, Donald. 1993. *Gender and Racial Inequality at Work: The Sources and Consequences of Job Segregation.* Ithaca, NY: Cornell University Press.

Tuan, Mia. 1999. *Forever Foreigners or Honorary Whites? The Asian Ethnic Experience Today.* New Brunswick, NJ: Rutgers University Press.

Ture, Kwame, and Charles V. Hamilton. 1992. *Black Power: The Politics of Liberation.* New York: Vintage.

Umoren, Imaobong D. 2018. *Race Women Internationalists: Activist-Intellectuals and Global Freedom Struggles.* Berkeley: University of California Press.

Unnever, James D., Francis T. Cullen and James D. Jones. 2008. "Public Support for Attacking the 'Root Causes' of Crime: The Impact of Egalitarian and Racial Beliefs." *Sociological Focus* 41(1), 1–33.

van Dijk, Teun A., ed. 1997. *Discourse as Social Interaction. Discourse Studies: A Multidisciplinary Introduction,* Vol. II. Thousand Oaks, CA: Sage Publications, Inc.

Wacquant, Loic. 2007. "Territorial Stigmatization in the Age of Advanced Marginality." *Thesis Eleven* 91(1), 66–77.

2010. "Prisoner Reentry as Myth and Ceremony." *Dialect Anthropology* 34(4), 605–20.

Walters, Pamela B. 2001. "Educational Access and the State: Historical Continuities and Discontinuities in Racial Inequality in American Education." *Sociology of Education* 74, 35–49.

Walters, R. 2007. "Barack Obama and the Politics of Blackness." *Journal of Black Studies* 38(1), 7–29.

Warnick, Brian. 2008. "Oppression, Freedom and the Education of Frederick Douglass." *Philosophical Studies in Education* 39, 24–32.

Waters, Mary. 1990. *Ethnic Options: Later Generation Ethnicity in America.* Berkeley: University of California Press.

Waytz, Adam, Kelly M. Hoffman and Sophie Trawalter. 2015. "A superhumanization bias in Whites' perceptions of Blacks." *Social Psychological and Personality Science* 6(3), 352–9.

Weber, Max. 1930. *The Protestant Ethic and the Spirit of Capitalism.* London: G. Allen and Unwin.

Weiman, David. 2007. "Barriers to Prisoners' Reentry into the Labor Market and the Social Costs of Recidivism." *Social Research* 74(2), 575–612.

Western, Bruce. 2006. *Punishment and Inequality in America.* New York: Russell Sage Foundation.

Western, Bruce, and Pettit, Becky. 2005. "Black–White Wage Inequality, Employment Rates, and Incarceration." *American Journal of Sociology* 111(2), 553–78.

Whitman, James. 2017. *Hitler's American Model: The United States and the Making of Nazi Race Law.* Princeton University Press.

Wilkerson, Doxey A. 1939. *Special Problems of Negro Education.* Washington, DC: Government Printing Office.

Williams, K. 2007. *Our Enemies in Blue: Police and Power in America.* Boston, MA: South End Press.

Williams-Witherspoon, Kimmika. 2013. "Blacks on Stage: Are We Still Replicating Stereotypes from the Legacy of Minstrelsy?" *Praxis: The Journal for Theatre, Performance Studies, and Criticism,* 1–12.

Wilson, David C., Paul R. Brewer and Phoebe Theodora Rosenbluth. 2014. "Racial Imagery and Support for Voter ID Laws." *Race and Social Problems* 6(4), 365–71.

Wilson, George, Vincent J. Roscigno and Matt Huffman. 2013. "Public Sector Transformation, Racial Inequality and Downward Occupational Mobility." *Social Forces* 91(3), 975–1006.

Wilson, William J. 1976. "Power, Racism, and the Theoretical Basis of Racial Conflict" [1973]. In Wilson, *Power, Racism, and Privilege: Race Relations in Theoretical and Sociohistorical Perspectives.* New York: Free Press.

1978. *The Declining Significance of Race: Blacks and Changing American Institutions.* University of Chicago Press.

1987. *The Truly Disadvantaged: The Inner City, the Underclass, and Public Policy.* University of Chicago Press.

2017. "Why Sociologists Matter in the Welfare Reform Debate." *Contemporary Sociology* 46(6), 627–34.

Winant, Howard. 2000a. "The Theoretical Status of the Concept of Race." In *Theories of Race and Racism,* ed. Les Back and John Solomos.

2000b. "Race and Race Theory." *Annual Review of Sociology* 26(1), 169–85.

2004. *The New Politics of Race: Globalism, Difference, Justice.* Minneapolis: University of Minnesota Press.

2009. "Just Do It: Notes on Politics and Race at the Dawn of the Obama Presidency." *Du Bois Review* 6(1), 49–70.

Wingfield, Adia Harvey. 2015. "Color-blindness is Counterproductive." *The Atlantic.* September 13.

Winter, Nicholas J. G. 2010. "Masculine Republicans and Feminine Democrats: Gender and Americans' Explicit and Implicit Images of the Political Parties." *Political Behavior* 32(4), 587–618.

Wooten, Melissa, and Enobong Hannah Branch. 2012. "Defining Appropriate Labor: Race, Gender, and the Idealization of Black Women in Domestic Service." *Race, Gender, & Class* 19(3–4), 292–308.

Wright, Michelle M. 2003. *Becoming Black: Creating Identity in the African Diaspora.* Durham, NC: Duke University Press.

Yancey, George. 2003. *Who is White? Latinos, Asians and the New Black/Nonblack Divide.* London: Lynne Rienner Publishers.

Young, Alford. 2004. *The Minds of Marginalized Men: Making Sense of Mobility, Opportunity, and Future Life Chances.* Princeton University Press.

Zuberi, Tukufu. 2001. *Thicker than Blood: How Racial Statistics Lie.* Minneapolis: University of Minnesota Press.

2004. "W. E. B. Du Bois's Sociology: The Philadelphia Negro and Social Science." *The ANNALS of the American Academy of Political and Social Science* 595(1), 146–56.

Index